Jane Austen's Novels
The Fabric of Dialogue

Jane Austen's Novels
The Fabric of Dialogue

By Howard S. Babb

Archon Books 1967

R69- 02658

Copyright © by the Ohio State University Press.
All rights reserved. Original Library of Congress
Catalog Card Number: 62-15101. Second printing,
1967, by Archon Books, by special arrangement
with the original publisher, the Ohio State University Press.

PR
4037
B 3

1967

Printed in the United States of America
Library of Congress Catalog Card Number: 67-28550

For

Hugh and Persis Babb

and

Alice Meyer

Preface

This book really originated in a sense of perplexity I had while reading that passage of dialogue at Rosings, in *Pride and Prejudice*, during which Darcy and Elizabeth talk of her piano-playing. Although their conversation struck me as intensely charged with personal feeling, and indeed as deeply moving, yet its surface appeared witty, restrained, suitably public. To resolve my perplexity, I turned back to study the speeches closely, and I seemed to find several linguistic devices serving to dramatize subtly the full behavior and emotions of the characters. So I began looking for comparable practices in the rest of *Pride and Prejudice* as well as in the other works by Jane Austen; and in trying to tie down the expressive values of these practices, I was led to investigate her style. The chief result of these explorations for me has been the growing conviction that Jane Austen's novels are not in fact so limited in range and in intensity as they are often thought to be. This is the thesis underlying the pages that follow, and I pursue it in the main by analyzing dialogues to show how, and how much, Jane Austen communicates in them.

Thus the book does not pretend to be either a general introduction to Jane Austen's writings, or a study of them in relation to the history of the novel, or an investigation of her irony—to name a few of the ways in which others have dealt tellingly with her fiction. In analyzing so much dialogue so intensively as it does, this book makes unusually heavy demands on the reader's attention, to say nothing of his fortitude, and for this I am sorry. But intensive treatment seemed to me required by the richness of Jane Austen's dialogue, and I felt the ex-

✳✳✳✳✳✳✳✳✳✳✳✳✳✳✳✳✳✳✳✳✳✳✳✳✳✳✳✳✳✳✳✳✳✳✳✳

tensive examples necessary to satisfy the reader that an occasional rabbit was not being pulled out of a hat. The reader's compensation for my method, I have to hope, is a sharpened insight into Jane Austen's art.

It is a pleasure to acknowledge how much this book owes to other persons. Every student of Jane Austen is indebted to R. W. Chapman for his magnificent edition of her writings, and I am grateful to the Oxford University Press for allowing me to quote so extensively from it. The Editor of *The Kenyon Review* has kindly given me permission to reprint, as part of Chapter V, a slightly different version of the essay published as "Dialogue with Feeling: A Note on *Pride and Prejudice.*"

In a more personal way, I am deeply indebted to Charles M. Coffin and John Crowe Ransom, who first acquainted me at Kenyon College with the study of literature. W. J. Bate of Harvard University introduced me to the ideas of the eighteenth century, and Andrews Wanning to the investigation of style. My friends Philip Finkelpearl, David Ferry, and Robert O'Clair stimulated me continuously when I was first thinking about Jane Austen. And Douglas Bush and Albert Guerard, Jr. read one version of this book with patience and care, making suggestions from which the final product has benefited greatly.

I owe much, as well, to my colleagues at the Ohio State University. Robert C. Elliott and Andrew M. Wright have given me help of various sorts. Roy Harvey Pearce has been a constant source of encouragement to me, as to others. And Robert M. Estrich not only read the final version of the book; he also made its preparation possible by giving me all the backing within the power of a department chairman and all the attentions of a friend.

But my greatest debt is to my wife: for her unwavering support while I was writing the book, as well as for her tact and literary judgment, which guided me on the way.

Howard S. Babb

Columbus, Ohio

Contents

-◦[1]◦- Jane Austen's Style:
The Climate of the Dialogues   3

-◦[2]◦- The *Juvenilia* and Fragments:
Toward Sustained Dialogue   33

-◦[3]◦- *Sense and Sensibility:*
Symmetrical Designs   51

-◦[4]◦- *Northanger Abbey:*
Parody, Pedagogy, and the Play of Feeling   86

-◦[5]◦- *Pride and Prejudice:*
Vitality and a Dramatic Mode   113

-◦[6]◦- *Mansfield Park:*
Ethical Rigor and an Emblematic Mode   145

-◦[7]◦- *Emma:*
Fluent Irony and the Pains of Self-Discovery   175

x CONTENTS

****

-•[8]•- *Persuasion:*
In Defense of Sensibility   203

-•[9]•- Conclusion   242

Jane Austen's Novels
The Fabric of Dialogue

1 Jane Austen's Style
The Climate of the Dialogues

It is not unfair to say that most of Jane Austen's critics are obsessed by a sense of her limitations. The germ of the bias is easy to find in her notorious references to "the little bit (two Inches wide) of Ivory on which I work with so fine a brush" and to "3 or 4 Families in a Country Village . . . the very thing to work on."[1] Charlotte Brontë supplied a catch phrase to go with "Ivory"—"There is a Chinese fidelity . . . in the painting"— while denouncing the novels as restricted in theme. To her they revealed only the most "distant recognition" of the "feelings" and no awareness of the "passions": ". . . what throbs fast and full, though hidden, what the blood rushes through, what is the unseen seat of life and the sentient target of death—this Miss Austen ignores."[2] It remained for Jane Austen's nephew to provide biographical support for the view by recording, "Of events her life was singularly barren . . . ."[3] These proved to be major strands of Jane Austen criticism, still plainly visible in a twentieth-century disapproval by H. W. Garrod: "Undoubtedly she is entitled to that praise which belongs to a writer who limits her theme and her style to the exact measure of her interests, knowledge and powers."[4] Technique, theme, and life have been confidently equated.

This kind of verdict has been passed so often on Jane Austen's work that sympathetic critics accept it almost without question. And even Mary Lascelles, in one of the most rewarding studies of Jane Austen, tends to settle for an uneasy truce. On the one hand she extenuates the limitations on the ground that they are intentional: ". . . Jane Austen's resolve to 'go on in her own way' means deliberate choice both of subject and of mood . . .

❋❋❋❋❋❋❋❋❋❋❋❋❋❋❋❋❋❋❋❋❋❋❋❋❋❋❋❋❋❋

she will take as subject for her art a certain region in the social world because it is . . . 'the delight of her life'—not, as her critics have loosely inferred, the safest thing for her to write about." But on the other hand she argues the limitations out of existence by a determined—and somewhat enigmatic—application of "scale": "By presenting her people in perspective, as none but a writer with an exact sense of scale can do, Jane Austen indicates recession, and so gives the impression of a limitless human world beyond her visible scene." [5] At best these claims seem to equivocate between the critic's sense of density in the novels and the usual opinion that they are highly restricted in manner and theme.

Reginald Farrer has taken a surer critical stance in emphatically differentiating between the surface of the works and their import. "Talk of her 'limitations' is vain," he insists, because "it must never be thought that limitation of scene implies limitation of human emotion": "Jane Austen's heroes and heroines and subject-matter are, in fact, universal human nature, and conterminous with it, though manifested only in one class . . . ." [6] His distinction is crucial in that it hints at the basic fallacy of the limitationists, their confusion of a novel's tone with its issues. For I suspect we have been hoaxed by the well-bred air of Jane Austen's characters, by the eminently social tone of their conversations, by the very stability of their moral universe. Because we can glide so easily over the surfaces of this fictional world, we have been tempted to ignore its substance. Thus the burden of the following chapters: that analysis of Jane Austen's dialogue reveals a richer substance in the novels, and a far greater range of expressiveness on the part of the characters, than has generally been allowed.

Probably we have been encouraged to undervalue her matter because it has so readily been classified as dealing in manners. How this could buttress the limitationist tradition may be suggested by Ernest Baker's remark about Jane Austen creating "a novel of manners in a narrower and truer sense" than Maria Edgeworth or Fanny Burney in that "She takes the morals for granted." [7] Such a comment leaves us, in effect, with manners

❋❋❋❋❋❋❋❋❋❋❋❋❋❋❋❋❋❋❋❋❋❋❋❋❋❋❋❋❋❋❋❋❋❋❋❋

operating in a kind of void. Marvin Mudrick, representing a more recent strain of Jane Austen criticism, moves to the opposite extreme. Concerned for the individualistic rather than the conventional, he relentlessly inverts Jane Austen's irony to argue that she was in bitter revolt against her society and really parodies its values.[8] We are now asked, it would seem, to discard the evidence of the manners and find the real significance of the novels in a psychological drive attributed to their author.

But both the revolutionists and the limitationists—though doubtless I have just formulated their positions too absolutely—appear to me to take, at bottom, too strait a view of manners. For manners are the very habits of man's being, social man or private man, and rooted in human experience. If as public gestures they are therefore formal to a degree and codify the values of society, we must never forget that they are at the same time inevitably charged with the values of the individual, because by means of them he expresses his private experience. Thus manners are neither readily subverted—men of straw for some deeper instinct—nor do they inhabit a vacuum. As Lionel Trilling has most handsomely assured us, we must take them seriously: "What I understand by manners, then, is a culture's hum and buzz of implication. I mean the whole evanescent context in which its explicit statements are made. It is that part of a culture which is made up of half-uttered or unuttered or unutterable expressions of value." "The great novelists," he adds, "knew that manners indicate the largest intentions of men's souls as well as the smallest and they are perpetually concerned to catch the meaning of every dim implicit hint." [9] Manners, then, if we read them as indexes to major cultural and personal values, may define a comprehensive and substantial reality. In Jane Austen's novels, we ignore gestures so significant at our peril.

Yet even supposing that manners are not a necessarily limited subject, we still need to face the charge that polite conversation must automatically be limited in its scope, intensity, and significance. This is the main problem dealt with through the chapters that follow. In them I shall be arguing that Jane Austen's dialogue actually reveals her characters in depth and shows them

✹✹✹✹✹✹✹✹✹✹✹✹✹✹✹✹✹✹✹✹✹✹✹✹✹✹✹✹✹✹

engaged in the most fundamental activities of personality: in bringing to bear the entire self, for instance, to sway someone else; or in evolving judgments about the behavior of others and of the self; or in winning through to insight into human beings and affairs, as well as lapsing into blindness, either process deeply conditioned by the nature of the character in question. Indeed the issues in these conversations are vital, although the tone of the speakers remains almost always decorously social. To discover these issues, we shall have to examine the very fabric of the dialogues—the implications woven into the language of the speakers themselves. And the first step in cultivating our awareness to these implications is to explore the linguistic context of the dialogues, Jane Austen's style; for in effect her style acts as the expressive norm in terms of which the verbal gestures of her characters become significant.

-◄[II]►-

Any writer's style, evidently, is determined in some measure by the culture from which he derives, by the kinds of words and linguistic structures that the culture makes especially available to him. And no one would question that Jane Austen, although her novels were published in the early nineteenth century, has her major affinities with the culture of the eighteenth century and with the stylistic modes that it fostered. As Mary Lascelles has observed, "To us Jane Austen appears like one who inherits a prosperous and well-ordered estate—the heritage of a prose style in which neither generalization nor abstraction need signify vagueness, because there was close enough agreement as to the scope and significance of such terms. Character and motive, for example, might be presented in them—a practice best illustrated, and very likely familiar to Jane Austen herself, in the *Lives of the Poets.*" [10] Indeed many traits that I shall be finding in Jane Austen's style—such as her dependence on conceptual terms, her ways with a particularized diction, her generalizations, her limited use of figurative speech—have their analogues in verbal practices common during the eighteenth century. Of course, any stylistic habit characteristic of a period carries the imprint of that age's attitudes. A typically eighteenth-century locution like "finny tribe"—to treat it oversimply in bringing out only these dimensions of its meaning—implies the outlines of a world view: the phrase minimizes the particularizing detail; it emphasizes universal aspects in referring to fish; it thus highlights the aspects accessible to man's reason; and, in the phrase's proportioning of general and particular, it observes a standard of decorum. It is attitudes like these, though Jane Austen happens not to use the sort of phrase cited, that come into play in her style when she does ground it in eighteenth-century practices.

As soon as we start talking about attitudes of any sort in relation to a style, whether a period or a personal style, we are likely to say that the style "expresses" them. Yet the word is misleading if it suggests that the attitudes are lying somewhere out behind the style, merely a part of its background. Rather, they are embedded in the style, which keeps bringing them immediately to bear, constantly projects these attitudes toward the reader (thus my frequent mention of the "audience" in describing Jane Austen's style). For language, and hence style, is inevitably transitive in that its essential function is to communicate. It communicates by shaping raw experience into a version shareable with others. An element of form inheres in all the items that go to make up language, in words themselves, syntactic patterns, rhetorical structures, and the like; that is to say, each of these is to some degree a convention, has some area of generally agreed upon significance, or communication could not take place. The inescapable formal dimension in language may discourage us from seeking out the man behind the style, inasmuch as the intervention of form would forbid us to match the contours of the reported experience with the initiating one. But this indigenous formality encourages us to conceive of a writer's style as a vehicle of persuasion: for it is the very essence of form to presume an audience, and, when a form is realized, it codifies an appeal to an audience. By this view of style, a thought shaped in language has already entered the realm of action; a sentence is a deed. And by this view, the style of an author is to be described in terms of the typical appeals that it makes, those signs that often suggest the writer's interpretation of the audience. Such are the theoretical assumptions that underlie the following analysis of Jane Austen's style, and I think that they allow us to define securely the particular world that she creates in her novels.

One mark of that world is its minimum of physical action. In place of physical event, the style records a series of intellectual, emotional, and moral states, implying that these—whether motives or consequences—make up the real importance of an action. The human mind and heart, in fact, are the major fields of activity in these novels. So verbs, traditionally active words, carry little weight. The passive voice, which insists on the static, is frequent, as is its equivalent, the impersonal construction. One example will be enough here, but I should preface it with two general remarks about the illustrations throughout this chapter. First, I have tried to choose—for obvious reasons—representative passages from as wide a range of Jane Austen's writing as possible. Second, the italics in these selections are mine unless otherwise noted, a way of setting off the stylistic trait in question, like the verbs in the present example:

> Elinor *had given* her real opinion to her sister. She *could not consider* her partiality for Edward in so prosperous a state as Marianne *had believed* it. There *was*, at times, a want of spirits about him which, if it *did not denote* indifference, *spoke* a something almost as unpromising. A doubt of her regard, *supposing* him *to feel* it, *need not give* him more than inquietude. It *would not be likely to produce* that dejection of mind which frequently *attended* him. A more reasonable cause *might be found* in the dependent situation which *forbad* the indulgence of his affection. She *knew* that his mother neither *behaved* to him so as *to make* his home comfortable at present, nor *to give* him any assurance that he *might form* a home for himself, without strictly *attending* to her views for his aggrandizement. With such a knowledge as this, it *was impossible* for Elinor *to feel* easy on the subject. (*Sense and Sensibility*, p. 22) [11]

These verbs do not portray vigorous physical action. Rather, they distinguish between basic categories of response: considering, believing, supposing, feeling, knowing. They further indicate presence or absence: giving, producing, attending, finding, forming —and being or not being. Yet what *is*, here, is "a want of spirits" or some other condition, and what *is not* is a capacity "to feel easy." The two strongest verbs, "spoke" and "forbad," activate concepts, not people: it is the "want of spirits" that "spoke" and "the dependent situation" that "forbad."

Indeed in Jane Austen's style such concepts are the real actors. She often handles these groups of nouns as if they need only step on the stage in order to convince the audience, but we must never doubt their power on that account.[12] For conceptual terms of this sort gain a kind of life of their own in that they seem to universalize whatever aspects of experience they name, treating them less as parts of a single configuration—the way the individual would encounter them in reality—than as absolutes. Since the words thus appear markedly abstract, they have a special air of being fixed by reason alone and therefore of being eminently shareable with others. Further, because these terms seem freed from the fluctuations of a merely personal opinion, they automatically command assent from an audience. One cue to their status for Jane Austen is that, in accordance with an eighteenth-century practice, she frequently capitalized such words in her manuscripts. But any page of the novels will witness the supreme role that these terms play: enunciating the general principles that underlie the individual variety, they embody enduring values.

The following passage shows how typically Jane Austen accumulates nouns referring to concepts, even when she describes the judgment of the light-hearted Henry Crawford:

Fanny's *beauty of face and figure,* Fanny's *graces of manner* and *goodness of heart* were the exhaustless theme. The *gentleness, modesty,* and *sweetness of her character* were warmly expatiated on, that *sweetness* which makes so essential a part of *every*

❋❋❋❋❋❋❋❋❋❋❋❋❋❋❋❋❋❋❋❋❋❋❋❋❋❋❋❋❋❋❋❋❋

woman's worth in the *judgment of man,* that though he sometimes loves where it is not, he can never believe it absent. Her
temper he had *good reason* to depend on and to praise. He had
often seen it tried. Was there one of the family, excepting Edmund, who had not in some way or other continually exercised
her *patience* and *forbearance?* Her *affections* were evidently
strong. To see her with her brother! What could more delight-
fully prove that the *warmth of her heart* was equal to its *gentle-*
ness?—What could be more encouraging to a man who had *her*
love in view? Then, her *understanding* was *beyond every suspi-*
cion, quick and clear; and her *manners* were the mirror of her
own modest and elegant *mind.* Nor was this all. Henry Crawford had too much *sense* not to feel *the worth of good principles*
in a wife, though he was too little accustomed to *serious reflec-*
tion to know them by *their proper name;* but when he talked of
her having such a *steadiness and regularity of conduct,* such a
high *notion of honour,* and such an *observance of decorum* as
might warrant any man in *the fullest dependence* on her *faith*
and *integrity,* he expressed what was inspired by the *knowledge*
of her being well principled and religious. (*Mansfield Park,*
p. 294)

The sentences present not so much a specific personality as a
configuration of concepts, because Fanny's qualities are, in a
sense, abstracted from her as absolutes of human nature. We
start with physical characteristics, which the broad terms "beauty
of face and figure" hardly touch on; move immediately to the
most general categories of personality with "manner," "heart,"
and "character"; go on to perhaps slightly more limited depart-
ments in "temper" and "affections"; but soon return to the larger
tracts of "understanding" and "manners." Here the dynamics of
behavior are less important than the conditions they illustrate:
the particular events implied by "He had often seen it tried" and
"To see her with her brother" merely prove that Fanny has a
"temper" one can "depend on" and "affections" which are
"strong."

It is not only these major conditions that stabilize Fanny's
character for us by absorbing it into a realm of established values.
By the typical genitive construction—as in "graces of manner"—
Jane Austen separates the attributes of concepts from the con-

cepts themselves, and these very attributes beget a new set of conditions.[13] Evidently "manners" can be graceful or not, a heart good or bad, "character" gentle, modest, and sweet or their opposites, "conduct" regular or irregular, "decorum" observed or neglected. The construction creates a world of immovable areas, each one capable of being subdivided into two—but rarely more —static regions. In "warmth of heart," the formulation detaches the emotional attribute from "heart" not merely in grammar but in idea, so that the heart's "warmth" can be equated with, measured against, its "gentleness." Likewise, "sweetness" is a unit of settled value in the sum of "woman's worth." It is hardly surprising that "love" should be "in view" in this world, not because "love" is simply an intellectual possibility—that is not true—but because it is another area to be analytically explored according to the postulates of character.

Yet if all these conceptual terms are especially stable in their detachment from too personal an emotion, the terrain they mark out is not therefore petrified. Clearly the "judgment of man" honors his emotional demand for "sweetness" in the "character" of the beloved. In the same way, a man of "sense" must instinctively "feel the worth of good principles." And apparently "knowledge" inspires one morally—even Henry Crawford for the moment. Of course, he meets Fanny in person, so he can respond fully to her qualities even though unable to call them "by their proper name." We meet her in the pages of a book, so Jane Austen must name Fanny's qualities for us. But we have already seen how the naming itself, if done with conceptual words, dramatizes value for the audience.

This stylistic habit is basic in Jane Austen's work, whatever the local job of the prose. For instance, conceptual terms pervade the introduction of each character, where they assess him against a scale of absolutes. And they turn up just as regularly in the most emotional scenes. But instead of following up these uses, we had better glance at another, noticing how Jane Austen employs a conceptual vocabulary to satirize—though she never turns against such words in themselves. Sometimes she creates parody by the wild disproportion between these naturally weighty terms and the commonplace situation they describe, in this case the departure of an indifferent man from the room: " . . . it is absolutely impossible that he should ever have left you but with Confusion, Despair, and Precipitation" (*Volume the Second*, p. 94). More often she writes ironically, using the conceptual words to render a smooth surface and a corrupt sense at the same time: "Flexibility of Mind, a Disposition easily biassed by others, is an attribute which . . . I am not very desirous of obtaining; nor has Frederica any claim to the indulgence of her whims, at the expense of her Mother's inclination" (*Lady Susan*, p. 294). All seems well until Lady Susan mentions her "inclination"; but this word, apparently so in tune with the rest, implies that her motives are no more dignified than the "whims" she objects to in her daughter—and so undermines the whole passage. This is no laughing matter, we might note in passing, for Lady Susan succeeds by manipulating society's terms. Yet Jane Austen also aims at effects nearer the comic, as in revising the pompous Mr. Parker's original statement, "My Plantations astonish everybody by their Growth," into "The Growth of my Plantations is a general astonishment" (*Sanditon*, p. 46).[14] Transforming the particular verb into the generic noun emphasizes his pretentiousness.

Indeed anyone studying the few revisions she has left us—for instance in R. W. Chapman's separate editions of *The Watsons*, a rather early fragment, and of *Sanditon*, her unfinished final work—will discover how frequently Jane Austen leans toward conceptual language. There is little or no satire in the following samples, simply the effects we saw before in the passage from *Mansfield Park*. She refixes action as an idea when she changes "am rather afraid of" to "have my fears in that quarter" (*The Watsons*, p. 16), "we have been doing" to "has been our Occupation" (*Sanditon*, p. 105), and "were beginning to astonish" to "were a moment's astonishment" (*Sanditon*, p. 114). Her revision of "particularly urged for" to "warmly offered his assistance" (*Sanditon*, p. 125) detaches the emotion from the action. Finally, she substitutes more pointedly conceptual terms, their vitality implicit in the capital letters, for rather flat assertions in replacing "was . . . of rather formal aspect" with "had a reserved air, & a great deal of formal Civility" (*The Watsons*, p. 21), or "truly gratified look" with "a look, most expressive of unexpected pleasure, & lively Gratitude" (*The Watsons*, p. 42), or "for want of something better to do" with "for want of Employment" (*Sanditon*, p. 70). No doubt many of these are colorless enough, but the recurrence of similar revisions betrays how fully Jane Austen relies on a conceptual vocabulary, one in which the abstractions become agents.

Another stylistic device with the same sort of reverberations is her use of general statements. No novelist can make these, unless in dialogue or perhaps in transcribing a character's private thoughts, without intruding—subtly or explicitly—into the fiction. In Jane Austen's novels the main purpose of such intrusions is clear: to remind the reader of common knowledge that he already shares or may share. For a generalization is a formula, presumably dependable because it applies to more than one case. More than that, its reliability is confirmed by the impersonal phrasing, which seems to promise us that the statement does not issue from any purely private judgment. Thus, a generalization, like its close relative the maxim, apparently brings to bear universal wisdom, so fundamental that we can all assume ourselves ready to call on it at any moment. And the form itself becomes a kind of guarantee because it automatically resurrects the sense of a trustworthy public community of views—even if the generalization really expresses a private opinion. So to generalize is to dramatize the unity of author and audience. Like the conceptual terms, this stylistic trait formulates a set of standards in such a way that they seem taken for granted, and thus it invites us to share them.

Jane Austen often generalizes in a light tone, simply prompting us to remember the basic facts of experience: " . . . where youth and diffidence are united, it requires uncommon steadiness of reason to resist the attraction of being called the most charming girl in the world" (*Northanger Abbey*, p. 50). Or she asks us to smile at a familiar human failing: "How quick come the reasons for approving what we like!" (*Persuasion*, p. 15). And, since the true values of human nature are constant, always secure, she may invert them for irony: "The business of self-command she settled very easily;—with strong affections it was impossible, with calm ones it could have no merit" (*Sense and Sensibility*, p. 104); "It is a truth universally acknowledged, that a single man in possession of a good fortune, must be in want of a wife" (*Pride and Prejudice*, p. 3).

But generalizations also serve—and this is crucial—for the most serious assessment of character. Representing the standards of society, either by irony or directly, they establish the terms in which we are to evaluate the behavior of the individual. In the following passage Jane Austen sounds like Swift for a moment as she reverses the values to make the bitterest of judgments:

> The whole of Lucy's behaviour in the affair, and the prosperity which crowned it, therefore, may be held forth as a most encouraging instance of what an earnest, an unceasing attention to self-interest, however its progress may be apparently obstructed, will do in securing every advantage of fortune, with no other sacrifice than that of time and conscience. (*Sense and Sensibility*, p. 376)

She may invigorate the generalizations with an intense rhetoric to castigate the moral abnormality of the marriage between Mr. Rushworth and Maria Bertram:

> She had despised him, and loved another—and he had been very much aware that it was so. The indignities of stupidity, and the disappointments of selfish passion, can excite little pity. His punishment followed his conduct, as did a deeper punishment, the deeper guilt of his wife. (*Mansfield Park*, p. 464)

Or Jane Austen, describing Emma's response to Mr. Knightley's proposal, will epitomize the issues of an entire novel in a sympathetic decree:

> Seldom, very seldom, does complete truth belong to any human disclosure; seldom can it happen that something is not a little disguised, or a little mistaken; but where, as in this case, though the

conduct is mistaken, the feelings are not, it may not be very material. (*Emma,* p. 431)

The rhetoric in all these passages is hardly chance: it suggests a firm conviction that society's judgments, the substance of the generalizations, are reliable.

Finally, and this is no less a matter of conviction, Jane Austen generalizes in the interests of propriety: to disengage us from particulars that are too highly emotional. Sometimes this propriety may seem mainly a technical contrivance, as in the comment on Harriet Smith's alarm at the gypsies: "A young lady who faints, must be recovered; questions must be answered, and surprises be explained. Such events are very interesting, but the suspense of them cannot last long. A few minutes made Emma acquainted with the whole" (*Emma,* p. 333). Here we must escape being seriously involved so that Emma can plot an attachment between Harriet and her savior, Frank Churchill, without appearing hatefully insensible. But there is more than mere contrivance to the propriety that Jane Austen usually seeks through generalizing. Perhaps the previous example gives us a clue when it implies that the most violent emotional effects are necessarily short-lived. For decorum is the realm of lasting values, where the too highly particular must be somewhat generalized so that it may reveal its relation with the universal. This assumption explains, I suspect, Jane Austen's notorious care to keep us at a distance from her hero and heroine when they finally declare their love. To take one scene, Elinor Dashwood

was oppressed, she was overcome by her own felicity;—and happily disposed as is the human mind to be easily familiarized with any change for the better, it required several hours to give sedateness to her spirits, or any degree of tranquillity to her heart. (*Sense and Sensibility,* p. 363)

As for Edward Ferrars,

it was impossible that less than a week should be given up to the enjoyment of Elinor's company, or suffice to say half that was to be said of the past, the present, and the future;—for though a few hours spent in the hard labour of incessant talking will dispatch more subjects than can really be in common between any two rational creatures, yet with lovers it is different. . . . no subject is finished, no communication is even made, till it has been made at least twenty times over. (*Sense and Sensibility,* pp. 363–64)

It may be true that Jane Austen can afford this distance by the novel's conclusion, when the characters have already made their emotional adjustments. Still, the generalizations deliberately create a tone of reserve, for reserve is the condition of decision and endurance—a proof of decorum.

This same cluster of preferences leads Jane Austen to avoid highly particular words on the whole. In a world stabilized by public agreement on certain concepts, we would hardly expect a vocabulary of evocative particulars to flourish. For the colors of sense and feeling, though of course providing local shading, can be by definition only briefly effective.[15] Moreover, a diction too richly suggestive may pose a threat to the author's control of his audience by exciting various reactions, some of them unpredictable.

When particular words do occur in Jane Austen's writing, they usually point out deviations from the norms of good breeding. The tendency appears in the *Letters:* ". . . she was highly rouged, & looked rather quietly and contentedly *silly* than anything else.—Mrs. Badcock . . . thought herself obliged . . . to *run round* the room after her *drunken* Husband" (I, 128). In the *Juvenilia* this diction sounds the tone of parody rather than of personal distaste, as in the following blatant reversal of the features conventionally attributed to young ladies in sentimental fiction: "Lovely & too charming Fair one, notwithstanding your forbidding Squint, your greazy tresses & your swelling Back . . . I cannot refrain from expressing my raptures, at the engaging Qualities of your Mind, which so amply atone for the Horror, with which your first appearance must ever inspire the unwary visitor" (*Volume the First,* p. 6).

After the *Juvenilia* particular terms are likely to be less extreme; yet they still emphasize what is alien to good form. On rare occasions in revising, Jane Austen adopts a more colloquial phrasing simply to ease expression. Thus "being always able by their vicinity, to" becomes "being always at hand to" (*Sanditon*, p. 36), or—an unusual reversing of the tendency we noted earlier—"a great increase of the Happiness" becomes "better & better" (*Sanditon*, p. 116). But more often she substitutes a particular phrasing to sharpen irony by delicate exaggeration. To insist on Margaret Watson's affected drawl, she changes "the words seemed likely never to end" to "she could hardly speak a word in a minute" (*The Watsons*, p. 87); in the same way, she points up Tom Musgrave's pretensions to fashion by writing "Dishabille" for "a state" (*The Watsons*, p. 107). This mode of intentional heightening is one staple of ridicule in the novels. So gossipy Mrs. Jenkins comes "hallooing to the window" (*Sense and Sensibility*, p. 106), and Elizabeth's curiosity is "dreadfully racked" about Darcy (*Pride and Prejudice*, p. 321). Or Jane Austen plays off particular terms against the generic to dramatize irregular behavior ironically: "Catherine . . . listened to the *tempest* with sensations of awe; and, when she heard it *rage* round a corner . . . and close with *sudden fury* a distant door, felt for the first time that she was really in an Abbey.—Yes, these were characteristic sounds" (*Northanger Abbey*, p. 166). The fun arises here from Catherine's sense that the singular is "characteristic."

But such diction need not be used ironically. It may simply intensify the departure from a rational standard. Jane Austen underlines the stupidity of Diana Parker and her friends by revising "mistakes" to "blunders" (*Sanditon*, p. 150). And she allows the insipid Lady Middleton to be pleased only by "four noisy children" who "pulled her about" and "tore her clothes" (*Sense and Sensibility*, p. 34). More strikingly, particular words make up a kind of backdrop to set off more permanent values when she celebrates the final understanding of Anne Elliot and Captain Wentworth:

> . . . as they slowly paced the gradual ascent, heedless of every group around them, seeing neither *sauntering* politicians, *bus-*

❋❋❋❋❋❋❋❋❋❋❋❋❋❋❋❋❋❋❋❋❋❋❋❋❋❋❋❋❋❋❋❋❋❋❋❋

tling house-keepers, *flirting* girls, nor nursery-maids and children, they could indulge in those retrospections and acknowledgments, and especially in those explanations of what had directly preceded the present moment, which were so poignant and so ceaseless in interest. (*Persuasion,* p. 241)

In this passage Jane Austen seems deliberately to contrast the transiently suggestive particulars with the fixed entities—"retrospections," "acknowledgments," and "explanations"—that confirm the endurance of the lovers' relationship and appeal reliably to an audience.

This movement from particular to generic is characteristic of the prose. Indeed most of the particular words are in effect absorbed into the generic terms that dominate the style. To take a single instance, a typical phrase describes Marianne Dashwood as "in violent affliction" (*Sense and Sensibility,* p. 75). The evocativeness of "violent" is blurred because the adjective merges with a state, "affliction"; further, Marianne is already "in," as the phrasing insists, the condition. At an exceptional moment, such as Anne Elliot's departure from Uppercross, Jane Austen may intensify the atmosphere with particulars:

An hour's complete leisure for such reflections as these, on a *dark November day,* a *small thick rain* almost *blotting out* the very few objects ever to be discerned from the windows, was enough to make the sound of Lady Russell's carriage exceedingly welcome; and yet . . . she could not quit the mansion-house, or look an adieu at the cottage, with its *black, dripping,* and *comfortless veranda,* or even notice through the *misty glasses* the last humble tenements of the village, without a saddened heart.— Scenes had passed in Uppercross, which made it precious. It stood the record of many sensations of pain, once severe, but now softened; and of some instances of relenting feeling, some breathings of friendship and reconciliation, which could never be looked for again, and which could never cease to be dear. (*Persuasion,* p. 123)

But even in this example the concrete landscape is replaced by a "record," something settled in the human mind, and Jane Austen translates the specific emotion, as we have come to expect, into a conceptual vocabulary, here only mildly animated by the subdued metaphor "breathings." It is not that she denies feeling; rather, she creates the terms in which it can be most meaningful for her characters and for her audience. In this world, evidently, feeling achieves significance when it escapes its natural domain of self-interest and attaches itself to a publicly recognized hierarchy of values like forgiveness, "friendship," and "reconciliation." The analogy to the danger of highly particular words is plain; because they propose only individual excitement, they may subvert decorum by preventing the reader from committing himself soberly to the publicly formulated values—or, worse, they may utterly divert the reader from those values by betraying him to a private emotion.

The same judgment of her audience determines the ways in which Jane Austen employs figurative language. The distrust of metaphor that arose around the middle of the seventeenth century—when the groundwork was laid for the dominant stylistic habits of the eighteenth century—has become a critical commonplace. Perhaps Dryden put the case most succinctly in the Preface to his "Religio Laici": "A man is to be cheated into passion, but to be reasoned into truth." [16] His remark implies the two standard complaints against figurative language. First, literally it lies because it likens or equates two things which are really not alike. Second, since its main purpose is to intensify, it invites an emotional response that may short-circuit our sensible alignment with reality. This distrust limited the possibilities of figurative expression rather sharply, as Jane Austen's prose makes clear.

It seems that the best insurance in using metaphor seriously is to choose figures so familiar that their meanings have been circumscribed and their emotions carefully subdued. Indeed, Jane Austen's usual metaphors are such old friends that we hardly notice them. Hearts are "at war" (Northanger Abbey, p. 99), "wounded" (Mansfield Park, p. 175), and "sinking" (Persuasion, p. 137). One's emotions often make one "blind" (Pride and Prejudice, p. 208). Hopes have been "harboured" (Mansfield Park, p. 175) or "hours flew" (Northanger Abbey,

❈❈❈❈❈❈❈❈❈❈❈❈❈❈❈❈❈❈❈❈❈❈❈❈❈❈❈❈❈❈❈❈❈❈

p. 120). One is "bound" to do something (*Sense and Sensibility*, p. 99), sees things "in the same light" (*Mansfield Park*, p. 36), feels "the full weight" of others' claims (*Emma*, p. 435), or is in a "glow" of spirits (*Persuasion*, p. 181). Expressions of this sort, appearing over and over again, are legitimate coin, worn smooth by long usage. Sometimes in her revisions we can see Jane Austen removing what might be thought counterfeit because of its glitter. Thus she changes "the disease of activity" to "a spirit of restless activity" (*Sanditon*, p. 130), and she dulls "we must not rip up the faults of the Dead" to "we must not find fault with the Dead" (*Sanditon*, p. 97).

But if figurative language, like particular diction, can be seriously employed only within strict limits, it may go beyond these to deflate or inflate for local satire, where there is no question of the figure deeply engaging the emotions of the audience. Some of the earlier examples are rather extravagant. The domestic Charlotte Lutterell pillories herself in calling her sister's face "White as a Whipt syllabub" (*Volume the Second*, p. 113). And Catherine Morland's romantic conception of herself is consciously exaggerated when Jane Austen dismisses her "heroine to the sleepless couch, which is the true heroine's portion; to a pillow strewed with thorns and wet with tears" (*Northanger Abbey*, p. 90). Later instances are likely to be farther from parody and nearer irony. In the sentence that follows, the figures are somewhat toned down by "seemed" and "almost," though they still accentuate Meryton's foolishness in judging Wickham: "All Meryton seemed striving to blacken the man, who, but three months before, had been almost an angel of light" (*Pride and Prejudice*, p. 294).

The extending of a figure, which obviously calls attention to it, also serves satiric purposes, and the added weight may be mercilessly used. At moments we can catch Jane Austen in the act of increasing the pressure. To preserve the military metaphor that belabors Margaret Watson's unpleasantness, the author substitutes "attacks" for "altercations" in "The Peace of the party for the remainder of that day . . . was continually invaded by her fretful displeasure, & querulous attacks" (*The Watsons*, pp. 115–16). In the novels as well, extended metaphors are a means to condemn. The longest of them—picked up again some forty pages after the sample given below—dramatizes Sir Thomas Bertram's attitude toward Fanny Price, whom he wants to become "sick" of her own home: "It was a medicinal project upon his niece's understanding, which he must consider as at present diseased. A residence . . . in the abode of wealth and plenty had a little disordered her powers of comparing and judging. . . . and he trusted that she would be the wiser and happier woman, all her life, for the experiment he had devised" (*Mansfield Park*, p. 369). The doctor, a judicious but sympathetic healer and professional precisionist, represents perfectly Sir Thomas' image of himself. Yet for us, who know how constantly and drastically he misjudges, every extension of the metaphor carries a new barb.

Whether sustained or not, then, the sharper figures of satire do not tempt us to surrender ourselves to them. It is as if Jane Austen feels that she can trust her audience in situations of this sort not to be fatuously blinded or intimately entangled. When she does design her figures to intensify emotionally, they are usually brief. On Marianne Dashwood's meeting with Willoughby, "the confusion which crimsoned over her face . . . had robbed her of the power of regarding him" (*Sense and Sensibility*, p. 43); Catherine Morland's "judgment was further bought off" (*Northanger Abbey*, p. 50); Fanny Price retreats from the "toils of civility" (*Mansfield Park*, p. 273); or—more startling because it occurs at a climax in the novel—"It darted through her, with the speed of an arrow, that Mr. Knightley must marry no one but herself" (*Emma*, p. 408). But even at these fairly intense moments, and others like them, the figures are so compressed, and so often conventional, that they hold the reader back from a deeply emotional involvement with the characters. And Jane Austen's normal use of figure is even safer, as in this description of Mary Crawford's discontent: "The assurance of Edmund's being so soon to take orders, coming upon her like a blow that had been suspended, and still hoped uncertain and at a distance, was felt with resentment and mortification" (*Mansfield Park*, p. 227). The "blow" itself refers to a condition; its force is dispersed by the account of its suspension, which is so indecisively figurative; and its impact is finally wasted when our attention is immediately shifted to the new conditions that the "blow" produces. We are back in the sphere of secure concepts, where judgments can be made because values are independent of the individual.

The last stylistic trait to be discussed is Jane Austen's rhetoric. The word is a risky one for my purposes because of itself it connotes almost automatically a kind of conscious splendor, and because the term, when mentioned in relation to the later eighteenth century, is all too likely to call up memories of such elaborately articulated structures as Burke's extended periods, Gibbon's massive irony, the emphatic idiom of Dr. Johnson— or even the pomposity of Fanny Burney.[17] But the two rhetorical structures that I want to single out in Jane Austen's prose are much less ostentatious and their effect relatively subdued. Yet I think that the basic tendencies which we have already noticed in her language—toward stability and restraint—are still visible. For a pattern of verbal groupings, however unobtrusive it may be, is by definition an organizing force, and thus dramatizes a basic order. Moreover, a formal arrangement, by selecting certain items for emphasis, marks a heightened tone—but not too heightened, for the very existence of the pattern implies emotional control. In Jane Austen's novels, one recurrent pattern is an essentially two-part structure: it may juxtapose its terms—sometimes for intellectual and moral distinctions, sometimes in the interest of irony—or it may double them for emphasis. The other pattern that she frequently calls on sets its terms in a straighter line, accumulating them for expressive power. In the case of either structure, the formality is indeed a gesture to move the audience, for to shape verbal patterns is both to ask for and to define a response. At the same time, though, the structures impersonalize emotion, temper it, by formulating it in such a way that it can be shared.

Perhaps I can make my sense of this emotive quality clearer

if we look at comparable sections from two of Jane Austen's letters to her brother Frank, each announcing her father's death (*Letters,* I, 144–46). The first excerpt runs:

> At nine this morning he [the family doctor] came again—& by his desire a Physician was called in;—Dr. Gibbs—But it was then absolutely a lost case—. Dr. Gibbs said that nothing but a Miracle could save him, and about twenty minutes after Ten he drew his last gasp.—Heavy as is the blow, we can already feel that a thousand comforts remain to us to soften it. Next to that of the consciousness of his worth & constant preparation for another World, is the remembrance of his having suffered, comparatively speaking, nothing. Being quite insensible of his own state, he was spared all the pain of separation, & he went off almost in his Sleep.

The letter recreates a flow of fact and sensation. The doctors arrive and judge; the death occurs; its effect on others is mentioned; but then the reader is returned to the authentic death. Everything happens in almost unmodulated sentences which contain a series of rather colloquial expressions—"a lost case," "nothing but a Miracle"—that culminates in the sharp "he went off almost in his Sleep." This is the intensity of actuality.

But Jane Austen sent the first letter to the wrong place, so the next day she wrote another. The difference between the two is not just a matter of distance from the event, though that has something to do with it. Rather, where the first presented a situation in all its immediacy, the second represents it rhetorically. This excerpt from the later version aims at creating a scene that will stimulate a perfectly conventional—though deeply felt—response:

> A Physician was called in yesterday morning, but he was at that time past all possibility of cure—& Dr. Gibbs and Mr. Bowen had scarcely left his room before he sunk into a Sleep from which he never woke.—Everything I trust & beleive was done for him that was possible!—It has been very sudden!—within twenty four hours of his death he was walking with only the help of a stick, was even reading!—We had however some hours

of preparation, & when we understood his recovery to be hopeless, most fervently did we pray for the speedy release which ensued. To have seen him languishing long, struggling for Hours, would have been dreadful! & thank God! we were all spared from it. Except the restlessness & confusion of high Fever, he did not suffer—& he was mercifully spared from knowing that he was about to quit the Objects so beloved, so fondly cherished as his wife & Children ever were.—His tenderness as a Father, who can do justice to?—My Mother is tolerably well; she bears up with great fortitude, but I fear her health must suffer under such a shock.

Here most of the sentences are carefully fashioned to arouse tension by their highly dramatic contrasts: the arrival of the new doctor vs. the impossibility of "cure"; the departure of help vs. the coming of death; the activities of life, such as "walking" and "reading," vs. the "sudden" onset of death (new material in this second letter, additionally exciting because it insists on the father's liveliness just before death); the hopelessness of "recovery" vs. the fervency of prayer; the suffering endured vs. the knowledge "mercifully spared." Even the exclamation marks formulate a plea for feeling, as does the narration of what "would have been dreadful" though it did not occur. But in all this shaping of the event, its actuality is idealized. The particular phrasings of the first letter become formulas in the second: "a Sleep from which he never woke," "the speedy release which ensued," and "the Objects so beloved, so fondly cherished as his wife & Children ever were." Indeed this later version gives us not so much the particular event in the Austen household as the proper death of a pious man in a pious family. Symbolic of this propriety are the exclamation "Everything I trust & beleive was done for him that was possible!" and the final rhetorical question, "His tenderness as a Father, who can do justice to?"

We can summarize in this way: the first excerpt is instinctively dramatic because it seems to record the event as personally perceived, while the second formulates both the event and the feeling appropriate to it. Thus the more formally heightened account strikes one as less intense than the first. But to regard this modulation of intensity as an abandonment of feeling on Jane Austen's part would be to misconceive one of her basic verbal methods. For it is only the formalizing of an emotion—the detaching it to some extent from the interested parties and the containing of it within a structure—that can give it an independent existence.

If we turn to Jane Austen's fiction, we find, quite predictably, patterns much more deliberate and detailed. It would be impossible to give examples here of all the local purposes that these patterns serve, so I shall bypass such matters as the many finely shaped parodic fragments in the *Juvenilia* and the mild rhetoric so often used later on simply to order a variety of materials without coloring them strongly. But I must illustrate the two basic structures that I referred to earlier, the one moving from side to side, the other going straight on. Either of them, to repeat, can be suited to any number of effects. My choice of an ironic passage to show the two-part movement and of an emotional passage to show the second pattern is purely arbitrary.

In the description of Sir John and Lady Middleton that follows, the rhetoric develops its pressure by distinguishing between two equally ridiculous extremes and balancing them against each other. Perhaps the main contours of the passage will stand out if it is typographically rearranged and only its major antithetic elements italicized, though this does no justice to the minor patterns of antithesis and parallelism that echo the main design:

The *house* was large and handsome;	and the Middletons lived in a *style* of equal hospitality and elegance.
The *former* was for Sir John's gratification,	the *latter* for that of his lady.
They were scarcely ever without *some friends* staying with them in the house,	and they kept *more company of every kind* than any other family in the neighbourhood.

❋❋❋❋❋❋❋❋❋❋❋❋❋❋❋❋❋❋❋❋❋❋❋❋❋❋❋❋❋❋❋❋

It was necessary to the happiness of both; for however dissimilar in temper and outward behaviour, they strongly resembled each other in that total want of talent and taste which confined their employments, unconnected with such as society produced, within a very narrow compass.

Sir John was a sportsman,	*Lady Middleton* a mother.
He hunted and shot,	and *she* humoured her children;

and these were their only resources.

Lady Middleton had the advantage of being able to spoil her children all the year round,	while *Sir John's* independent employments were in existence only half the time.

Continual engagements at home and abroad, however, supplied all the deficiencies of nature and education;

supported the good spirits of *Sir John,*	and gave exercise to the good-breeding of *his wife.*

(*Sense and Sensibility,* p. 32)

The rhetoric both organizes and energizes an adverse judgment of the Middletons. The structural oppositions define extremes which the pattern periodically unites for more explicit attacks. The closing sentence recapitulates the structure and the sense, distinguishing Sir John from his wife but confirming the foolishness of both.

Jane Austen's rhetoric moves in a straighter line when she represents Catherine Morland's anguish at being dismissed from Northanger Abbey, especially in those emotional series, indicated by italics, that characterize the middle section of the passage:

> Catherine's swelling heart needed relief. In Eleanor's presence friendship and pride had equally restrained her tears, but no sooner was she gone than they burst forth in torrents. Turned from the house, and in such a way! —Without any reason that could justify, any apology that could atone for the *abruptness,* the *rudeness,* nay, the *insolence* of it. Henry at a distance—not able even to bid him farewell. *Every* hope, *every* expectation from him suspended, at least, and *who* could say how long?— *Who* could say when they might meet again?—And all this by such a man as General Tilney, *so* polite, *so* well-bred, and heretofore *so* particularly fond of her! It was as incomprehensible as it was mortifying and grievous. From what it could arise, and where it would end, were considerations of equal perplexity and alarm. (*Northanger Abbey,* p. 226)

The climactic series are not the only traditional device used here for dramatizing excitement. The incomplete sentences, variation in sentence length, exclamation marks, and rhetorical questions all accumulate to express powerful feeling in the body of the selection. But this passage has a quite different facet that also deserves attention: the doubled units with which Jane Austen opens and closes it. The first pairs—"friendship" and "pride," "any reason . . ." and "any apology . . ."—mark as it were the initial restraint that is released in the series of the middle section. And the final pairs dam up the flow of emotion in the reservoirs of reason and condition so carefully articulated by "incomprehensible" vs. "mortifying and grievous," "From what . . ." vs. "where . . . ," and "perplexity" vs. "alarm." By the end of the passage, emotion has been safely consolidated in "considerations," and the rhetoric has controlled even while it has heightened.

This containing of emotion, as I earlier suggested, is the recurrent effect of Jane Austen's rhetoric. Whatever the pattern she chooses and whatever its inherent power, she employs it to define, and thus evoke, a decorous public response.

❊❊❊❊❊❊❊❊❊❊❊❊❊❊❊❊❊❊❊❊❊❊❊❊❊❊❊❊❊❊

❧[III]❧

All Jane Austen's linguistic habits, I have been maintaining, dramatize attitudes that are presumed to have automatic public appeal. Her style, that is, constructs a version of reality. And it is her own stylistic practices that establish the possibilities of meaning for the verbal gestures of her characters, their gestures revealing, in turn, how these persons resist or adjust to the reality projected by Jane Austen's style. The clues to their behavior lie in the deeds of their language, even when the verbal surface is unruffled, or hardly ruffled. In thus suggesting that we come at the characters through their styles, let me add, I am not implying that these persons can be considered as absolutely real (although for the sake of simple expression, I shall often refer to them as if they were living). Plainly the characters in a novel retain only a virtual life. Yet as parts of the writer's total dramatic enterprise, as embodiments of what he wants to communicate, these figures must show their innermost qualities to us. In the case of a character, then, we are peculiarly justified in interpreting the style as the man.

Throughout Jane Austen's novels, indeed, it is especially necessary for us to examine how the characters speak, because what we learn about them otherwise is commonly filtered through the mind of a heroine who has biases of her own. If we would see them truly, we must look at the dialogue, for that is where the characters define themselves. They may do so by various verbal traits, which acquire their significance, as I have already said, through the values implicit in Jane Austen's own style. Perhaps the usual diction of a character gives him away. Does he simply recite concrete facts? or does he intensify what he refers to with particular terms that dramatize his own excitement? or does he use conceptual terms—and reliably or unreliably? Maybe the key to a character lies in his figurative language. Does he tend to avoid it, conceivably distrusting its fictitiousness and intensity? or does his too violent commitment to figures prove that he is emotionally obsessed? or does his control of metaphor suggest that he is emotionally disengaged? Often a character's speech rhythms are indicative. Does he chatter breathlessly? or is he easily agitated? When does he use rhetoric, and what kind of rhetoric is it? Even more significant are the character's habits in generalizing. Does he generalize inductively or deductively, and in either case properly or improperly? What kind of norms do his generalizations betray, the wisdom of common experience or the merely personal disguised as the universal? These are some of the major means by which dialogue may represent behavior itself. Then there is a further technique that appears periodically in Jane Austen's novels: she will set up a trivial enough social situation, yet allow her characters to talk of it in such a way that it becomes a kind of metaphor dramatizing much vaster areas of human experience, though the literalness of the situation preserves decorum. By analyzing practices like these in the following chapters, I shall try to suggest that the novels present characters more intensively human and explore a greater range of experience than the limitationists, put off by the decorous tone, have admitted.

All this is not to say that Jane Austen consciously plotted out her characters' verbal habits and then meticulously patterned them in dialogue, nor that her characters can be reduced to a few traits verbally expressed—impressions which I fear the following analyses may give. But it is to say that in her own style Jane Austen's habits are so significant and so precisely sustained as to create a context in which minute stylistic variations on the part of her characters are charged with import. Because such slight variations are expressive, she can maintain a tone of propriety; indeed decorum is the condition of communication in this society, what makes society possible and meaningful. Yet the conversations will show us that language dramatizes the terms on which the individual participates in society—and that those terms may be anything but decorous. Profoundly human motives, in short, are revealed in the dialogue, which makes up the very real action in these novels that notoriously lack incident.

✻✻✻✻✻✻✻✻✻✻✻✻✻✻✻✻✻✻✻✻✻✻✻✻✻✻✻✻✻✻✻✻✻✻

1. *Jane Austen's Letters,* ed. R. W. Chapman (Oxford, 1932), II, 469, 401. (Cited hereafter as *Letters.*)

2. *The Brontës: Life and Letters,* ed. Clement Shorter (London, 1908), II, 127–28.

3. James E. Austen-Leigh, *A Memoir of Jane Austen,* ed. R. W. Chapman (Oxford, 1926), p. 1.

4. "Jane Austen: A Depreciation," *Essays by Divers Hands,* ed. Lawrence Binyon (London, 1928), VIII, 31.

5. *Jane Austen and Her Art* (Oxford, 1939), pp. 123, 197. (Cited hereafter as *Jane Austen.*)

6. "Jane Austen, *ob.* July 18, 1817," *The Quarterly Review,* CCXXVIII (1917), 6. (Cited hereafter as "Jane Austen.")

7. *The History of the English Novel* (London, 1935), VI, 71. (Cited hereafter as *History.*)

8. *Jane Austen: Irony as Defense and Discovery* (Princeton, N. J., 1952), *passim.* (Cited hereafter as *Jane Austen.*) See also D. W. Harding, "Regulated Hatred: An Aspect of the Work of Jane Austen," *Scrutiny,* VIII (1940), 346–62. Mudrick's view, I should add immediately, seems to me to falsify the plot of every novel, which shows its major characters discovering freedom, not in the anarchy of self-will, but in willingly adjusting to and living through the conventions of their society.

9. "Manners, Morals, and the Novel," *The Liberal Imagination* (New York, 1950), pp. 206, 211–12.

10. *Jane Austen,* p. 107. Two other critics discuss Jane Austen's materialistic language as expressive of her historical environment: Mark Schorer, "Fiction and the 'Matrix of Analogy,'" *The Kenyon Review,* XI (1949), 539–60; Dorothy Van Ghent, *The English Novel: Form and Function* (New York, 1953), pp. 99–111. (Hereafter I refer to Schorer's article by its full title and to the book by Dorothy Van Ghent as *The English Novel.*)

11. I take my quotations of Jane Austen's fiction from, and give page references to, R. W. Chapman's third edition of *The Novels of Jane Austen* (5 vols.; Oxford, 1933) and the sixth volume he edited comprising her *Minor Works* (London, 1954)—with the exceptions noted in my first two chapters, where at times I use Chapman's separate editions of *The Watsons* (Oxford, 1927) and of the *Fragment of a Novel* (Oxford, 1925).

12. Oblique evidence for the vitality of conceptual terms during the eighteenth century itself is perhaps provided by the age's notorious readiness to personify them, to endow them verbally with life. Earl R. Wasserman has explored this habit fully—in "The Inherent Values of Eighteenth-Century Personification," *PMLA,* LXV (1950), 435–63—and he is underlining the particularization implicit in the mode when he says: "Indeed, the eighteenth century recognized the personified abstraction, not as a device for abstracting and universalizing, but as a means of clothing the universal in imagery effective to the senses, of transferring the abstraction from the intellect to the imagination"

(pp. 456–57). The sentence also makes clear, of course, that the things animated by personification were universals, abstractions; and it is the latent life of such terms when they appear in Jane Austen's style—as distinct from their actual personification—that I want to emphasize.

13. William K. Wimsatt has said of Dr. Johnson's style that "if he is interested in generality, in the classes to which things belong, the aspects which unify groups of objects, he becomes at moments even more interested in these aspects as things in themselves, as metaphysical realities. Allowing the physical objects to be pressed out of sight, he erects the metaphysicalities or abstractions into the substantives of his discourse" (*The Prose Style of Samuel Johnson* [New Haven, 1941], pp. 55–56). The universe of Johnson's "discourse" which these sentences define seems to me analogous to the universe which I am claiming that Jane Austen's style creates, one structured by fixed qualities. In the local matter of the genitive construction, Wimsatt finds Johnson favoring a type of *"appositional* genitive in which one noun is abstract, or both"; and the critic traces the duplications of sense in a phrase like "excitements of fear, and allurements of desire": "The notion 'fear' (itself perhaps abstract) has the quality of exciting pulled out of it and formed into a second abstraction; so 'allurements' is pulled out of 'desire'; and the pairs of abstractions float in unstable expansion, each ready to collapse into one" (p. 57). My guess would be that this sort of appositional genitive does not turn up frequently in Jane Austen's writing. At any rate, the genitives I cite in my text—such as "graces of manner"—function rather to subdivide Jane Austen's universe in the way that I go on to describe.

14. R. W. Chapman prepared separate editions of all Jane Austen's minor works except *Volume the Second,* including within them canceled phrasings and sentences. Many of these original versions he omitted, however, in his collected edition of the *Minor Works.* Thus whenever, in this and in the next chapter, I cite a revision, the page references will be to his separate edition of *The Watsons* (Oxford, 1927) or of the *Fragment of a Novel* (Oxford, 1925), commonly called *Sanditon.*

15. The same sort of claim about the attitude of the eighteenth century itself toward the particular has been voiced by Bertrand H. Bronson in his eloquent essay "Personification Reconsidered," *ELH: A Journal of English Literary History,* XIV (1947), 163–77. Speaking of the age's poets, Bronson observes: "They were neither humanly incurious of, nor emotionally insensitive to, particulars, as almost any page of Boswell will prove; but personal statements gained force, conviction, vaster horizons, when lifted to the plateau of the general consensus" (p. 165).

16. *The Works of John Dryden,* ed. Sir Walter Scott (Edinburgh, 1821), X, 32.

17. The prose of Fanny Burney is worth a glance here because of the various links between her work and Jane Austen's. She was one of Jane Austen's immediate predecessors, of course, as a woman novelist writing stories about courtship which concern themselves to some extent with manners; and her novels were evidently read and reread by Jane Austen. In the matter of style, Fanny Burney is generally conceded to derive

from Dr. Johnson. And there is a Johnsonian ring to many passages of even her first book, before her manner further stiffened. In the following excerpt, I think we can hear the tones of her master most clearly in the nearly equal articulation of both members in a parallel or antithetic structure, this even weighting of the parts making the structure especially emphatic, while the recurrent equalizing leaves us with the impression of a highly patterned prose: "In all ranks and all stations of life, how strangely do characters and manners differ! Lord Orville, with a politeness which knows no intermission, and makes no distinction, is as unassuming and modest, as if he had never mixed with the great, and was totally ignorant of every qualification he possesses; this other Lord, though lavish of compliments and fine speeches, seems to me an entire stranger to real good-breeding; whoever strikes his fancy, engrosses his whole attention. He is forward and bold, has an air of haughtiness towards men, and a look of libertinism towards women, and his conscious quality seems to have given him a freedom in his way of speaking to either sex, that is very little short of rudeness" (*Evelina* [Everyman's Library ed.; New York, 1951], p. 106).

Certainly the basic organization here is firm enough: the contrast between Lord Orville and "this other Lord," between the real "politeness" expressed through an "unassuming" manner in the one, and the essential "rudeness" exhibited in the presuming manner of the other. But some of the minor structures are less convincing. The careful parallelism in "all ranks and all stations" would appear to imply that the second member should somehow significantly advance the meaning of the first; yet in this context "stations" actually tells us no more than "ranks," and indeed the repeated "all" comes to seem excessive when both the examples we arrive at are lords. One wonders, too, how much "modest" adds to "unassuming," or "bold" to "forward"—or even whether "makes no distinction" in fact conveys much more than "knows no intermission," since a continuing "politeness" can hardly be thought to lapse in any way. The effect of these less than satisfying minor structures is to make the prose feel inflated, as if Fanny Burney were writing with her ear on the pattern of sound rather than with her mind strictly on the sense. While Dr. Johnson's prose is likely to be at least as carefully shaped, his structures commonly rest on much surer logical foundations. And the effect of verbal flabbiness is as alien to Jane Austen's style as to Dr. Johnson's, though of course her prose is not so consistently patterned, her constructions not so equally weighted in their parts, as his or Fanny Burney's. What Jane Austen herself may owe to the style of Dr. Johnson—the prose moralist she liked best, according to her brother—is hard to tie down. The particular indebtedness mentioned by Mary Lascelles is to Johnson's "coining" of "pregnant abstractions," a practice echoed in such a phrase as the "desultory good-will" ascribed to Miss Bates (*Jane Austen*, p. 109). But, as Mary Lascelles also suggests, the similarities between Jane Austen's style and Dr. Johnson's are very general; so much so, I think, that we are justified in viewing Johnson rather as a part of the eighteenth century's legacy to Jane Austen than as a more specific stylistic model.

2 The Juvenilia and Fragments

Toward Sustained Dialogue

Before we go on to inspect Jane Austen's novels in separate chapters, it may be worthwhile to glance here at a smattering of dialogues from three of the fragments: "Catharine or the Bower," found in the *Juvenilia; The Watsons,* a later piece; and *Sanditon,* the story Jane Austen was writing at the time of her death. Whatever the risk in thus grouping together fictions from different creative periods, there are certain clear advantages. For one thing, the unfinished works exhibit some of the conversational devices I have mentioned in their starkest and least complex form. Also, the persistence of the devices over a span of time should suggest that they are basic to Jane Austen's technique.

The *Juvenilia,* of course, are rather barren hunting grounds for the controlled brilliance of Jane Austen's mature conversational effects. One reason is that she casts many of these pieces in an epistolary form, the narrative convention so familiar to her from eighteenth-century fiction, and this form clearly does not encourage dialogue. More important, the prevailing mode of the *Juvenilia* is burlesque, Jane Austen taking off on practically every feature of the sentimental novel so popular at the time, from its cult of sensibility to its narrative techniques. And for purposes of burlesque, speech itself need only contradict, or grossly exaggerate, or otherwise strongly underline an extreme: "Alas! (exclaimed I) how am I to avoid those evils I shall never be exposed to? What probability is there of my ever tasting the Dissipations of London, the Luxuries of Bath, or the stinking Fish of Southampton? I who am doomed to waste my Days of Youth and Beauty in an humble Cottage in the Vale of Uske" (*Volume the Second,* p. 79). For the most part, what flourishes in the dialogues of the *Juvenilia* is excess of every sort, which is plainly Jane Austen's target.

But a few of the *Juvenilia*, notably "Catharine or the Bower," do contain conversations that seem nearer in tone to the finished novels. The fragment tells of a naïve and pleasant young girl who lives in the country with a watchful aunt; fashionable city relatives visit them, the son of the family soon arriving unexpectedly and undertaking a courtship of Kitty. So far as it goes— and in this the story anticipates *Northanger Abbey*'s juxtaposing of the young Thorpes and Catherine Morland—"Catharine or the Bower" depends upon contrasting the modish Miss Stanley and her brother with the essentially sensible Kitty. To some extent the verbal habits of the characters realize this distinction.

Camilla Stanley, for example, on learning that the neighbors she has readily abused are going to give a ball, shows her demanding giddiness in brief declarative rhythms that treat anything concerning herself with equal intensity:

> ". . . —We are all the happiest Creatures in the World . . . . What Charming People they are! I had no idea of there being so much sense in the whole Family—I declare I quite doat upon them—. And it happens so fortunately too, for I expect a new Cap from Town tomorrow which will just do for a Ball—Gold Net—It will be a most angelic thing—Every Body will be longing for the pattern—" . . . . (*Volume the Third*, p. 207)

Clearly, she conceives of every private emotion or idea as an absolute, so she utters her personal whims here as public generalizations. Her tendency to generalize indiscriminately is at moments counterpointed to Kitty's genial sense: when Camilla gushes, ". . . I am always in love with every handsome Man in the World," Kitty replies with "There you outdo me . . . for I am only in love with those I *do* see" (p. 223). Their dialogues also reveal Camilla resorting, under emotional pressure, to vehemently particular diction: "Well, I declare it is quite a pity that they should be suffered to live. I wish my Father would propose knocking all their Brains out" (p. 204). Kitty, on the contrary, evaluates with reliable concepts when she is displeased with Camilla for not recognizing the plight of an indigent friend dispatched to India to get a husband:

> "But do you call it lucky, for a Girl of Genius & Feeling to be sent in quest of a Husband to Bengal, to be married there to a Man of whose Disposition she has no opportunity of judging till her Judgement is of no use to her, who may be a Tyrant, or a Fool or both for what she knows to the Contrary." (p. 205)

As this conversation continues, Kitty further differentiates herself from Camilla by distinguishing between the real and the apparent—the abiding theme in Jane Austen's writings. When the thrilling appearances of such a "quest" incite Camilla to say, "I declare I should think it very good fun if I were as poor," Kitty retorts with the truth: "I beleive you would think very differently *then*" (p. 205). But conversational effects of this sort, though they often pointedly contrast Kitty with Camilla, are not really sustained throughout the story.

Another kind of irresolution somewhat undermines Jane Austen's effort at representing Edward Stanley in dialogue. She intends him, we finally make out, to be as foolish as his sister, but frequently his speech contradicts this. When Edward first appears, finding everyone except Kitty gone to the ball, he introduces himself in a scene that develops a real sense of controlled give and take within a standard social situation (p. 216). Perhaps his detachment in the following is a trifle overdone:

> "You do me too much honour Ma'am, replied he laughing, in supposing me to be acquainted with M^r & Mrs Stanley; I merely know them by sight; very distant relations; only my Father & Mother. Nothing more I assure you."
> "Gracious Heaven!" said Kitty, are *you* Mr Stanley then?—I beg a thousand pardons—Though really upon recollection I do not know for what—for you never told me your name—"

Edward need not have strained the joke by "very distant relations." But, when Kitty instinctively retreats from the emotional "Gracious Heaven!" to the safety of "recollection" and then

✳✳✳✳✳✳✳✳✳✳✳✳✳✳✳✳✳✳✳✳✳✳✳✳✳✳✳✳✳✳✳✳✳✳✳✳✳

transforms her initial surprise into the attack of "you never told me your name," he modulates his reply as delicately:

> "I beg your pardon—I made a very fine speech when you entered the room, all about introducing myself; I assure you it was very great for *me*."
> "The speech had certainly great Merit, said Kitty smiling; I thought so at the time; but since you never mentioned your name in it, as an *introductory one* it might have been better."

Edward's social sense is absolutely sure when he stands apart from his speech to pass ironic judgment on it, the stance permitting him to belittle himself appropriately. This is precisely the controlled tone which, without giving himself away, may invite Kitty to pay a compliment. And she as carefully attends to the "speech" rather than the personality, for it allows her to praise him indirectly, by "great Merit," yet without betraying a socially indecorous or personally excessive emotion. Both of them observe the rules of such an encounter beautifully. So far so good.

But apparently we must believe that the man who can make so strong a showing on one page will, two pages later, utterly give himself away as a ridiculous fop by saying, after taking "above half an hour" to make minor preparations in his dress for the ball, "Well . . . have not I been very quick? I never hurried so much in my Life before." There is no trace of irony here. And he is as completely enveloped in himself when he goes on to tell Kitty that it "will be a most agreable surprize to everybody to see you enter the room with such a smart Young Fellow as I am" (p. 218). Yet a moment later Edward is once more in witty control, though Kitty's conventionality leads her to protest against his plan. He has proposed that they compound the offense of traveling to the ball without chaperon by making an unannounced entrance:

> "Do not you think your Aunt will be as much offended with you for one, as for the other of these mighty crimes."
> "Why really said Catherine [*sic*], I do not know but that she

may; however, it is no reason that I should offend against Decorum a second time, because I have already done it once."

"On the contrary, that is the very reason which makes it impossible for you to prevent it, since you cannot offend for the *first time* again."

"You are very ridiculous, said she laughing, but I am afraid your arguments divert me too much to convince me." (p. 219)

The play with "reason" here and the occasionally sinuous movement of the conversations look forward to the later novels. But on the whole, the dialogue of "Catharine or the Bower" remains marked by the abrupt exaggerations and the minor inconsistencies in representing character that are usual in the *Juvenilia*. The flashes of Jane Austen's mature rhythms are too intermittent to dramatize a really consistent body of attitudes.

◄[II]►

It might be possible, though very risky, to apply the same sort of verbal analysis to the epistolary *Lady Susan*. Perhaps one could discern the central conflict between Lady Susan and society in the difference between her verbal habits and Mrs. Vernon's: on the one hand, a willful misuse of conceptual terms and of the standards they embody; on the other, a proper use of such words and an allegiance to public norms, both of which enable Mrs. Vernon to see through Lady Susan. But letters are not dialogue, and they can hardly be treated as such. Moreover, the epistolary convention is one that Jane Austen abandons in her major novels (an early version of *Sense and Sensibility* was a novel in letters)—abandons in part, I suspect, because the convention traditionally required that the characters spell out their motives quite clearly from time to time. And throughout Jane Austen's mature works, as we know, she prefers a convention in which most of the characters are seen from the outside and may speak equivocally, a convention which locates dialogue in a social setting. So it would be better for our purposes to turn to *The Watsons,* a work written after she had discarded the epistolary genre and one in which we have a fairly sustained attempt to dramatize characters and issues by conversation alone.

This fragment concerns the difficulties of the Watson sisters, hampered by the lack of money, in attracting serious suitors. Emma Watson, after living for fourteen years in comparative luxury and refinement with her aunt, is forced, by her aunt's second marriage, to return to her own home. Emma finds her eldest sister, Elizabeth, caring for their invalid father; her brother proudly married to a woman with £6,000; another sister, Margaret, away on a visit to her brother in hopes that Tom Musgrave will miss her; and a third sister on another visit in pursuit of an elderly man. The prime catch in the neighborhood is Tom Musgrave, on whom all the sisters, except Emma, have designs, but he is more interested in tending on Lord Osborne and the ladies at Osborne Castle. All the characters whom we hear either busily define a private, and therefore false, decorum or otherwise deviate from valid norms; thus the fragment seems constantly to shift its grounds, arbitrarily mooring its standards of behavior first in one character and then in another.

The first pages, for example, use the almost vulgar yet naturally agreeable Elizabeth to point up Emma's over-refinement. Elizabeth may expose a commonplace mind in her talk, which often runs on monotonously from fact to fact:

> "But first of all Nanny shall bring in the dinner. Poor thing!— You will not dine as you did yesterday, for we have nothing but some fried beef.—How nice Mary Edwards looks in her new pelisse!—And now tell me how you like them all, & what I am to say to Sam." (p. 341)

But she is fundamentally in touch with reality, and her plain speech is quite deliberately contrasted with Emma's rather blind commitment to delicacy of feeling. Emma will protest against another sister's conduct:

> "—To be so bent on Marriage—to pursue a Man merely for the sake of situation—is a sort of thing that shocks me; I cannot un-

derstand it. Poverty is a great Evil, but to a woman of Education & feeling it ought not, it cannot be the greatest.—I would rather be Teacher at a school (and I can think of nothing worse) than marry a Man I did not like." (p. 318)

But Elizabeth takes the measure of Emma's opinion in replying,

"I would rather do any thing than be Teacher at a school . . . . I have been at school, Emma, & know what a Life they lead; *you* never have.—I should not like marrying a disagreable Man any more than yourself,—but I do not think there *are* many very disagreable Men;—I think I could like any good humoured Man with a comfortable Income." (p. 318)

The mildly ironic touches near the close here should not obscure Elizabeth's almost compassionate sense of actuality. It crops up again and again, as in her praise of Emma for refusing a drive with Tom Musgrave—and in her clear-sighted judgment of herself: "You did very right; tho' I wonder at your forbearance, & I do not think I could have done it myself" (p. 341). Indeed Jane Austen explicitly weighs Emma against Elizabeth in describing their reactions to an unexpected call by Lord Osborne: Emma, thrown into a flutter of excessive propriety, "felt all the inconsistency of such an acquaintance with the very humble stile in which they were obliged to live," whereas "—Of the pain of such feelings, Eliz: knew very little;—her simpler Mind, or juster reason saved her from such mortification—& tho' shrinking under a general sense of Inferiority, she felt no particular Shame" (p. 345).

Yet the somewhat precious Emma, without apparently undergoing any change in the fragment, becomes our standard for gauging the deviations of the other characters from a true decorum. She is a means to set off the nearly vacuous elegance of the Edwards family, or, more strikingly, to light up the moneyed vulgarity of her brother and his wife. Mrs. Robert Watson continually hints at a decorum founded on £6,000, whether she tells of being "as particular as ever" in always having her little girl "properly attended to" by a private maid (p. 350), or accepts the limited accommodations in the Watson home: "I hope I can put up with a small apartment for two or three nights, without making a peice of work. I always wish to be treated quite 'en famille' when I come to see you" (p. 351). Her patronage insists that she is superior to the Watsons. Of course, her contrived superiority cracks at the slightest provocation because it does not conventionalize significant emotion, so she is heard snapping at Margaret, "You are a sad shabby girl.—I have been quarrelling with you all the way we came" (p. 350). Robert Watson's language shows him to be as naturally irascible and quite as concerned with money. Of the aunt's second marriage, which has thrown Emma back on the care of her own family, he snarls, "I hope the old woman will smart for it" (p. 352). His anger and devotion to money combine to produce so emotional a generalization as "A woman should never be trusted with money" (p. 351), or one even more self-interested, about the aunt keeping Emma "at a distance from your family for such a length of time as must do away all natural affection among us" (p. 352), a generalization that justifies Robert's utter lack of feeling for Emma. To this couple's egotism posing as rationality, Emma opposes her unselfish loyalty to her aunt: "Do not speak disrespectfully of her—She was very good to me; & if she has made an imprudent choice, she will suffer more from it herself, than I can possibly do" (p. 352). Her judgment, if it is a judgment, is carefully formalized: it tolerates no interference by the impertinent and it minimizes her private emotion.

In similar fashion Emma, though she hardly addresses Tom Musgrave, at least provides the major occasions that provoke his indecorousness, and she later serves as a foil to bring out Lord Osborne's impropriety. The socially artful Tom, who plays Master of the Revels to Lord Osborne, is the most intriguing character in the fragment for anyone analyzing dialogue. The problem—solved more delicately in Jane Austen's later management of Frank Churchill—is this: How can the clever fop's speech dramatize his cleverness and foppishness at the same time? Here she undertakes a solution by allowing Tom to manipulate a conventional decorum for his own purposes in the conversations. But, as if not yet quite certain of her dramatic control, Jane

Austen immediately insures our disapproval by letting Emma overhear Tom when he agrees to lay the groundwork for the taciturn Lord Osborne's introduction to her: "Very well my Lord—. If she is like her Sisters, she will only want to be listened to" (p. 333).[1]

Only after we have been thus alerted, apparently, can we be trusted with Tom speaking to Emma (pp. 334–35). She has earlier danced with a little boy, Charles Blake, to make up for Miss Osborne's incivility in breaking her promise to be his partner. Emma's act gives Tom his opening after she has refused his own invitation to dance:

> "My little friend Charles Blake, he cried, must not expect to engross you the whole evening. We can never suffer this—It is against the rules of the Assembly—& I am sure it will never be patronised by our good friend here Mrs E.; She is by much too nice a judge of Decorum to give her license to such a dangerous Particularity."

Note how quickly in his joking tone Tom erects a code of behavior out of "rules," "Decorum," and "Particularity." But he does not do so because he considers these to be stable social values in whose interest he acts. On the contrary, he cites them only to establish his distance above the boy and Emma; his very creation of the code mocks Emma's generous deed as singular. Having proven his social superiority by this trick, Tom seems for just a moment on the verge of exploring Emma herself when he goes on to inquire for her sisters: "How comes it, that we have not the pleasure of seeing your Sisters here this Evening? —Our Assemblies have been used to be so well treated by them, that we do not know how to take this neglect." The impersonality of "your Sisters" and "Our Assemblies" could be read as accepted social practice, leading up to the more emotional, perhaps more personal, tone implicit in "neglect." But no; Tom's interest is really confined to himself, as is plain when he hears with feigned surprise that two sisters have long been absent from home: "But I am afraid I have been a very sad neighbour of late. I hear dreadful complaints of my negligence wherever

✻✻✻✻✻✻✻✻✻✻✻✻✻✻✻✻✻✻✻✻✻✻✻✻✻✻✻✻✻✻✻✻✻✻

I go, & I confess it is a shameful length of time since I was at Stanton." It might seem at first glance as if Tom disparages his departure from the conventional by such emotive terms as "sad," "dreadful," and "shameful," but of course he actually intends them to elevate him above convention. In this initial meeting with Emma, Tom demonstrates his power first by formulating convention and then by insisting that it does not apply to himself. Here and throughout the fragment he bends every effort to convincing others that he belongs to the fashionable world of Lord Osborne.

Tom has one other resource, figurative language, for exhibiting his stylishness, and we should notice quickly how it works before passing on to Lord Osborne himself. On the day after the ball, Tom turns up to offer Emma a ride back to Stanton, bringing her a message from Elizabeth that the Watson carriage is delayed:

> "I received that note from the fair hands of Miss Watson only ten minutes ago . . . I met her in the village of Stanton, whither my good Stars prompted me to turn my Horses heads—she was at that moment in quest of a person to employ on the Errand, & I was fortunate enough to convince her that she could not find a more willing or speedy Messenger than myself—. Remember, I say nothing of my Disinterestedness." (pp. 338–39)

Tom's chivalric figure consciously exaggerates, as he proves by deliberately fracturing it in the last clause to stress its weight, to make a parade of his simulated feeling. The impression he wants to create is not of sincere emotion but of his verve in formulating so pretentious a figure. His access to the terms and his control of them display his superiority again.

Unlike Tom Musgrave, Lord Osborne has no need to manufacture little verbal structures that lay claim to rank, for he is a noble by birth. His fashionable heritage expresses itself to some extent in the indecorously particular comments which, given his rank, he can afford. Yet the most interesting thing about Lord Osborne is how quickly Jane Austen has changed him under Emma's pressure. The first time we hear him at any length is with Emma, near the end of the fragment, when he and Tom pay an unprecedented visit to the Watsons (pp. 345–47). Lord Osborne starts out ungraciously enough when he finds that bad weather has kept Emma from a morning walk:

"You should wear half-boots." . . . "Nothing sets off a neat ankle more than a half-boot; nankin galoshed with black looks very well.—Do not you like Half-boots? [Emma answers,] "Yes—but unless they are so stout as to injure their beauty, they are not fit for Country walking."—"Ladies should ride in dirty weather. . . . I wonder every Lady does not.—A woman never looks better than on horseback.—" "But every woman may not have the inclination, or the means." "If they knew how much it became them, they would all have the inclination, & I fancy Miss Watson—when once they had the inclination, the means w^d soon follow."

His disrespectfully specific talk of ankles, his generalizations that concern themselves only with appearances—both of these avow Lord Osborne's unwarranted sense of superiority. And they are refuted by Emma's grasp of reality—first in her distinction between the beauty and utility of "half-boots," then in her rational generalization that politely but positively differentiates between "inclination" and "means." Originally the conversation continued with Lord Osborne becoming more and more affronting, till Emma cuts him off with a "cold monosyllable & grave look"; then Lord Osborne "had too much sence, not to take the hint— & when he spoke again, it was with a degree of courteous propriety which he was not often at the trouble of employing." [2] But Jane Austen changes all this, adding on a separate sheet the following material in order to continue the talk with Emma's firm rebuttal and a rather different insight into Lord Osborne:

". . . there are some circumstances which even *Women* cannot controul.—Female Economy will do a great deal my Lord, but it cannot turn a small income into a large one." . . . Her manner . . . made his Lordship think;—and when he addressed her again, it was with a degree of considerate propriety, totally unlike the half-awkward, half-fearless stile of his former remarks.—It was a new thing with him to wish to please a woman; it was the first time that he had ever felt what was due to a woman, in Emma's situation.—But as he wanted neither Sense nor a good disposition, he did not feel it without effect. (pp. 79–80)

Now there is a sharp change of heart on the part of Lord Osborne, which Jane Austen intervenes firmly to detail.

And a few pages later she revises a speech of his to Emma—the original phrasings are in brackets following the clauses that were substituted for them—to convert it into the most decorous of invitations:

"My Hounds will [I shall] be hunting this Country next week —I beleive they will throw off at Stanton Wood on Wednesday at 9 o'clock. I mention this, in hopes of y^r being [I hope you will be] drawn out to see what's going on.—If the morning's tolerable, pray do us the honour of giving us your good wishes in person [do not be kept at home]." (p. 82)

Without exception, the revisions replace the dominantly personal tone of Lord Osborne's earlier remarks with that calculated impersonality which characterizes intercourse between equals. His observance of propriety is almost fierce. So pointed a transformation of Lord Osborne may lead us to wonder, incidentally, whether we can be positive that the fragment would have continued as the Austen family predicted, with Emma ultimately refusing him for Mr. Howard, clergyman to the parish including Osborne Castle.

But however *The Watsons* might have proceeded, the fragment itself has one last dialogue that we should observe because it shows Jane Austen struggling with a technique which she uses more frequently and with greater finesse in the later novels. I mean her method of letting the characters treat an actual situation as a kind of sustained metaphor in their conversation, thus speaking with socially appropriate indirection while in fact revealing strong personal emotion. How demanding the method is we can see in the scene that follows between Margaret Watson and Tom Musgrave, where Jane Austen revises to heighten the metaphoric effect (the original phrases are printed in brackets), forcing Margaret to plead her case by indirection for a time, though the structure finally cracks.

Margaret has just returned to Stanton from a month's visit with her brother, ostensibly coming to greet Emma, really because she is much taken with Tom. Through most of their dialogue (pp. 105–7), she pretends to talk of Emma, though basically she is exploring her own relation with Tom. He has appeared at the home of the Watsons bent on viewing Emma, not even knowing that Margaret is back; but of course, he recognizes immediately what she is up to and gives her small satisfaction. Tom begins the dialogue by professing great surprise that Margaret has been so long absent, carefully detaching himself from her and attaching himself to the fashionable world by such modishly emotional generalizations as "All hours are alike to me" and " 'tis amazing how Time flies."

> "You may imagine, said Marg^t in a sort of Whisper, what are my Sensations [how great my enjoyment] in finding myself once more at Stanton. You know what a sad visitor I make.—And I was so excessively impatient to see Emma;—I dreaded the meeting, & at the same time longed for it.—Do you not comprehend the sort of feeling?"—"Not at all, cried he aloud. I could never dread a meeting with Miss Emma Watson,—or any of her Sisters." It was lucky that he added that finish.

It is clear that Margaret is really talking about her emotion for Tom, with Emma a convenient surrogate. The first revision intentionally subdues Margaret, substituting a lover's ambiguity, by which she hopes to arouse Tom, for the outright declaration of pleasure. Yet to find herself at Stanton is to be near Tom, and she guardedly begs him to admit what she implies that she has felt: sadness, impatience, dread, longing. Tom understands perfectly well what she wants, so he refuses, seizing the occasion to emphasize a particular interest in Emma. The "any of her Sisters" is a kind of controlled afterthought, designed actually to pacify Emma, who overhears her name, rather than Margaret.

Jane Austen has deleted Margaret's "Oh! you Creature!" after the word "finish," for this expression of emotion would again be too pointed. And Margaret goes on to probe Tom's feeling for her metaphorically by compelling him to appraise Emma's "complexion":

> "—Did you ever see anything more perfectly beautiful?—I think even *you* must be a convert to a brown complexion."—He hesitated; Margaret was fair herself, & he did not particularly want to compliment her; but Miss Osborne & Miss Carr were likewise fair, & his devotion to them carried the day. ". . . You have seen Miss Osborne?—she is my model for a truly feminine complexion, & she is very fair."—"Is she fairer than me? [She is about as fair as I am, I think]"—Tom made no reply.

Tom once more evades her, as usual assigning himself to a higher social status. By the final change Jane Austen tries hard to sustain the metaphorical effect by substituting a question for the blunt emotion of Margaret's original demand. But Margaret's "me" protrudes itself to shatter the metaphorical structure, and this conversation comes to an end. The artistic strain is noticeable in the revisions, and it is evident as well in Jane Austen's intervention to explain Tom's attitude explicitly. Later on she will trust the structure to carry its own weight.

This uncertainty, like her failure to mediate surely between Elizabeth and Emma in linking a sense of reality with a sense of decorum, or like her irresolution about Lord Osborne after placing him and Tom for us so securely, seems symptomatic of Jane Austen's inexperience with a narrative convention to which she was probably only beginning to adjust, that convention which she makes triumphantly her own in the completed novels.

⊰[III]⊱

It is much more difficult to pass any decisive judgments on *Sanditon,* the work interrupted by Jane Austen's death, than on *The Watsons.* For though this final fragment is slightly longer, its apparent heroine, Charlotte Heywood, is hardly more than a name, and Jane Austen spends most of its pages in sketching a gallery of eccentrics, the Parkers and the Denhams, who are caught up in promoting Sanditon as a health resort. There is too little evidence here, at least to my mind, for us to determine what the major lines of force in the completed story might have been. All we can safely say is that the mode of the fragment as we have it, for whatever reasons, is largely parody. Thus the conversations are not very interesting technically, because in the main each character exists in a single dimension.

Most often in the dialogues of *Sanditon*, Jane Austen depends more on an exaggerated matter than a dramatic verbal manner to expose her figures for us. The busybody Diana Parker, for instance, speaks every dull item in her mind straight out:

> "—You must have heard me mention Miss Capper, the particular friend of *my* very particular friend Fanny Noyce;—now, Miss Capper is extremely intimate with a Mrs Darling, who is on terms of constant correspondence with Mrs Griffiths herself. —Only a *short* chain, you see, between us, & not a Link wanting. Mrs G. meant to go to the Sea, for her Young People's benefit—had fixed on the coast of Sussex, but was undecided as to the where . . . ." (p. 408)

On and on she goes, for another page or so, finally stopping with "Am I clear?—I would be anything rather than not clear." Poor Miss Bates never sank to this. Jane Austen exercises no selectivity to represent the bore in this passage; she just reproduces her talk. Like much of the dialogue in the fragment, the passage is not formed.

Only two characters, Mr. Parker and Sir Edward Denham, are somewhat more successfully represented: at least each possesses a typical verbal manner that dramatizes him to some extent. Mr. Parker, as *Sanditon* everywhere makes clear, has no conception of fact. The first chapter shows him in a locale utterly unknown to him, disputing with a resident about where he is and who lives down the road, convinced that the native is wrong about his own neighborhood. In short, Mr. Parker has transformed his wish into a "fact," and the pattern recurs again and again in the fragment. If he does happen to start from a fact, he reverses the process, distorting the actuality until it accords only with his wish. So his new home on a cliff is much more advantageous than his old home in a comfortable valley, for now *"We* have all the Grandeur of the Storm, with less real danger, because the Wind meeting with nothing to oppose or confine it around our House, simply rages & passes on—while down in this Gutter—nothing is known of the state of the Air, below the Tops of the Trees . . ." (p. 381). In similar fashion, his private desires are always the basis of his generalizations, which he takes to be literally true: ". . . but Sanditon itself—everybody has heard of Sanditon,—the favourite—for a young & rising Bathing-place, certainly the favourite spot of all that are to be found along the coast of Sussex;—the most favoured by Nature, & promising to be the most chosen by Man" (p. 368).

Evidently habits of mind like these hopelessly confuse reality with appearance. For example, when Mr. Parker receives a letter from his hypochondriac relations, he describes, before opening it, how the sensible Sidney Parker would react: "—Sidney laughs . . . but it really is no Joke—tho' Sidney often makes me laugh at them all in spite of myself.—Now, if he were here, I know he w^d be offering odds that either Susan Diana or Arthur w^d appear by this letter to have been at the point of death within the last month" (p. 385). Yet in spite of his reflection, when the letter does make just such extravagant claims, Mr. Parker is completely taken in: "Seriously, a very indifferent account" (p. 386). As always, he is quite absurd—and very good-hearted.

Sir Edward Denham, the other character who establishes himself by his verbal manner, is also absurd, so far as we can tell from the fragment, though in a very different way. Jane Austen reports that he has fallen under the spell of the passionate scenes in the books he has read, and she thus scores off the excessively emotional strain in fiction again, as well as the confusion of novels with life. Obviously Sir Edward's sensibility has run wild, for he violates every linguistic propriety. Often he seems to wallow in the intensities of figurative language, the token of a diseased mind overwhelmed by feeling. Thus of Robert Burns, in whose poetry "there is Pathos to madden one," Sir Edward gushes, "His Soul was the Altar in which lovely Woman sat enshrined, his Spirit truly breathed the immortal Incence which is her Due" (p. 397). In the same way, his addiction to highly evocative particular terms marks a gratuitous sensationalism: "—It were Hyper-criticism, it were Pseudo-philosophy to expect from the soul of high toned Genius, the grovellings of a common mind.—The Coruscations of Talent, elicited by impassioned feeling in the breast of Man, are perhaps incompatible with some of the prosaic Decencies of Life" (p. 398). If Sir Edward builds on conceptual terms, as in recounting his taste in fiction, they inflate what he wants to say beyond all sense, so we are not surprised when he finally abandons them in large part, surrendering himself again to metaphor:

> "You will never hear me advocating those puerile Emanations which detail nothing but discordant Principles incapable of Amalgamation, or those vapid tissues of ordinary Occurrences from which no useful Deductions can be drawn. . . . The Novels which I approve are such as display Human Nature with Grandeur—such as shew her in the Sublimities of intense Feeling—such as exhibit the progress of strong Passion from the first Germ of incipient Susceptibility to the utmost Energies of Reason half-dethroned,—where we see the strong spark of Woman's Captivations elicit such Fire in the Soul of Man as leads him— (though at the risk of some Aberration from the strict line of Primitive Obligations)—to hazard all, dare all, atcheive all, to obtain her." (p. 403)

His rhetoric in this passage is the appropriate counterpart to Sir Edward, the parallelism, climactic series, and suspension developing an intensity reckless of consequences.

Yet even though Sir Edward and Mr. Parker are dramatized by their verbal mannerisms, they emerge as caricatures rather than portraits; and in truth, they strike us as little closer to rounded persons than the characters in the novel to whom Jane Austen assigns a parodic matter only. For greater subtlety, or more finished workmanship, we must turn to the major novels, where Jane Austen has smoothed the jagged outlines of the *Juvenilia, The Watsons,* and *Sanditon.* In the completed works we will find the dialogue more precisely structured and much more revealing.

1. There is a similar uneasiness on Jane Austen's part when she tries to regulate the story's point of view in relation to Tom Musgrave, a natural enough difficulty if much of her previous experience had been with the epistolary convention. Through most of the fragment she is driven to such evasions as "Emma's calm curtsey in reply must have struck him . . . & gave him probably the novel sensation of doubting his own influence" (p. 335) or "As Tom Musgrave was seen no more, we may suppose his plan to have succeeded, & imagine him mortifying . . . in dreary solitude" (p. 336). Not until the fragment is almost over does she drop the mood of supposition to speak more directly—in the customary way of the later novels—with the authority of an author: "He loved to take people by surprise, with sudden visits at extraordinary seasons" (p. 355).

2. From now on in this chapter, the page references to *The Watsons* will be to R. W. Chapman's separate edition of the work, for I shall be glancing in one way or another at Jane Austen's revising.

3 Sense and Sensibility
Symmetrical Designs

Everyone would agree that *Sense and Sensibility* creates the impression of being extremely rigid. The title itself announces the main antithesis, yet it can hardly suggest how diligently Jane Austen distinguishes between the mode of sense and the mode of feeling in the novel's plot, style, and theme. To review these quickly, before we look into the linguistic habits of the characters, may remind us how uncompromising *Sense and Sensibility* is, and how insistently it resolves—though readers sometimes overlook this—the initial antithesis.

In its broadest outlines, the plot sets up a series of comparable situations in which we are to watch the sense of Elinor Dashwood and the sensibility of Marianne, her younger sister, at work. The novel's first phase opposes the restrained courtship of Elinor by a despondent Edward Ferrars to Willoughby's ebullient relationship with Marianne, and, more important, contrasts Elinor's relative composure during Edward's long absences with Marianne's distraction at being separated from Willoughby. In the second stage, when both attachments seem impossible because of Edward's engagement to Lucy Steele and Willoughby's sudden marriage, Elinor's stoicism is reckoned against Marianne's wild despair. By the end of the novel, though, these extremes approach each other: the sisters agree in judging Willoughby's character, and Elinor, after suffering through Marianne's illness, Willoughby's self-vindication, and what appears to be Edward's marriage to Lucy, is finally united with Edward, while Marianne subdues herself to the point of accepting the warmhearted Colonel Brandon.

An outline like this, however, cannot indicate how deeply the distinction between sense and feeling is embedded in the non-conversational prose of the novel. It is this prose, of course, that fixes the climate in which the action takes place, and passages like the one that follows, a simple description of how Elinor reacts on finding herself on the road to London with Marianne and her "objections" to the trip overruled, turn up on almost every page:

SENSE	FEELING
But these *objections* had all,	with that happy *ardour* of youth which Marianne and her mother equally shared, been *overcome* or *overlooked*;
and Elinor, in spite of every occasional *doubt* of Willoughby's constancy, could not witness	the *rapture of delightful expectation* which filled the whole soul and beamed in the eyes of Marianne,
	without *feeling how blank* was her own prospect, *how cheerless* her own state of mind in the comparison,
	and *how gladly* she would engage in the solicitude of Marianne's situation to have the same *animating* object in view, the same possibility of *hope*.
A short, a very short time however must now *decide* what Willoughby's intentions were; *in all probability* he was already in town.	Marianne's *eagerness* to be gone declared her dependance on finding him there;
and Elinor was *resolved* not only upon gaining every new light as to his character	

which her own *observation*
or the *intelligence* of others
could give her, but likewise
upon watching his behaviour
to her sister . . . .

(p. 159; italics mine)

Although the diagram cannot reproduce all the discriminations that the passage makes, it brings out the main antithesis between Elinor's sense and Marianne's sensibility: in contrasting the sisters, the rhetoric of course evaluates them to some degree. Little wonder, with the distinction between sense and sensibility so woven into the texture of the narrative, that the novel feels inflexible.

But we would be wrong if we regarded the previous passage as purely antithetic, a mere treasuring of Elinor's reason at the expense of Marianne's feeling, for both the structure and the words declare that Elinor also has emotions. In lodging this claim, the passage at least points our way toward *Sense and Sensibility*'s theme, and about this, no matter how strait-laced it feels, we must make no mistake. The novel contends that the individual can morally engage himself in the social organism, of which he is necessarily a part, only when he achieves an appropriate balance between sense and feeling. Both are necessary: sense to formulate his relation with society, feeling to vitalize it. This is the meaning that Jane Austen enforces throughout the novel by its action, structure, and especially by her patterned groups of characters. We must defer considering the leading men and the minor figures until later in this chapter, but here we may glance again at Elinor and Marianne, who express the theme most plainly by their development in contrary directions as the novel continues. For *Sense and Sensibility* finally insists—though awkwardly at moments—on Marianne's capacity to reason and on Elinor's capacity to feel in making decisions.

Each sister has the necessary potential from the start. Marianne, to take her first, is described as "sensible" at her introduction (p. 6)—and indeed never strikes the reader as the kind of character oversimplified to sheer sensibility which he might actually find in the novels of sentiment, or might expect to find in an anti-sentimental novel. But through most of this story Marianne's sensibility is in the ascendant, with the result that her definitions, and the actions they lead to, are quite in error. For her, morality is sheer emotion: ". . . if there had been any real impropriety . . . I could have had no pleasure" (p. 68). And so is reason itself: ". . . the restraint of sentiments . . . appeared to her . . . a disgraceful subjection of reason" (p. 53). Thus decorum, the meeting ground of sense and feeling that society has established, is a fraud in Marianne's eyes because it somewhat restricts the free play of the individual: ". . . I thought it was right," she jibes at Elinor, "to be guided wholly by the opinion of other people" (pp. 93–94). Although Elinor answers that her own "doctrine" of propriety has never countenanced "the subjection of the understanding" and adds what amounts to a warning against abandoning one's mind to the grip of personal feeling, the truth of her reply is not borne in on her sister until the last section of the novel. By then, however, Marianne's reason is no longer at the mercy of her sensibility. Rather, the qualities unite, enabling her to appraise Willoughby's behavior morally and to decide against her own "most shamefully unguarded affection" (p. 345). With sense as sensibility's partner rather than its slave, Marianne attains the perspective essential to living meaningfully within society.

The novel charts a course for Elinor precisely the opposite of Marianne's, though the case of the elder sister is slightly complicated by the fact that she serves as our point of view in much of the story. In this early work, at least, Jane Austen apparently felt that she could not risk—as she frequently does later on— tying her reader to a mind liable to distort the world it perceives, so Elinor must see clearly for the most part.[1] Although we are told at her introduction that "her feelings were strong" (p. 6), she is primarily allied with sense through the first two-thirds of the book in trying to guide Marianne toward reason. But once Marianne is relatively safe from Willoughby, Elinor's capacity to feel is stressed again and again. Jane Austen's touch is not always sure: she treats Elinor's emotional flutters arising from Willoughby's final visit (pp. 333, 334, 339, 349) as she had Elinor's earlier palpitations over the lock of hair in Edward's ring (pp. 98–99)—with a kind of embarrassed irony, as if the reader cannot quite be trusted to recognize when the feelings betrayed by his point of view are excessive, given the situation, and self-indulgent. Elinor strikes a deeper note, though her passionate emotion is still to some extent self-centered, when she blames herself for having formerly decided so coolly that Marianne's illness could not be serious (pp. 312–14) or when she is shaken to the core at the news of Edward's supposed marriage despite all that her sense can do (pp. 353–58). In her finest moment, however, Elinor shows Marianne, and us, what the proper quality of intense feeling is, how it may suitably inform judgment and behavior, when she explains how she has been "supported" in her disappointments: "By feeling that I was doing my duty.—My promise to Lucy, obliged me to be secret. I owed it to her, therefore, to avoid giving any hint of the truth; and I owed it to my family and friends, not to create in them a solicitude about me, which it could not be in my power to satisfy" (p. 262). She feels as deeply as Marianne, yet she expresses it in her obligation to others, thus controlling her emotion and charging it with extra-personal significance. As all these instances declare, however differently Jane Austen manages them, sense alone is not enough.

Indeed the entire novel argues that the "duty" to which Elinor has just referred—and its social counterpart is decorum—marks the highest achievement of the individual in compelling him to relate himself both sensibly and emotionally to others.[2] The risk of the excessive feeling which the novel mainly, though not exclusively, attacks is that the individual in its grasp cannot escape himself sufficiently to discover what his personal or social duty is. And sheer self, of course, is the antithesis of society, which is the condition of man. One may well feel that Marianne's conversion is a little strained and that Elinor is handled even more arbitrarily at moments. Still, Jane Austen's very forc-

ing of her materials testifies to her concern that the theme of
Sense and Sensibility should represent a mean valuable because
it has a foot in either camp. The argument remains utterly conventional, and Jane Austen's pursuit of it by tracing what might
be called the double allegiance of each sister makes the novel
none the less rigid—though perhaps somewhat more inclusive
in its claims than has sometimes been maintained.

-◄[II]►-

In order to discover how the dialogues of *Sense and Sensibility*
dramatize its meaning, we had best start with a few speeches by
Elinor and Marianne, not only because the sisters represent the
dominant principles in the novel, thus conditioning our approach to the other characters, but because the modes of sense
and sensibility vent themselves in sharply contrasting verbal
habits. Marianne is always bent on asserting her intense inner
life, often favoring particular terms to lay bare her energetic responses: "That is an expression, Sir John . . . which I particularly dislike. I abhor every common-place phrase by which
wit is intended; and 'setting one's cap at a man,' or 'making a
conquest,' are the most odious of all. Their tendency is gross and
illiberal" (p. 45). Every charged word dramatizes the distance
that she feels between herself and the gregarious Sir John Middleton. She certainly does not avoid conceptual terms, yet she
uses them in such a way that they reflect her emotional commitments rather than more objective standards. When she hears
from Sir John that Willoughby once danced for eight hours
without a break, she ardently replies, "Did he indeed? . . . and
with elegance, with spirit?" and continues, "That is what I like;
that is what a young man ought to be. Whatever be his pursuits, his eagerness in them should know no moderation, and
leave him no sense of fatigue" (p. 45). Here Marianne's conceptual language first exalts an extreme which she finds attrac-

tive and then helps consolidate the extreme as a generalization, something valid for a class. That the diction is applied eccentrically and the generalization unreliable because it expresses the view of a single citizen only—none of this bothers Marianne at all, for her world is herself. It is a world in which "like" becomes "ought" without any strain, not only in language but in fact, as she later proves by defending as decorous her unchaperoned visit with Willoughby to Allenham.

For Marianne, plainly, a generalization is emotionally dictated, expressing something like an act of faith in herself. For Elinor, a generalization is the reverse: it means separating oneself from the fallibilities of private feeling and appealing to knowledge that is sure in its universal applicability. At one point, for instance, she carefully qualifies her mother's fervent praise of Colonel Brandon as Marianne's suitor, praise which Mrs. Dashwood—whose sensibility is so much like her younger daughter's—delivers quite in the mode of Marianne: "But his coming for me as he did, with such active, such ready friendship, is enough to prove him one of the worthiest of men." Although Elinor's feelings are all on the side of Colonel Brandon, she in effect warns her mother against the dangers of hasty induction:

> "His character, however . . . does not rest on *one* act of kindness, to which his affection for Marianne, were humanity out of the case, would have prompted him. To Mrs. Jennings, to the Middletons, he has been long and intimately known; they equally love and respect him; and even my own knowledge of him, though lately acquired, is very considerable; and so highly do *I* value and esteem him, that if Marianne can be happy with him, I shall be as ready as yourself to think our connection the greatest blessing to us in the world." (p. 337)

Elinor explores the very foundations of Colonel Brandon's "character" before arriving at her closing generalization. In her usual fashion, she builds her case on conceptual terms, here stable because she uses them to minimize personal emotion: "kindness" is assessed in the light of "affection" and "humanity,"

❋❋❋❋❋❋❋❋❋❋❋❋❋❋❋❋❋❋❋❋❋❋❋❋❋❋❋❋❋❋

just as "love" is measured against "respect." At the same time, Elinor secures her case further by citing other witnesses; only after they have testified does she offer her own judgment. It is this movement of mind, which justifies emotion rather than denies it, that characterizes her durable relation to the society of the novel.

The contrast between the sisters is carried out in the matter of rhetoric as well, though each is driven at last to use the mode of the other, which again suggests that Marianne is ultimately able to discriminate and that Elinor can feel. Elinor's usual rhetoric, however, is just what we would guess: emotionally low-pressured, controlled, it devotes itself mainly to articulating a series of distinctions. When Edward's engagement to Lucy Steele is made public, for example, Elinor explains her own reaction to Marianne in a thoroughly typical passage, typical in that her rhetoric divides sense and feeling into antithetic compartments, typical in that she allows an emotional series only at the close, and then in the interests of reason and propriety:

SENSE	FEELING
"I am not *conscious* of having provoked the disappointment by any imprudence of my own,	
	and I have *borne* it as much as possible without spreading it farther.
I *acquit* Edward of all essential misconduct.	
	I *wish* him very happy;
and I am so *sure* of his always doing his duty,	
	that though now he may harbour some *regret,* in the end he must become so.
Lucy does not want *sense,* and that is the foundation on which every thing good may be built.	
	—And after all, Marianne, after all that is *bewitching* in

the idea of a single and constant attachment, and all
that can be said of *one's happiness depending entirely* on
any particular person,

it is not meant—it is not fit
—it is not *possible* that it
should be so."

(p. 263; italics mine)

But Elinor's scrupulous antitheses here between reason and
feeling give way for once when Marianne accuses her of not
being upset by the engagement because she does not care for
Edward. In the face of this most serious challenge to her sensibility, Elinor responds with a passionate rhetoric that convinces
even Marianne:

"—It was told me,—it was in a manner forced on me by the very
person herself, whose prior engagement ruined all my prospects;
and told me, as I thought, with triumph.—This person's suspicions, therefore, I have had to oppose, by endeavouring to appear
indifferent where I have been most deeply interested;—and it
has not been only once;—I have had her hopes and exultation
to listen to again and again.—I have known myself to be divided
from Edward for ever, without hearing one circumstance that
could make me less desire the connection.—Nothing has proved
him unworthy; nor has any thing declared him indifferent to me.
—I have had to contend against the unkindness of his sister, and
the insolence of his mother; and have suffered the punishment of
an attachment, without enjoying its advantages." (pp. 263–64)

The fundamental movement of the passage is straight ahead,
generating its power mainly through the anaphoric structure:
"It was told," "it was . . . forced," "told . . . with triumph";
"I have had . . . to listen," "I have known," "I have had to
contend." And the antitheses—"indifferent" vs. "interested," "divided" vs. "less desire," "unworthy" vs. "indifferent," "contend"
vs. "suffered," "unkindness" vs. "insolence," "punishment" vs.
"advantages"—their primary purpose is not at all to differentiate
but to intensify, for they accumulate all that Elinor has endured.
This is far indeed from Elinor's normal style, but it lets us look

for once below the disciplined surface that almost always conceals the depth of her attachments.

Marianne's typical rhetoric sounds very like the second speech by Elinor. It would be unfair to judge the younger sister by the purple passage in which she takes leave of "Dear, dear Norland!" (p. 27), even though the energetic movement of the lines straight ahead characterizes many other speeches by Marianne. But perhaps her essential difference from Elinor will come clear if we watch Marianne exert a charged rhetoric, as she habitually does, to support a precarious generalization, here in defense of her "intimacy" with Willoughby:

> "I have not known him long indeed, but I am much better acquainted with him, than I am with any other creature in the world, except yourself and mama. It is not time or opportunity that is to determine intimacy;—it is disposition alone. Seven years would be insufficient to make some people acquainted with each other, and seven days are more than enough for others. I should hold myself guilty of greater impropriety in accepting a horse from my brother, than from Willoughby. Of John I know very little, though we have lived together for years; but of Willoughby my judgment has long been formed." (pp. 58–59)

She generalizes on the basis of her particular feeling for Willoughby. In the antitheses—between "insufficient" and "more than enough," between her brother and Willoughby—she establishes extremes, not to search out a secure middle ground, in the manner usual with Elinor, but to validate the extremes themselves by drastically juxtaposing them. So she ends, with a kind of charming inconsequence, by claiming in effect that she has "long" known Willoughby when she began by denying it. For Marianne, the antithetic structure is normally a means to augment feeling rather than to make sensible distinctions.

Indeed, in terms of the novel one thing she must learn is a rhetoric that plainly differentiates between sense and feeling, a rhetoric that will prove her fully capable of evaluating personality by demonstrating that she can stand outside herself. Thus in her climactic speeches, when she looks back on her past with Willoughby, Marianne takes over a style like the one that Elinor practices most often:

SENSE	FEELING
	"—Do not, my dearest Elinor, let your *kindness* defend
what I know your *judgment* must censure. My illness has made me *think* . . . . I con-*sidered* the past; I saw in my own behaviour since the beginning of our acquaintance with him last autumn, nothing but a series of *imprudence* towards myself,	
	and *want of kindness* to others. I saw that my own *feelings* had prepared my sufferings, and that my want of fortitude under them had almost led me to the grave. . . .
I did not *know* my danger till the danger was removed;	but with such *feelings*
as these *reflections* gave me,	I wonder at my recovery,—wonder that the very *eagerness of my desire* to live, to have time for atonement to my God, and to you all, did not kill me at once. Had I died,—in what *peculiar misery* should I have left you, my nurse, my friend, my sister!—You, who had seen all the *fretful selfishness* of my latter days; who had known all the *murmurings of my heart!* . . . —My mother too! How could you have consoled her!—I cannot express my own *abhorrence* of myself.

❋❋

Whenever I looked towards
the past, I saw some *duty*
neglected,   or some *failing indulged.*"

(pp. 345–46; italics mine)

The entire passage—and my omissions would not alter its fundamental shape—issues from Marianne's newly found sense. One
mark of it is what we might call her double vision, which now
allows her to balance off observations about her reason, or earlier lack of reason, against comments on her emotions. Her
antitheses here seem designed less to intensify than to distinguish meaningfully, and it might be added that Marianne's
speech goes on to outline her future in a similarly stable two-
part structure. This is not to say that all her feeling has evapo-
rated. On the contrary, the emotional terms and broken clauses
of her Norland rhetoric reappear in the second half of the quotation, when she speaks of her illness, but now they dramatize her
fervently unselfish commitment to others. Taken as a whole,
the passage suggests that Marianne can achieve a viable norm,
the sort of norm we saw figured earlier in the fusion of sense
and sensibility that governs Elinor's behavior.

⊸[III]⊱

Jane Austen carries on the theme of the novel by her characterization of its leading men, each one revealing an individual blend of sense with sensibility and a particular relationship
with society that results from it. They are placed just as cate-
gorically for us as Elinor and Marianne: Edward Ferrars in the
middle, flanked on one side by Colonel Brandon and on the
other by Willoughby.

Edward's main trait is his self-control, not as steely as Elinor's,
but as consistent. It shows itself through most of the extraor-
dinarily few speeches granted this conventional "hero" in his
tendency to stand apart from himself, gauging his capabilities, as

it were, from a responsibly objective vantage point. Sometimes
he does so in a wittier guise than we may remember, given
Elinor's somber picture of him that haunts the novel, but his
underlying diffidence about himself is very real. If he commands
a rhetoric of intensity, he will use its series and antitheses
ironically, against himself:

> "It has been, and is, and probably will always be a heavy misfor-
> tune to me, that I have had no necessary business to engage me,
> no profession to give me employment, or afford me any thing like
> independence. But unfortunately my own nicety, and the nicety
> of my friends, have made me what I am, an idle, helpless being.
> . . . I always preferred the church, as I still do. But that was not
> smart enough for my family. They recommended the army. That
> was a great deal too smart for me. . . . and, at length . . .
> idleness was pronounced on the whole to be the most advanta-
> geous and honourable, and a young man of eighteen is not in
> general so earnestly bent on being busy as to resist the solicita-
> tions of his friends to do nothing. I was therefore entered at Ox-
> ford and have been properly idle ever since." (pp. 102–3)

Edward's antitheses proclaim his distance from his family, but
largely at another irresponsible extreme, and his final generalizations resolve them only to hoot at the foolishness of himself
and his family. In short, the rhetoric passes judgment on him in
the light of perceived responsibility—and Edward creates the
rhetoric himself.

He may also employ an intense vocabulary, but again it mocks
himself, this time from the perspective of Marianne and her
enthusiasm about a "picturesque" landscape:

> "I shall call hills steep, which ought to be bold; surfaces strange
> and uncouth, which ought to be irregular and rugged; and dis-
> tant objects out of sight, which ought only to be indistinct
> through the soft medium of a hazy atmosphere. You must be sat-
> isfied with such admiration as I can honestly give. I call it a very
> fine country—the hills are steep, the woods seem full of fine tim-
> ber, and the valley looks comfortable and snug—with rich mead-
> ows and several neat farm houses scattered here and there."
> (p. 97)

This is no attack on Marianne; rather, Edward is taking his usual belittling measure of himself, admitting that he prefers the verifiable contents of the landscape to its privately affective qualities. Typically, he recognizes the claims of the other side while staking out his own to define himself.

Yet Edward's recurrent need to evaluate himself publicly, whether by a sometimes ironic rhetoric, by generalizations turned against himself, or by his diction, signals only his self-distrust, not any doubt about the virtues that he holds in view. And his distrust of himself is ultimately unfounded, for—like the highly emotional Captain Wentworth in *Persuasion,* to take a more obviously sympathetic figure—he is moved to act with the strictest honor when put to the test, standing by his engagement to Lucy Steele though disinherited for doing so and though he has long stopped loving her. "I thought it my duty," he says, "independent of my feelings, to give her the option of continuing the engagement or not, when I was renounced by my mother, and stood to all appearance without a friend in the world to assist me" (p. 367). This firm self-denial, even the words themselves, might come from the lips of the staunch Elinor.

If Edward usually observes decorum in what he says by restraining emotion unless it can be discharged against himself, Colonel Brandon is very different. It is his fate to see the decorum he clutches at on the verge of slipping through his fingers again and again—an early method on Jane Austen's part, it would seem, to dramatize acute feeling. He expresses his character fully during his first conversation, when he queries Elinor about Marianne's distaste for second attachments (pp. 56–57). Elinor tells him that Marianne's attitude is wholly unreasonable, yet Colonel Brandon gives away his liking for the younger sister by defending her: ". . . there is something so amiable in the prejudices of a young mind, that one is sorry to see them give way to the reception of more general opinions." Probably he hopes that the generalization will make him appear suitably disengaged, but clearly it arises only from his private feeling. And sheerly private feeling, at least Marianne's, as Elinor quickly points out, bears little relation to sense or "propriety." However, the Colonel's affection for Marianne urges him on, though he still masks it with the indirection of "those who" and a conceptual diction: "Does your sister make no distinction in her objections against a second attachment? . . . . Are those who have been disappointed in their first choice, whether from the inconstancy of its object, or the perverseness of circumstances, to be equally indifferent during the rest of their lives?" But when Elinor reports the adamantine view of Marianne, who has "never yet" considered a second attachment "pardonable," Colonel Brandon's façade of objectivity breaks down:

> "This . . . cannot hold; but a change, a total change of senti-
> ments—No, no, do not desire it,—for when the romantic refine-
> ments of a young mind are obliged to give way, how frequently
> are they succeeded by such opinions as are but too common, and
> too dangerous! I speak from experience. I once knew a lady who
> in temper and mind greatly resembled your sister . . . but
> who from an inforced change—from a series of unfortunate cir-
> cumstances"—Here he stopt suddenly; appeared to think that he
> had said too much . . . .

He tries to hold himself back by the generalization, emotionally based though it is, about the change of "a young mind." But his feelings, for the girl like Marianne and indeed for Marianne herself, are so strong that they threaten to burst through in too particular a revelation. Sensing his danger, he stutters into silence, his only way of retaining a perilous grip on propriety. This is the verbal pattern that Colonel Brandon enacts almost every time he speaks: in discussing Willoughby's supposed engagement to Marianne (p. 173) or Willoughby's marriage to Miss Grey (p. 199). And the pattern finds its analogy in the action of the Colonel when, stirred by Edward's loyalty to Lucy, he will not himself offer Edward the living of Delaford but commissions Elinor to do so.[3]

Willoughby has by all odds the most attractive manner of the three suitors, which means here, as so often in Jane Austen's novels, that he is the one whose language we must study most carefully if we want to get at his real character. In terms of the pattern formed by the leading men, he is stationed on Edward's other flank, occupying a position opposite Colonel Brandon. While the Colonel's acceptance of decorum constrains him to shroud his feelings in silence, Willoughby's rejection of anything conventional spurs him to advertise his emotions, often at the top of his voice. Yet in spite of his vivacity, the nature of his feelings differs sharply from the nature of Marianne's. What is a religion with her is more of a profession with Willoughby. This is what makes him dangerous in the world of the novel, and what Elinor intuits by her sense. For he does not utterly surrender himself to emotion in the mode of Marianne; rather, he seems to practice feeling as a means of gratifying himself momentarily. But to practice feeling is to be essentially detached, which denies the very basis of emotion. Willoughby plainly makes this point about himself when, in reporting to Elinor that he tried to attach Marianne while planning a marriage for money with Miss Grey, he questions whether he has "ever known" what it is to love: "for, had I really loved, could I have sacrificed my feelings to vanity, to avarice?—or, what is more, could I have sacrificed her's?—But I have done it" (pp. 320–21). Yet Willoughby need not have told us openly about this emotional discrepancy, for his linguistic habits reveal it over and over.

Consider his rhapsody on the Dashwoods' home (pp. 72–73). It seems at first the passionate cry of a sensibility like Marianne's, a celebration of picturesque detail by extravagantly emotional generalizations: "Improve this dear cottage! No. *That* I will never consent to. Not a stone must be added to its walls, not an inch to its size, if my feelings are regarded." But his fervor must be quite conscious, for his continuation and conclusion prove that all his remarks are calculated to praise Marianne, using the cottage as a metaphor for her. To take a single example, ". . . this place will always have one claim on my affection, which no other can possibly share," at which point Mrs. Dashwood underlines his meaning for us by looking "with pleasure at Marianne." His whole speech, in short, amounts to a work of art, which is to say that it no longer expresses raw feeling, the kind that reveals itself in Marianne's talk.

Perhaps this basic distinction between Willoughby and Marianne will become clearer in their different uses of figurative language. Here is Marianne, denouncing marriage by any woman over twenty-seven because, according to her standards, it could not be for love: "It would be a compact of convenience, and the world would be satisfied. . . . To me it would seem only a commercial exchange, in which each wished to be benefited at the expense of the other" (p. 38). Marianne gives herself up to the figure—commerce is completely antipathetic to her idea of love —to pour out her disgust with the world's opinion. But here is Willoughby, trying to convince Elinor of his love for Marianne by describing what he felt on receiving her letters:

> "When the first of her's reached me . . . what I felt is—in the common phrase, not to be expressed; in a more simple one—perhaps too simple to raise any emotion—my feelings were very, very painful.—Every line, every word was—in the hackneyed metaphor which their dear writer . . . would forbid—a dagger to my heart. To know that Marianne was in town was—in the same language—a thunderbolt.—Thunderbolts and daggers!—what a reproof she would have given me! . . . . " (p. 325)

Apparently for him metaphor is largely a problem of expression with attendant dangers, not an instinctive translation of feelings into words. Willoughby makes fun of the metaphors, yet uses them anyway, because to mock and then use them is a way of pledging their intensity and thus his own. But this marks a deliberate recreation of the vitality of language; the double attitude of the artist, at the same time in and outside of his work, remains. The ultimate effect is of Willoughby's detachment, and the irony is its symptom.[4]

Indeed he controls his conversation as industriously as Edward does, though for very different purposes. Where Edward puts his detachment to work in judging himself, Willoughby's detachment allows him to contrive his own intensification. We can hardly avoid the sense that he is constantly performing, that his rhetoric is often a stratagem designed for the specific occasion—especially in that long scene near the end of the novel when he accounts to Elinor for his behavior toward Marianne. One might argue that Willoughby's objectivity would be natural here inasmuch as he is looking back on the past, but mainly he is striving to convince Elinor of his past and present integrity: he engages himself directly in self-vindication. Thus it may appear at first surprising—though in the last analysis it is deeply typical—that he should be found constructing so careful an artifice as his reply to Elinor after she reproaches him with the seduction which she has discovered through Colonel Brandon. His rhetoric is brilliantly conceived throughout. He begins by claiming that Colonel Brandon is partial, and so by implication that he himself is impartial. Then he acts out a supposedly fair judgment of himself and the girl in a series of antitheses:

> "Remember," cried Willoughby, "from whom you received the account. Could it be an impartial one? I acknowledge that her situation and her character ought to have been respected by me. I do not mean to justify myself, but at the same time cannot leave you to suppose that I have nothing to urge—that because she was injured she was irreproachable, and because I was a libertine, *she* must be a saint. If the violence of her passions, the weakness of her understanding—I do not mean, however, to defend myself. Her affection for me deserved better treatment, and I often, with great self-reproach, recal the tenderness which, for a very short time, had the power of creating any return. I wish —I heartily wish it had never been. But I have injured more than herself; and I have injured one, whose affection for me— (may I say it?) was scarcely less warm than her's; and whose mind—Oh! how infinitely superior!" (p. 322)

But Willoughby has no rationally sound defense, so he must insist, as he does in the last half of the speech, on his strong feelings and his inviolable attachment to Marianne, energizing these declarations by a rhetoric that moves straight on. He is certainly not carried away; in fact, he remains supremely conscious of his audience, for he bows to Elinor's propriety with "may I say it?" and hopes to placate her sense by praising the "mind" of Marianne. His whole effort is very winning, but the meticulous formulation of his defense unmasks its policy. And sentiment is no longer sheer sentiment if one makes a production of it.

All this is not to say that we should take Willoughby as a mere faker who feels nothing for Marianne, but the quality of his feeling differs radically from the quality of hers. For him emotion is something to be professed by means of rhetoric, irony, and diction—they are tools to indulge it—but not to be thoroughly acted upon.

◄[IV]►

The minor characters fill out the theme by taking positions along a line stretching from the extreme of emotion to the extreme of sense, either limit marking a complete self-interest. The novel proposes, we remember, that one ought to mediate between the claims of the rival camps, sense determining one's adjustment to society and unselfish feeling animating it. What the minor characters reveal, each in his different way, is a series of failures in mediation, therefore a variety of uncreative social adjustments, some less serious, some more. It is unfair to them as individuals to categorize them roughly in four groups, but perhaps such an arrangement will throw the dominant motifs of the novel into higher relief.

At one extreme is a cluster of figures whose feelings perpetually run riot in their talk, divorcing it from sense. Charlotte Palmer's exclamatory bursts flatten all she mentions to the dead level of the superlative, obliterating any distinction between the particular and the general, thus annihilating rationality. Her absolutism has driven Mr. Palmer to one just as drastic, though the reverse of hers in that he invariably voices his disgust. And if Miss Steele's grammatical errors seem a rather nasty insistence on the part of the author that Anne is underbred, still her

✳✳✳✳✳✳✳✳✳✳✳✳✳✳✳✳✳✳✳✳✳✳✳✳✳✳✳✳✳✳✳✳✳✳

vocabulary implies that she is almost as witlessly intense as Mrs. Palmer: everything is "monstrous," "plaguing," "vast," the energetic counters proving, so Anne hopes, that she belongs to the fashionable world. The three characters in the second group are somewhat more subdued, and the novel presents them as essentially good-hearted, even though their conversation usually shows sense at the mercy of warmly private feeling. The talk of Sir John Middleton brims with generalizations, all of them based on his own pleasure, whether in hunting or in getting up a party to gratify himself and others. The vigorous emotions of Mrs. Jennings often confuse her thinking—witness her many false inductions—and sometimes make her as careless with her words, as in her indecorous reference to Colonel Brandon's "love child"; but when faced with the reality of Marianne's rejection by Willoughby and subsequent illness, Mrs. Jennings shows herself wholeheartedly sympathetic. With the last member of this group, Mrs. Dashwood, we approach Marianne's position on the scale, for the mother has an active sensibility of her own; though it tempts Mrs. Dashwood into a number of false inductions, still her sensibility is triggered by her unselfish love for her daughters. Lucy Steele has a post all to herself, out beyond Elinor's and not yet at the limit of sense: as we shall see in a moment, she almost always calculates her relation to society shrewdly, but her calculations do not square with her real feelings. As for the John Dashwoods and Robert Ferrars, who are placed at the extreme of sense, they brandish their reason in everything they say, but their version of reason consists of the ugliest self-interest.

Most of these minor characters reveal themselves so transparently in their remarks that they need not detain us. Yet we might linger briefly with Lucy Steele and then the John Dashwoods, for they are playing a deeper linguistic game. Lucy is convinced in her heart that she is the equal of anyone and jealously guards her success with Edward as a token of her value. But she also recognizes that society regards her as an inferior. In much of the novel she turns this fact to her advantage, playing the role of the inferior for all it is worth. However, the conflict between the role she assumes and her real self breaks into the open toward the end of her two long talks with Elinor.

Throughout them Lucy is warning Elinor to leave Edward alone, most of the time with her usual astuteness. For instance, she parades her inferiority by drawing attention to her indecorums, thus in effect neutralizing her opponent by making Elinor over into a social arbiter (although of course the maneuver also serves Lucy by implying that she feels delicately enough to know her breaches for what they are). At the same time, she alleges a special fondness for Elinor, thus tying her rival's hands. Moreover, Lucy proclaims her passion for Edward at every turn, which automatically entitles her to the pity of the world for lovers in difficulties. These facets of Lucy's role are caught together in a speech near the end of her first encounter with Elinor:

> "I was afraid you would think I was taking a great liberty with you . . . in telling you all this. . . . but . . . as soon as I saw you, I felt almost as if you was an old acquaintance. Besides . . . I am so unfortunate, that I have not a creature whose advice I can ask. . . . I only wonder that I am alive after what I have suffered for Edward's sake these last four years." (pp. 132–33)

With ammunition like this, Lucy wins the first battle hands down.

But her tone changes, as does Elinor's, after they meet again. Elinor is under a special obligation to preserve the forms of decorum because she has been cast as the social superior; yet she has also been personally attacked by Lucy and can return the fire only by manipulating those forms so obviously that Lucy will understand her. Thus Elinor resorts, quite uncharacteristically, to generalizations loaded with ambiguity, such as "If the strength of your reciprocal attachment had failed, as between many people and under many circumstances it naturally would during a four years' engagement, your situation would have been pitiable indeed" (p. 147). And Lucy, fully alive to Elinor's implication that the "attachment" may have "failed," feels driven to speak out herself—not at all in the manner that her role demands—when she replies with a generalization that authoritatively measures her power as a person: "I can safely say that he has never gave me one moment's alarm on that account from the first." By the end of their talk Lucy may again convert Elinor into a judge, but now the strain on her temper shows through her sentences:

> "'Tis because you are an indifferent person," said Lucy, with some pique, and laying a particular stress on those words, "that your judgment might justly have such weight with me. If you could be supposed to be biassed in any respect by your own feelings, your opinion would not be worth having." (p. 150)

The personal venom here, however obliquely she may express it, and her assumption of equality, even superiority, in judging Elinor make it plain that Lucy's private sense of herself is wholly at odds with her normal public pose as the docile social inferior. Evidently Jane Austen wants us to make no mistake about this, for her own words strain, in the previous passage and throughout the two conversations, to fix Lucy's unpleasantness for us.

In treating the John Dashwoods, though, Jane Austen stands at a greater distance, trusting her irony and their dialogue to interpret them for us. They differ from most of the other minor characters in being perfectly aware that it is improper to generalize on the basis of personal feeling alone; thus, though they always do so, they scrupulously insist that they are not acting out of private prejudice but in an enlightened way, according to a community of opinion.

Their behavior is outlined at the opening of their first talk (p. 9), which dramatizes their allegiance to society, but to an utterly private version of it. The conversation begins with John reminding Fanny that he has promised his dying father to "assist" Mrs. Dashwood and her daughters, John himself having settled on an amount of three thousand pounds. This prospect irritates Fanny because she is entirely selfish, but of course she cannot admit such an indecorous motive. So she sets about erecting a supposedly reasonable standard of behavior, first by assuming that the father was insane, although she propitiates her husband with "I dare say," then by citing the probability of "ten to one" to justify her assumption: "He did not know what he was talking of, I dare say; ten to one but he was light-headed at the time. Had he been in his right senses, he could not have thought of such a thing as begging you to give away half your fortune from your own child." A norm so patently rational, Fanny presumes, should appeal automatically to John. Still, she refuses to take any chances, pushing on to color her father-in-law's departure from the norm by the emotive "begging." Her husband hesitates momentarily: though admitting his father's aberration, "He could hardly suppose I should neglect them," John yet sees himself as a man of honor who must behave according to the letter of decorum's law, "The promise, therefore, was given, and must be performed." But a way out begins to glimmer in the generalization with which he closes: "Something must be done for them whenever they leave Norland and settle in a new home." It sounds pompous and authoritative enough to satisfy propriety, yet is unparticular enough to evade any rashly concrete promises.

Fanny, however, is still not content. She takes over his generalization to avoid provoking him, but she feels impelled to qualify it, even at the risk of mentioning the specific sum, though she minimizes this breach of decorum by keeping her phrasing as impersonal as possible: "Well, then, *let* something be done for them; but *that* something need not be three thousand pounds. Consider . . . that when the money is once parted with, it never can return." And she immediately fortifies her position by calling up the maxim about "money . . . once parted with." By the end of her speech she is seeking additional support in another emotive reminder of "our poor little boy," but she hardly needs it, for her husband has already caught sight of the grounds on which he can turn against the Dashwoods. Though acknowledging that his boy may some day "regret" the giving up of "so large a sum," John can make out what appears a much more objective case by following up Fanny's maxim with an appeal of his own to a community of opinion: "If he should have a numerous family . . . it would be a very convenient addition." Now safely allied with a public attitude, John can pronounce on the particular case, and of course start cutting down the amount of his assistance: "Five hundred pounds would be a prodigious increase to their fortunes!" His "prodigious" is wonderfully hypocritical, less congratulating him on his own kindness than expressing what he takes to be a normal public view of the Dashwoods' situation. And this hypocrisy typifies his character as well as Fanny's throughout the novel. Both subscribe to a presumably enlightened community of opinion, but it is one that utterly perverts social value because it twists reason into the service of merely selfish feeling. Thus, they provide the sharpest ironic statement of *Sense and Sensibility*'s theme.

ᐧᐧᑥ V ᑖᐧᐧ

Having glimpsed the characters pretty much in isolation so far, we might look finally at two scenes in which some of the major figures sustain their behavior in dialogue, interweaving their verbal habits to dramatize basic human conflicts. There is a sense of metaphoric indirection in each conversation, stronger in the second than in the first, though such scenes do not really flourish until the later works. Thus in the first example (pp. 50–52) Willoughby, Marianne, and Elinor represent themselves initially by their attitudes toward the absent Colonel Brandon, but, as their talk goes on, they often break the metaphoric tissue by commenting on each other more openly.

Willoughby starts the ball rolling with a well-bred sneer: "Brandon is just the kind of man . . . whom every body speaks well of, and nobody cares about; whom all are delighted to see, and nobody remembers to talk to." He controls his dislike for the Colonel by shaping it in witty antitheses, yet he refuses any personal responsibility for it by generalizing. Marianne is ready enough to agree with his verdict: "That is exactly what I think of him . . . ." But she accepts her responsibility, both by "I" and by her flat statement. Now Elinor speaks up, trying to keep feeling separate from sense in the antithesis of her first sentence: "Do not boast of it . . . for it is injustice in both of you. He is highly esteemed by all the family at the park, and I never see him myself without taking pains to converse with him." And her second antithesis, between "all the family" and "I," seeks to steady an opinion by balancing it on different authorities.

Willoughby is right on his toes to exploit Elinor's modesty, taking over her antithesis to use it against her:

> "That he is patronized by *you* . . . is certainly in his favour; but as for the esteem of the others, it is a reproach in itself. Who would submit to the indignity of being approved by such women as Lady Middleton and Mrs. Jennings, that could command the indifference of any body else?"

The antithesis serves his purpose in two ways: first, by setting Elinor apart with a show of deference from those he wishes to attack; second, by intimating—because "patronized" echoes the feeling latent in her phrase "taking pains"—that Elinor's judgment of Colonel Brandon is emotionally biased. Since Willoughby has apparently disproved her sense by the rhetoric of his first sentence, he then feels free to assert his own opinion, though again he formulates it impersonally, this time with all the power of a rhetorical question behind it. Of course the antithesis of his closing sentence does not mark out, as the shape of Willoughby's speech would imply, a more truly rational scale than Elinor's; rather, he aims at an emotional intensity that will dislocate the balanced view she has offered. However, Elinor knows how to restore an equilibrium: "But perhaps the abuse of such people as yourself and Marianne, will make amends for the regard of Lady Middleton and her mother. If their praise is censure, your censure may be praise, for they are not more undiscerning, than you are prejudiced and unjust." Now her antitheses take over his adverse judgments, only to lay them off, point by point, against the recklessness with which he and Marianne have made up their minds.

This is too much for Marianne: "In defence of your protegé you can even be saucy." Her assault with a particular diction is characteristic, and she implies, as Willoughby has, that Elinor's opinion really rests on aroused emotions. Elinor replies, though not in kind, by diagramming the validity of her view. The generalization in her first sentence carefully attaches her feelings to sense:

> "My protegé, as you call him, is a sensible man; and sense will always have attractions for me. Yes, Marianne, even in a man between thirty and forty. He has seen a great deal of the world; has been abroad; has read, and has a thinking mind. I have found him capable of giving me much information on various subjects, and he has always answered my inquiries with the readiness of good-breeding and good nature."

The rest of her speech documents the opening generalization with evidence that always distinguishes precisely between Colonel Brandon's qualities and her own response to them. It is a powerful retort that drives Marianne to sheer mockery: "That is to say . . . he has told you that in the East Indies the climate is hot, and the mosquitoes are troublesome." She wants a series rather than an antithesis to pile up the specific items that express her contempt. And Elinor can vanquish petulance only by insisting on the integrity of her previous claim: "He *would* have told me so, I doubt not, had I made any such inquiries, but they happened to be points on which I had been previously informed." Willoughby, of course, takes the part of the younger sister: "Perhaps . . . his observations may have extended to the existence of nabobs, gold mohrs, and palanquins." But he converts Marianne's instinctive scorn into conscious parody by juxtaposing highly exotic particulars to the sober Colonel Brandon.

Elinor's reply brings the fundamental issue directly into the open: "I may venture to say that *his* observations have stretched much farther than *your* candour. But why should you dislike him?" Again she relocates Willoughby's disparagement in a clarifying context, this time weighing the Colonel's "observations" against Willoughby's obtuseness. More important, she goes on by asking Willoughby to accept responsibility for his feelings by declaring their cause. But Willoughby will not speak for himself honestly. At first he simply reverts to the kind of antithesis and generalization that he employed earlier to censure Colonel Brandon:

> "I do not dislike him. I consider him, on the contrary, as a very respectable man, who has every body's good word and nobody's notice; who has more money than he can spend, more time than he knows how to employ, and two new coats every year."

Halfway through, though, Willoughby abandons his previous methods for a climactic series to show his disdain. Yet if he were to arrive at a serious climax after what Elinor has said, Willoughby might justify her attack by betraying too much feeling. So he expresses his detachment by the bathetically particular close, which suspends his rhetoric between a witty joke and a disagreeable sneer. Marianne can command no such finesse. She simply heaps up conceptual terms that designate emotion because she is convinced that feeling alone has value: "Add to which . . . that he has neither genius, taste, nor spirit. That his understanding has no brilliancy, his feelings no ardour, and his voice no expression." Her final phrase rings with irony only for us; for her it is truly climactic, a fit indictment of Colonel Brandon's lackluster personality. In short, Marianne's feelings engage her completely, and her essential difference from Willoughby comes clear again.

Elinor cannot combat emotions of this order with mere argument:

> "You decide on his imperfections so much in the mass . . . and so much on the strength of your own imagination, that the commendation I am able to give of him is comparatively cold and insipid. I can only pronounce him to be a sensible man, well-bred, well-informed, of gentle address, and I believe possessing an amiable heart."

She may cite the main errors of Marianne and Willoughby once more: "mass" perhaps refers to their intense rhetoric, especially their series, and "imagination" suggests that their judgment is illogical. But Elinor's reason has made no headway against her opponents, so she ends—with conscious irony—by shaping an explicitly personal judgment in a series of her own. Willoughby pounces on Elinor's opinion, first professing to find a slight breach of decorum in it, but then pretending, like a true gallant, to overlook the breach by exaggerating his own willfulness:

> "Miss Dashwood . . . you are now using me unkindly. You are endeavouring to disarm me by reason, and to convince me against my will. But it will not do. You shall find me as stubborn as you can be artful. I have three unanswerable reasons for disliking Colonel Brandon: he has threatened me with rain when I wanted it to be fine; he has found fault with the hanging of my curricle, and I cannot persuade him to buy my brown mare. If it will be any satisfaction to you, however, to be told, that I believe his character to be in other respects irreproachable, I am ready to confess it. And in return for an acknowledgment, which must give me some pain, you cannot deny me the privilege of disliking him as much as ever."

His exaggerated antitheses now seem designed to mock his emotion. But only in parody will he state his real feelings about Colonel Brandon, which is not to bear their moral weight. If Willoughby assumes the role of a social hero who will sacrifice himself for the comfort of a lady, yet his rhetoric derides the distinctions of reason throughout the passage.

The conversation itself generates a sense of speed which verbal analysis of this sort pretty mercilessly destroys, a sense that arises from one person putting the previous speaker's words or structure to a new use. But the dancelike movement, if it can be called that, is rigidly patterned: the dancers go through a series of prescribed groupings rather than improvise fluently. Although this first dialogue is the more brilliant, the second (pp. 288–90) is less mechanical, dramatizing the gravely restrained emotions of Elinor and Edward. Again an absent Colonel Brandon serves as the metaphoric vehicle by which deep personal feelings may be obliquely expressed. He has commissioned Elinor to present the living of Delaford to Edward, so she finds herself in the predicament of offering the man she loves the means to marry Lucy. Edward, of course, has been avoiding Elinor since the publication of his engagement, and when he learns of the Colonel's plan from her, he becomes convinced that she must have an understanding of some sort with his patron.

At the start of their talk, however, he has simply dropped in to say goodbye, embarrassment at his own situation halting his delivery:

> "Mrs. Jennings told me . . . that you wished to speak with me, at least I understood her so—or I certainly should not have intruded . . . though at the same time, I should have been extremely sorry to leave London without seeing you and your sister; especially as it will most likely be some time—it is not probable that I should soon have the pleasure of meeting you again."

In spite of his shyness, Edward wants "extremely sorry" to prove his special interest in Elinor, though he also mentions "your sister" so as not to offend. And his personal regret lies even nearer the surface in the colloquial "it will most likely," too near, he evidently feels, for he replaces it with the more formal, more firmly general "it is not probable."

Elinor also defines her feeling by what she excludes, striving to appear impersonal in her remarks. At first she does so, following Edward's cue, by the "our" and "we" that seem to speak for Marianne as well as herself; in similar fashion, the phrase "good wishes" suggests an emotional temperature suitable to friendship and no more:

> "You would not have gone, however . . . without receiving our good wishes, even if we had not been able to give them in person. Mrs. Jennings was quite right in what she said. . . . I am charged with a most agreeable office, (breathing rather faster than usual as she spoke.) Colonel Brandon . . . has desired me to say that . . . he has great pleasure in offering you the living of Delaford . . . . Allow me to congratulate you on having so respectable and well-judging a friend, and to join in his wish that the living . . . were much more considerable, and such as might better enable you to—as might be more than a temporary accommodation to yourself—such, in short, as might establish all your views of happiness." [5]

Although she makes a gesture of putting Edward at ease by verifying Mrs. Jennings' statement, Elinor immediately withdraws even further, into the anonymity of an "office." Naturally she has to call it a "most agreeable" one because everyone must pretend that Edward knows what he is about with Lucy; but, much more important, by transforming herself into a mere agent, Elinor can tender the living without being thought to comment herself in any way on Edward's engagement. All the emotions behind the offer belong explicitly to the Colonel; for her part, Elinor will only "join in his wish." Since good breeding demands some expression of feeling, however, she brings herself to congratulate Edward on his "friend," not on his good fortune (which might come too close to Lucy), nor, of course, on his fiancée. She stumbles so at the end, I suspect, less because she despises Lucy than because to speak the word "engagement" would bring her own emotional relationship with Edward too directly into the open. Her desperate evasions all the way through betray her real passion.

Edward responds with two words—"Colonel Brandon!"—which are highly ambiguous. Perhaps they merely repeat the name of an unexpected benefactor. Or maybe they express a conviction—tinged with surprise? with regret?—that Elinor has urged Colonel Brandon to the act, which raises all sorts of doubts about her present feelings for Edward himself. Or possibly they signal a dawning suspicion on his part of an intimacy between her and the Colonel. Elinor sets out to be impersonal again in her reply, but her sympathy can be detected in the emotional terms with which she describes Edward's position:

> "Yes . . . Colonel Brandon means it as a testimony of his concern for what has lately passed—for the cruel situation in which the unjustifiable conduct of your family has placed you—a concern which I am sure Marianne, myself, and all your friends must share; and likewise as a proof of his high esteem for your general character, and his particular approbation of your behaviour on the present occasion."

And she is aware that her feelings show, for she hurries on to make the "concern" a general one and to bury herself in the category of "friends." Yet we may question whether Elinor succeeds in obliterating herself completely in her conclusion. Of course, she again ascribes the praise to Colonel Brandon, and it is moral praise, thus not dangerously private in its emotion, whoever may be its source. But in the zealous approval of Edward's stand against his family is there not a hint of Elinor's own contempt for the family which has disapproved of a match between Edward and herself?

However this may be, Edward's answer—"Colonel Brandon give *me* a living!—Can it be possible?"—sets up the same reverberations as before, ranging from sheer surprise to a suspicion that Elinor is close to Colonel Brandon. This time her response obviously transcends her "office": "The unkindness of your own relations has made you astonished to find friendship any where." Though her phrasing is impersonal and though she still mentions "friendship," only keen sympathy could make such a remark possible. Edward senses this and tries to break through to her personal feelings: "No . . . not to find it in *you*; for I cannot be ignorant that to you, to your goodness I owe it all.—I feel it—I would express it if I could—but, as you well know, I am no orator." His emphatic *"you"* is instinct with emotion, even if he somewhat weakens its force in going on to speak of her as his benefactor rather than his beloved. Moreover, Edward refers directly to his own feelings, though denying his ability to "express" them.

Elinor tries to escape involvement by stepping back toward her earlier role, and on the surface, at least, she is successful:

> "You are very much mistaken. I do assure you that you owe it entirely, at least almost entirely, to your own merit, and Colonel Brandon's discernment of it. I have had no hand in it. I did not even know . . . that the living was vacant . . . . As a friend of mine, of my family, he may perhaps—indeed I know he *has*, still greater pleasure in bestowing it; but, upon my word, you owe nothing to my solicitation."

Ironically enough, however, her most positive confession of regard for Edward lurks behind her talk of the Colonel's pleasure in befriending the Dashwoods: Elinor's logic can only be that Colonel Brandon owes his good opinion of Edward to her family and herself. But Edward sees no further than the surface,

> which probably contributed to fix that suspicion in his mind which had recently entered it. . . . at last, and as if it were rather an effort, he said,
> "Colonel Brandon seems a man of great worth and respectability. I have always heard him spoken of as such, and your brother I know esteems him highly. He is undoubtedly a sensible man, and in his manners perfectly the gentleman."

At first glance he seems simply to reflect on the character of his good Samaritan and perhaps to compliment Elinor on having such a man for a friend. Actually he is bringing himself—in hopes of pleasing Elinor—to praise the man whom he believes she has chosen to love instead of himself. After all, Edward has heard her deny his own plea for personal feeling by admiring Colonel Brandon.

Presuming now that she is to marry the Colonel, Edward completely mistakes her reply:

> "Indeed . . . I believe that you will find him, on farther acquaintance, all that you have heard him to be; and as you will be such very near neighbours, (for I understand the parsonage is almost close to the mansion-house,) it is particularly important that he *should* be all this."

He interprets her meticulousness in referring to Colonel Brandon alone to be a sign that she has so entirely rejected himself (and his future wife) as to forbid him her presence. In the same way, Elinor's insistence that the Colonel *"should* be all this" seems to command Edward to take over a favorable opinion of his patron. And for her to recall the nearness of the "parsonage" to the "mansion-house" must appear to Edward a gratuitous cruelty. From his point of view there is indeed nothing left for him to do but leave Elinor and go to thank Colonel Brandon.

Most of these motives that I have been spelling out are

intuited readily enough, of course, by anyone who reads *Sense and Sensibility*. But translating the dialogue in such detail seems the only way of showing precisely how Jane Austen manages, even in this early novel, to communicate urgent emotional tensions within a superficially narrow tonal range. At any rate, the scene between Elinor and Edward proves that the very restraint of language—when the characters speak impersonally or decoorously about a particular situation—may itself be a device for intensification. In proving this, the scene again reflects the theme of the novel, that sense and sensibility must interpenetrate, and warns us to keep a sharp lookout for similar effects, or more subtle ones, in the novels to come.

1. One symptom of Jane Austen's immaturity in the matter of point of view is that her manipulation of it sometimes produces narrative effects which are highly suspect, to say the least. What are we to make of that curious passage in which we are transferred into the mind of Mrs. Jennings while Elinor and Colonel Brandon, as we later learn, discuss the offer of a living to Edward Ferrars (pp. 280–82)? If we are meant to share momentarily Mrs. Jennings' supposition that the Colonel is courting Elinor, the less likely alternative, surely Jane Austen should sustain the ambiguity longer. But if, as seems much more probable, she designs the shift in point of view to make us laugh at Mrs. Jennings' absurd speculation, surely the old lady's foibles have been sufficiently underlined earlier—and to tease the joke through ten pages is nearly tedious. Also dubious is the novel's climax, where we learn with Elinor of Lucy Steele's marriage to a Mr. Ferrars, but it turns out to be Robert, not Edward: the final effect is less dramatic than coy.

2. In my opinion, several critics have been misled by the major emphasis on Elinor's sense to interpret the novel as rejecting all emotion. Thus Marvin Mudrick, who puts the case most forcefully, finds the author contending that "Not merely *false* feeling, but feeling itself, is bad . . . . because it is a personal commitment" (*Jane Austen*, pp. 90–91). But I think the novel differentiates more firmly between excessive and appropriate emotion than the critic will allow. Surely the speech about "duty" just cited insists that Elinor's sense of what is proper is deeply informed by her feeling, that she makes an intensely "personal commitment." Mudrick is hampered, to my mind, by his reluctance to concede that one may express personal emotion in adhering to social forms—or even that these forms may have any meaningful content. The split that he assumes between private and social code lurks behind a remark like "Elinor has misgivings about Willoughby, but they exclusively concern his failure to attend to social forms" (p. 83). Yet the

implicit distinction here between a personal and a social judgment would be inconceivable to Elinor—and in the world of the novel.

3. Colonel Brandon's most interesting variation of his technique, or violation of it, occurs when he tells Elinor about the seducing of his ward by Willoughby (pp. 204–10). Although the Colonel's emotions lead him into one of his typical verbal morasses at the outset, and though he periodically lunges at the cloak of decorum with explanations like "I *will* be more collected," most of his remarks beg openly for tears: indeed Jane Austen has him describing such items as a "spunging-house," a former beloved "in the last stage of a consumption," and "a little girl, the off-spring of her first guilty connection" in the sort of stock rhetoric and trite language that she could ridicule unmercifully in the *Juvenilia*. I think we may fairly wonder whether these verbal monstrosities really represent the flowering of Colonel Brandon's personality—in which case we can be thankful that we hear no more from him than we do—or a collection of pressures on Jane Austen. It seems to me that the latter is more likely, that she temporarily forces him out of character, making him abandon his habitual retreat to the decorum of silence so that he can speak in behalf of the novel. For the course of *Sense and Sensibility* demands that Willoughby's past come clear; Colonel Brandon is the only character in anything like a position to tell a story of this sort; and I suspect that Jane Austen, in her inexperience, felt it necessary to treat such a revelation in absolutely unambiguous moral terms—though the result here is stylistically gross. This is the kind of overeagerness, I think, that we have seen before: when Jane Austen shifts our point of view to make fun of Mrs. Jennings or underlines the irony at Elinor's excessive feeling.

4. A distinction such as I have suggested between the use of figurative language by Marianne and by Willoughby appears as well in Samuel Richardson's *Clarissa,* where he sustains it to dramatize a similar clash of personality: between Clarissa, who is always in the grip of her ideals, speaks her figures from the bottom of her heart, and Lovelace, who is playing a part and remains in control of his figures. But I doubt that one should think of this as a technical device which Jane Austen discovered while reading Richardson and later employed herself. Rather, it seems to me the sort of dramatic vehicle that any author might happen on when imagining his characters intensively. Of course, Willoughby does strike one as deriving, at some remove, from Lovelace, but Marianne and Clarissa feel worlds apart. If it is true that Jane Austen should be regarded as a distant follower of Richardson in treating to some extent the interior of personality, still the novels of the two create radically different impressions. Richardson proceeds—and no one can doubt the power of the method—by suffocating the reader through enveloping him in the minutest details of personality and event; Jane Austen keeps us further off from her characters, even those with whom her point of view identifies us, and the air is always plentiful, its temperature more various.

5. Mary Lascelles has noted that for the type of the parenthetical

intrusion here—"(breathing rather faster than usual as she spoke.)"— Jane Austen is ultimately indebted to Samuel Richardson, who discovered that "a parenthetical phrase, most often built upon a present participle, if introduced abruptly into the midst of a speech . . . gives the air of eyewitness" (*Jane Austen*, p. 110). According to the critic, this trick was also taken over by Fanny Burney and Boswell.

4 Northanger Abbey
Parody, Pedagogy, and the Play of Feeling

Northanger Abbey is a much gayer affair than *Sense and Sensibility*. Not that its essential subject is any less weighty: the novel pits reality against Catherine Morland's imagination as uncompromisingly as *Sense and Sensibility* contrasts Elinor with Marianne. Nor does the element of parody, which of itself would be brittle enough, account for *Northanger Abbey*'s gaiety. Rather, the delicately light tone of the whole and especially the wonderful suppleness of the conversations between Catherine and Henry Tilney fill the novel with a spirit of *joie de vivre*. *Northanger Abbey* has a far richer flavor than its genesis as a parody of those Gothic tales which came to enthrall the eighteenth century would suggest, and, I believe, a firmer body.[1]

It is surely, at bottom, a novel about education, one which Jane Austen might well have subtitled "The Dangers of the Imagination," for Catherine skirmishes with the same enemy throughout the book. During its first half she naïvely misinterprets many of the social actualities at Bath because, imposed upon by Isabella Thorpe, she tends to view them according to notions of friendship and honor that derive ultimately from novels of sentiment. But while those novels treat sentiment as a means of insight, in *Northanger Abbey* it is associated with a lack of perception. Thus Catherine, under the spell of her apparently intimate companionship with Isabella, completely misjudges the rise and fall of her friend's supposed attachment to James Morland; determined to find nothing but fidelity in Isabella, Catherine simply overlooks such facts as her friend's irritation on learning that James is not rich or her subsequent flirtation with Captain Tilney. In the second half of the story, Northanger Abbey itself gives Catherine all the encouragement she needs to transform life into a piece of Gothic fiction—to read the natural death of General Tilney's wife as a bizarre murder that he has plotted. Whether Isabella or the Abbey supplies the local stimulus for Catherine, the source of her difficulties remains her own gullible imagination, which seizes on novels as statements of fact and therefore distorts the reality surrounding her. It is this strand of meaning that ties the halves of the story together, even though the parodic episode at the Abbey seems strained in comparison with the earlier, more realistic scenes at Bath.

Of course parody and realism exist side by side throughout *Northanger Abbey* because of the particular narrative device that Jane Austen has chosen to dramatize her theme. This device consists of providing the reader with two bearings, as it were, on Catherine's actions: Jane Austen takes one of these herself, masquerading as an author who champions the behavior recommended by sentimental novels; the other she takes from inside the story by means of the sensitively rational Henry Tilney, whose opinions are solidly grounded in reality. In her own role Jane Austen talks of Catherine and a typical sentimental heroine in the same breath, when describing, for instance, a reconciliation with Henry:

> Feelings rather natural than heroic possessed her; instead of considering her own dignity injured by this ready condemnation—instead of proudly resolving, in conscious innocence, to shew her resentment towards him who could harbour a doubt of it . . . and to enlighten him on the past only by avoiding his sight, or flirting with somebody else, she took to herself all the shame of misconduct, or at least of its appearance, and was only eager for an opportunity of explaining its cause. (p. 93)

Passages of this sort, many of them sounding a much stronger note of parody, recur throughout the story and answer several purposes. They serve to remind us that Catherine has her own problems with novels, and in doing so they keep the theme of *Northanger Abbey* before us. But they also mark the real difference between the fundamentally honest, good-natured Catherine and the egotistical, exaggeratedly sensitive heroine of the sentimental novel, as is evident in the lines I have quoted. This difference needs to be maintained, because Catherine must develop and reform as the story goes on. Obviously Jane Austen's pose as commentator restricts her in the main to speaking parodically and forbids her to show Catherine any way out of her difficulties. That job is turned over to Henry Tilney, who for all his wit performs in a basically realistic fashion. This remains the dominant tone of the novel, far outweighing the element of parody, and fittingly enough, for Catherine must finally come to terms with a real world.

Although Henry courts Catherine with verve from the beginning of *Northanger Abbey* to the end, he offers her at the same time a complete course of instruction in sensible behavior. During the scenes at Bath he aims primarily at discovering the nature of society to her, whereas at the Abbey he concerns himself largely with enlightening her about herself. But a distinction of this sort should really not be made, for in either case he tries to free Catherine's imagination from the errors bred in it by reading novels. Perhaps the shape, import, and texture of the story will come clearer, however, if I first sketch the major influences to which Catherine is exposed, then present a typical conversation in which Henry plays the pedagogue, and finally—to suggest *Northanger Abbey*'s vivacity and subtlety— explore a dialogue in which the feeling of Henry and Catherine for each other is transmitted through a gracefully modulated verbal surface.

II

The most important fact that Catherine must be brought to recognize in the world at Bath is the duplicity of Isabella and John Thorpe, both of whom make a practice of showing off their individuality by manipulating fashionable communities of opinion. (I shall always be using *community of opinion* pejoratively: to mean a view which appears the property of a select group and thus suggests the social exclusiveness of the person professing it.) To be sure, the young Thorpes are not the only bad angels whom Catherine encounters. But neither Mrs. Allen nor Mrs. Thorpe—the one of them proving her utter self-concern by habitually generalizing about dress, the other by generalizing about the virtues of her own family—wields real influence over Catherine. And even General Tilney does not pose any sustained threat to her while she remains at Bath. John and Isabella do, however; and, though the brother is too openly a boor to gain much ground in his suit for Catherine, she needs all the help she can get from Henry Tilney to protect her sensibility against the sister.

Plainly Isabella models the role that she usually adopts in *Northanger Abbey* on the conduct celebrated by sentimental novels. Her air of intimacy with Catherine in the following passage, which occurs during the first conversation that we hear between them, may serve to remind us how quickly such friendships flourished in the sentimental tradition. But more directly, her vigorous diction, extravagant figures, and intensive generalizations are designed to publish a most spirited set of feelings—presumably to convince Catherine, here, of how warmly Isabella regards her:

> "There is nothing I would not do for those who are really my friends. I have no notion of loving people by halves, it is not my nature. My attachments are always excessively strong. I told Capt. Hunt at one of our assemblies . . . that . . . I would not dance with him, unless he would allow Miss Andrews to be as beautiful as an angel. The men think us incapable of real friendship you know, and I am determined to shew them the difference. Now, if I were to hear any body speak slightingly of you, I should fire up in a moment:—but that is not at all likely, for *you* are just the kind of girl to be a great favourite with the men."
>
> (pp. 40–41)

Actually, Isabella has her eye not on Catherine but on herself.

In the opening sentences she cuts a figure by generalizations that flaunt her emotional integrity. Then she summons up a community of opinion—a kind of generalization that she momentarily affects to share with Catherine, yet immediately turns to her own advantage—about the "real friendship" that exists between young ladies despite what men may say. Of course the mere content of this advances Isabella's cause to some extent, because it obviously applies to elegant young ladies only. But she exalts herself more spectacularly by the way in which she manages the generalization: minimizing its communal aspects, she treats it as a springboard to catapult her into new revelations of her strenuous loyalty—"I should fire up in a moment" —and of her personal insight in recognizing Catherine's attractions. In sum, Isabella enjoys all the social convenience of calling on what seems a community of opinion about "real friendship" while in fact she restricts the community to herself, appropriating the public power of the view to a display of her own uniqueness. (This fundamental self-centeredness in Isabella does in fact ally her, whether she realizes it or not, with the cult of sensibility celebrated in novels, which itself promotes egocentricity in exalting the feelings of the individual.) The cited passage is characteristic in the sense that Isabella is driving to gratify herself in whatever she utters, whether she assumes the intensely sentimental pose that she does here or speaks, as we shall hear a little later, with a more than hard-headed practicality.

John devotes himself as avidly as Isabella to pursuing his own pleasure and performing with dash. His execution is much less subtle than hers, in fact sometimes crudely profane, yet like Isabella he tries to impress his superiority on Catherine by exploiting a community of opinion, whether he talks with her about horses, his usual subject, or "drinking":

"There is no drinking at Oxford now, I assure you. Nobody drinks there. You would hardly meet with a man who goes beyond his four pints at the utmost. Now, for instance, it was reckoned a remarkable thing at the last party in my rooms, that upon an average we cleared about five pints a head. . . . *Mine* is famous good stuff to be sure. You would not often meet with any thing like it in Oxford—and that may account for it." (p. 64)

John derisively sets up a fashionable norm of "four pints" with his first generalizations, thrusting right on from them to make his deviation from the standard known. The intensive "remarkable" and "famous" advertise his supremacy, while in effect he substantiates his claim by the reliable impersonality of "it was reckoned" and the apparently cautious "not often" or "may account." Again the power of generalizations has been misappropriated to the service of the individual.

John, then, zealously plays up to his idea of a "sport" in his abortive efforts to court Catherine—too engrossed by his role to realize how little it appeals to her. And Isabella casts herself as the kind of spirited young lady popularized by novels when she wins Catherine's friendship, attracts James Morland into an engagement, breaks with James to try her luck with Frederick Tilney, and at last, jilted by him, seeks a reconciliation with James through Catherine. It is the sort of style practiced by the Thorpes, with its giddy magnification of the trivial and its parade of intensity, that Henry Tilney sets out to undermine in his first conversation with Catherine (pp. 26–27). There he works by mimicking the style, either feigning not to believe that Catherine keeps no "journal"—"How are your various dresses to be remembered, and the particular state of your complexion, and curl of your hair to be described in all their diversities, without having constant recourse to a journal?"—or mocking a smart emotionalism:

Then forming his features into a set smile, and affectedly softening his voice, he added, with a simpering air, "Have you been long in Bath, madam?"

"About a week, sir," replied Catherine, trying not to laugh.

"Really!" with affected astonishment.

"Why should you be surprised, sir?"

"Why, indeed!" said he, in his natural tone—"but some emotion must appear to be raised by your reply, and surprize is more easily assumed, and not less reasonable than any other.—Now let us go on. Were you never here before, madam?"

Clearly Henry objects to the style itself on the ground that the feeling it lavishes on details exaggerates them beyond all reason. But his "assumed" hints at another objection, that the style may become a means of disguise. His hint is borne out when the Thorpes appear in *Northanger Abbey*, for, as we have already seen, they exploit the style mercilessly, using the social code that it reflects as a modish façade while contriving to aggrandize themselves.

The impropriety of the Thorpes is not a matter of style alone; it extends to their behavior as well. The novel shows them twisting social forms as ruthlessly as linguistic ones to serve their own ends. Without a qualm John lies to Catherine about seeing Henry drive away with Eleanor Tilney and later lies to them about Catherine having a previous engagement, all for the purpose of clearing his own path to Catherine and to the fortune that he believes her to possess. It is ironically fitting that John's self-absorption should doubly frustrate him in the end: when he attempts to propose, he is so busy managing his own role to create this new community of opinion that he fails to perceive Catherine's total ignorance of what he intends; and he brags to General Tilney of Catherine's wealth in order to glorify himself, with the result that the General encourages Henry's suit, which makes John's hopeless.

As for Isabella, whether she intrigues with Catherine, James Morland, or Frederick Tilney, she presses after money as single-mindedly as John, and as indecorously. But she achieves a climax richer in fraud than anything he can manage. It occurs when she has already decided to abandon James, because he turns out to be poorer than she had thought, for Frederick Tilney, and just after she has been fostering an attachment between Catherine and John, only to find that Catherine feels no attraction to him. "Since that is the case," replies Isabella, "I shall not tease you any further"; "I thought it a very foolish, imprudent business, and not likely to promote the good of either," for "it is not a trifle that will support a family now-a-days; and after all that romancers may say, there is no doing without money" (pp. 145–46). She cheerfully repudiates the sentimental community of opinion with which she has constantly plied Catherine as a "tease," something "romancers may say," and replaces it with tough financial judgments. Even this new sense, however, is laid down by her with an eye to her own benefit, not Catherine's. Isabella is really engaged, as the continuation of the dialogue shows, in making out a case for her rejection of James before hinting at her change of mind to Catherine. For she readily perverts Catherine's reference to morality—"You *do* acquit me then of any thing wrong?"—to trap her into another community of opinion, one which is in fact grounded in Isabella's entirely selfish concern with her own situation, although the impersonal phrasing lends a specious air of authority to what she says and even pretends to regard the case of Catherine:

> "Oh! as to that . . . . A little harmless flirtation or so will occur, and one is often drawn on to give more encouragement than one wishes to stand by. . . . All those things should be allowed for in youth and high spirits. What one means one day, you know, one may not mean the next. Circumstances change, opinions alter." (p. 146)

The generalizations are strictly controlled to prepare Catherine for Isabella's turn to Frederick Tilney and to justify it. All the earlier intensities of manner have disappeared, but Isabella's dedication to self-interest remains, which suggests that she is always playing a part, never committing herself in and through her speech.

A distinction of this sort between words and deeds is exactly what Catherine's general naïveté and specific fascination with novels prevent her from recognizing adequately. Henry Tilney keeps trying to open her eyes whenever they meet, to the Thorpes in particular, though he never judges them personally for Catherine, as well as to social uses and abuses as a whole. Sometimes he employs the mimicry we noticed earlier, and often he speaks out more directly; but he never, in contrast to the

Thorpes, imposes his views on Catherine. The job he under-takes is of instructing her how to form her own opinions ra-tionally. So if she badgers him to explain how his brother could think of making up to an already engaged Isabella, Henry at first arranges his replies to shed a clear light on her friend: "Is it my brother's attentions to Miss Thorpe, or Miss Thorpe's admission of them, that gives the pain?" or "I understand: she is in love with James, and flirts with Frederick" (p. 151). But when Catherine demands that he "guess" at his brother's mo-tives, Henry refuses:

> " . . . —Nay, if it is to be guess-work, let us all guess for our-selves. To be guided by second-hand conjecture is pitiful. The premises are before you. My brother is a lively, and perhaps sometimes a thoughtless young man; he has had about a week's acquaintance with your friend, and he has known her engage-ment almost as long as he has known her." (pp. 151–52)

After the powerful generalization about "conjecture," he insists that she decide for herself and then summarizes the evidence on which she may act. This is Henry's invariable goal—to teach Catherine sensible processes of thinking and to make her accept responsibility for them.

In the second half of the story, it is Catherine's fevered mis-interpretation of General Tilney brought on by her exposure to the Abbey that needs curing. Certainly the General stands as a bad enough angel in his own right, yet he hardly measures up to her vision of him—more appropriate in something like *The Mysteries of Udolpho*—as the murderer of his wife. The worst he can do is peremptorily dismiss Catherine from his home when he discovers that she lacks the fortune credited to her by John Thorpe. Many readers have objected that this act seems dramatically unconvincing; without denying the charge, we might nevertheless observe that the General's earlier re-marks betray the same kind of indecorous self-indulgence. In-deed he is a somewhat toned-down version of the Thorpes, pushing forward himself and his desires as assiduously as they do, though he accomplishes this by reversing their technique, that is, by constantly feigning to minimize or censure himself. His first real speech in the novel stamps his nature for us, when he characteristically intrudes to take over what his daughter has begun and invite Catherine to the Abbey himself:

> "My daughter, Miss Morland . . . has been forming a very bold wish. We leave Bath . . . . And could we carry our selfish point with you, we should leave it without a single regret. Can you, in short, be prevailed on to quit this scene of public triumph and oblige your friend Eleanor with your company in Gloucestershire? I am almost ashamed to make the request, though its presumption would certainly appear greater to every creature in Bath than yourself. Modesty such as your's—but not for the world would I pain it by open praise. If you can be induced to honour us with a visit, you will make us happy beyond expression." (p. 139)

Although the General seems to shower Catherine with consideration here, true decorum would hardly sanction so lushly emotional an address or the florid self-deprecation of "our selfish point" and "almost ashamed." Nor would it allow him the direct mention of her "modesty," which he has all the satisfaction of pointing to before he pretends to retreat decently. The whole passage is overripe, as if he were more interested in publicizing his own sense of propriety and his own capacity to feel than in actually persuading Catherine, even though her visit is much to his purpose. And in fact General Tilney never, here or elsewhere, really projects himself into others. Whatever he says discloses how self-indulgent he is, whether in half-covertly calling attention to himself and his possessions or in bending everyone else to his wishes.

Eleanor Tilney is the opposite of her father. One of *Northanger Abbey*'s good angels, she works side by side with the more vivacious Henry in the service of reason and decorum. Thus she provides a contrast to the selfish Isabella Thorpe and to the egocentric General Tilney—and never more dramatically than when she is charged with the General's command to banish Catherine from the Abbey. In her talk with Catherine (p. 225),

Eleanor demonstrates the warmest sympathy and, what is more impressive, an integrity founded in the deepest feeling:

> "I could hardly believe my senses, when I heard it;—and no displeasure, no resentment that you can feel at this moment, however justly great, can be more than I myself—but I must not talk of what I felt. . . . Good God! what will your father and mother say! After courting you from the protection of real friends . . . to have you driven out of the house, without the considerations even of decent civility!"

Thoroughly upset herself by what her father has done, she can yet ignore her own pain for, or translate it into, the effect of the incident on Catherine and the Morlands. Because of Eleanor's relationship to the General she cannot denounce him outright: "Alas! for my feelings as a daughter, all that I know, all that I answer for is, that you can have given him no just cause of offence." But the claims of decorum weigh far more heavily with her than loyalty to her father, as she shows in her closing judgment of Catherine's hurried departure: "I hope, I earnestly hope that to your real safety it will be of none; but to every thing else it is of the greatest consequence; to comfort, appearance, propriety, to your family, to the world." Eleanor's generalization brings the conceptual terms to life by insisting on their value. And she proves herself emotionally committed to these values by pleading with Catherine to write her, even though General Tilney has forbidden all correspondence between them.

At this narrative climax of *Northanger Abbey*, it is up to Eleanor to stand by Catherine and give what aid she can, for Henry is away from home. But he has already guided Catherine through the thematic climax of the story, which occurs before the General has any thought of forcing her to leave. One day at the Abbey, Henry surprises Catherine as she comes from the room of his dead mother, where she has been searching for proof of the monstrous crimes that she imagines General Tilney to have perpetrated. Learning her suspicions, Henry discovers that all his earlier efforts to educate her in the nature of the world have hardly helped, and he proceeds to offer her his plainest lesson in logic and its moral consequences. He needs to do so, less because her misconception libels his father than because it is a sin against her own faculties. Thus, after carefully spelling out his father's innocence in the affair, Henry turns directly to Catherine at the culmination of the dialogue, reproving her more openly than ever before for the impropriety into which her abuse of reason has led her:

> "If I understand you rightly, you had formed a surmise of such horror as I have hardly words to—Dear Miss Morland, consider the dreadful nature of the suspicions you have entertained. What have you been judging from? Remember the country and the age in which we live. Remember that we are English, that we are Christians. Consult your own understanding, your own sense of the probable, your own observation of what is passing around you—Does our education prepare us for such atrocities? Do our laws connive at them? Could they be perpetrated without being known . . . ? Dearest Miss Morland, what ideas have you been admitting?" (pp. 197–98)

He asks her to view the reality about her reasonably rather than imaginatively, that is, to correct the very processes of her thought. Now he uses the novelistic language of intensity—the "horror" and "dreadful" of which Catherine has been so fond— not parodically but literally, as an accurate measure of her moral aberration. And Henry's rhetoric is just as forthright, aligning the series of facts that she has forgotten and accumulating the rhetorical questions to develop an intensity quite unusual for him, but one justified because Catherine has outraged morality. Even at a moment like this, however, he expresses his feeling for her by "Dearest Miss Morland," though she is too morti- fied to notice it.

Still, Catherine has finally been shocked into seeing herself and the world clearly. So the General's violence, when it comes, stirs her emotions but not her imagination, as Jane Austen de- clares: "Her anxiety had foundation in fact, her fears in prob- ability; and with a mind so occupied in the contemplation of

✻✻✻✻✻✻✻✻✻✻✻✻✻✻✻✻✻✻✻✻✻✻✻✻✻✻✻✻✻✻✻✻

actual and natural evil, the solitude of her situation, the dark-
ness of her chamber, the antiquity of the building were felt and
considered without the smallest emotion" (p. 227). And Catherine can return to her own home, convinced of her blameless-
ness and recognizing the genuine guilt of General Tilney. There
she may wonder restlessly what Henry really thinks of her and
chafe under the rather prosaic sense of her mother—that lady
who might well make Henry's instruction unnecessary if she
were with Catherine throughout the story. But Henry soon arrives to put an end to her suspense and to gain the consent of
her parents to their marriage.

⊣[III]⊢

The theme of the novel is expressed most obviously in its main
action, then, which shows Catherine making a morally secure
discovery of herself at the Abbey, arriving at a fuller understanding of her enemies, whether the Thorpes or General
Tilney, and finally winning Henry, the champion of reason.
It is through the dialogues between Catherine and Henry, however, that Jane Austen dramatizes her theme most richly, rendering in them the very process of education. We have already seen
Henry teaching his pupil by open mockery and earnest warn-
ings, but his usual mode is closer to the lively irony that runs
through his talk with Catherine when she accompanies him and
Eleanor on a walk out from Bath (pp. 106–10). Indeed he holds
forth with so much wit here that for me to concentrate on
dredging up the serious purposes in what he says must seem an
overly solemn affair. Yet perhaps such an analysis can be justified if it suggests how thoroughly a representative passage in the
novel is imbued with its theme. And the passage is representative, not only of Henry's charming educational methods but of
Northanger Abbey's whole movement: for rather as Catherine
turns from literature to life in the story, so this conversation be-

gins with the case of literature and ends in considering life itself.

The dialogue gets under way with Henry a bit puzzled when his protégée, admiring a cliff outside of Bath, seems to equate reading with reality:

> "I never look at it," said Catherine . . . "without thinking of the south of France."
> "You have been abroad then?" said Henry, a little surprized.
> "Oh! no, I only mean what I have read about. It always puts me in mind of the country that Emily and her father travelled through, in the 'Mysteries of Udolpho.' But you never read novels, I dare say?"
> "Why not?"
> "Because they are not clever enough for you—gentlemen read better books."

But when Catherine apparently separates herself from him by these last generalizations, Henry's reply shows him in perfect control. His words stand both as a compliment, declaring that there is no distance between them, and as an ironic reminder of the violent sensibility cultivated by fiction of this sort in its devotees:

> "The person, be it gentleman or lady, who has not pleasure in a good novel, must be intolerably stupid. I have read all Mrs. Radcliffe's works, and most of them with great pleasure. The Mysteries of Udolpho, when I had once begun it, I could not lay down again;—I remember finishing it in two days—my hair standing on end the whole time."

The opening generalization about the "pleasure in a good novel" looks firmly sensible—as if Henry shares and approves of Catherine's taste—except for his "intolerably," which pushes a trifle too far, making the whole sentence sound like the claim of a too intense partisan. But perhaps the ambiguity of his tone comes through more clearly in the last clause, where the exaggeration about "my hair standing on end" may warrant how completely he belongs to Catherine's party or caricature the agitation of novel readers.

Henry continues in this equivocal vein with the deft extension of a legal metaphor when he next speaks, after Eleanor has described his impatience to finish *The Mysteries of Udolpho*:

> "Thank you, Eleanor;—a most honourable testimony. You see, Miss Morland, the injustice of your suspicions. Here was I, in my eagerness to get on, refusing to wait only five minutes for my sister; breaking the promise I had made of reading it aloud, and keeping her in suspense at a most interesting part, by running away with the volume, which, you are to observe, was her own, particularly her own. I am proud when I reflect on it, and I think it must establish me in your good opinion."

By "testimony," "injustice," and "opinion" Henry invokes the law and its implications of authority—to give Catherine a sober guarantee, it would seem, of his enthusiasm for novels. But of course the behavior which he dwells on, of himself as a novel-reader, is a series of improprieties, if not illegalities. While the ironic value of the figure becomes clearest in Henry's closing reference to "your good opinion," it is also true that the last sentence continues to express his desire of having a place in Catherine's "good opinion." His use of the metaphor throughout the passage epitomizes Henry's attitude: his control of it suggests the detached superiority of a judge, yet he controls it to demonstrate his liking for Catherine.

But she destroys the delicate balance of his two speeches, if she has ever really been aware of it, by taking what he has said of novels at face value and then delivering an even more extreme version of her previous statement about men and books. Catherine's generalization now typifies the whole sentimental mode that he has been covertly attacking, her new formula abandoning the moderate language of reason for the jargon of emotional intensity:

> "I am very glad to hear it indeed, and now I shall never be ashamed of liking Udolpho myself. But I really thought before, young men despised novels amazingly."

"It is *amazingly;* it may well suggest *amazement* if they do—
for they read nearly as many as women. I myself have read hundreds and hundreds. Do not imagine that you can cope with me
in a knowledge of Julias and Louisas. If we proceed to particulars, and engage in the never-ceasing inquiry of 'Have you read
this?' and 'Have you read that?' I shall soon leave you as far behind me as— . . . I want an appropriate simile;—as far as your
friend Emily herself left poor Valancourt when she went with
her aunt into Italy."

While Henry still allies himself with her to some extent by
speaking so knowingly about Catherine's favorite subject, he
seizes on her "amazingly" to dramatize the peril of her ways.
For one thing, he relocates the word in a new, a factual context,
as if to show her the conditions under which such an intense
expression can meaningfully survive. More than that, he offers
her a model of valid generalizing, in effect, by countering her
assertion with a proposal of his own about how much men read
and then going on to document it. Although the legal metaphor
reappears in "particulars" and "inquiry," it no longer seems so
equivocal: perhaps a tone of the former irony persists, but in the
main the figure now calls up the sense of a reliably rational
process. And in truth, the body of Henry's speech reveals him
engaged in weighing evidence, backing up his generalization
with specific instances before he allows himself the luxury of
"an appropriate simile" to clinch his argument.

So when Catherine, learning nothing from his demonstration,
repeats her error in referring to "Udolpho" as "the nicest book
in the world," he makes his point even more directly:

"Very true . . . and this is a very nice day, and we are taking a
very nice walk, and you are two very nice young ladies. Oh! it is
a very nice word indeed!—it does for every thing. Originally perhaps it was applied only to express neatness, propriety, delicacy,
or refinement;—people were nice in their dress, in their sentiments, or their choice. But now every commendation on every
subject is comprised in that one word."

Impudent as Henry's comments are, they add up to a solid lesson in intellectual precision, and it is just possible that they also hint at a moral critique of the sentimentally intense mode with which Catherine has associated herself. He at least proves by his climactic generalizations—in which "nice" serves "for every thing" and includes "every commendation on every subject"—that verbal commitment to the mode prohibits one from making distinctions, the very basis of thinking. And an obvious analogy suggests itself: that a personal commitment to the mode, which would mean responding with the same intensity to every stimulus, perverts the nature of human experience.

Eleanor now breaks in to chide Henry for his impertinence, then sympathetically engages Catherine in a discussion that soon turns to other reading. Although Eleanor's gentle manner changes the tone of the dialogue for the time being, the issues remain essentially the same. History is mentioned, which Catherine can peruse "a little as a duty," but

> "The quarrels of popes and kings, with wars or pestilences, in every page; the men all so good for nothing, and hardly any women at all—it is very tiresome: and yet I often think it odd that it should be so dull, for a great deal of it must be invention. The speeches that are put into the heroes' mouths, their thoughts and designs—the chief of all this must be invention, and invention is what delights me in other books."

Apparently Catherine views the facts of history as a drag on "invention," that imaginative vitality which makes fiction so compellingly real for her. Distinguishing inadequately between the genres, she blurs their separate claims to reality. Eleanor's reply, however, makes exactly the distinctions that her friend has glossed over:

> "Historians, you think . . . are not happy in their flights of fancy. They display imagination without raising interest. I am fond of history—and am very well contented to take the false with the true. In the principal facts they have sources of intelligence in former histories and records, which may be as much depended on, I conclude, as any thing that does not actually pass

under one's own observation; and as for the little embellishments you speak of, they are embellishments, and I like them as such. If a speech be well drawn up, I read it with pleasure, by whomsoever it may be made—and probably with much greater, if the production of Mr. Hume or Mr. Robertson, than if the genuine words of Caractacus, Agricola, or Alfred the Great."

For Eleanor, history is primarily factual, but it also makes use of art ("embellishments") to enhance the facts without radically distorting them; once the distinction is recognized, both orders of reality can be enjoyed. But we must still do justice to Eleanor's rhetoric here, which is as winningly deferential as it is firm. After she has generalized Catherine's position by the phrasing of her first sentences about "historians"—which serves in part to prevent her own disagreement, when it comes, from seeming a personal attack on Catherine—Eleanor quickly admits that she herself is emotionally biased (by "fond") before going on with her analysis. In the body of her argument she is scrupulous about separating facts, carefully assessing their credibility, from ornamentation. And her differentiation between the artistic and the "genuine," now applied to some specific cases, runs through the closing sentence, even while Eleanor professes her partiality again. Unlike Henry, she sustains decorum precisely by insisting on her bias, and the whole speech shows how competent an instructor she is in her own right.

Yet still Catherine resists their logic. She may now count up five people who approve of history, but she converts these "instances" into a new emotional assertion:

"So many instances within my small circle of friends is remarkable! At this rate, I shall not pity the writers of history any longer. If people like to read their books, it is all very well, but to be at so much trouble in filling great volumes, which, as I used to think, nobody would willingly ever look into, to be labouring only for the torment of little boys and girls, always struck me as a hard fate; and though I know it is all very right and necessary, I have often wondered at the person's courage that could sit down on purpose to do it."

Perhaps in opposing "all very well" to "a hard fate" or "know" to "wondered" Catherine is struggling to distinguish between what is reasonable and what she feels. But her most ringing generalizations about history here, hardly qualified by "as I used to think," remain clearly emotional in origin. Henry recognizes this and responds with some exciting pedagogy, simultaneously parodying both her claims and the illogic of her "method":

> "That little boys and girls should be tormented . . . is what no one at all acquainted with human nature in a civilized state can deny; but in behalf of our most distinguished historians, I must observe, that they might well be offended at being supposed to have no higher aim; and that by their method and style, they are perfectly well qualified to torment readers of the most advanced reason and mature time of life. I use the verb 'to torment,' as I observed to be your own method, instead of 'to instruct,' supposing them to be now admitted as synonimous."

Her claims themselves Henry undermines largely by exaggeration. First he announces it a matter of principle that all children should be mortified—his ironic clashing of "civilized" with "tormented" further dramatizing Catherine's vehemence—and then stretches her generalization until historians are harrassing the "mature" as well as the young. With his last sentence Henry points out the logical fallacy in her performance. It is in the brilliant rhetoric of his reply, though, that he mimics Catherine's procedure most instructively. We may recall how her conviction that everything historians write is dull immediately begot another generalization, even more hopelessly subjective, to the effect that tormenting children with dullness is the whole motive of historians. No wonder Henry begins by sorting out two of the ideas that she has so thoroughly entangled, the first third of his opening sentence treating the vexation of "little boys and girls," and the second third allowing historians some "higher aim." But in the closing third—as if he would now re-enact Catherine's folly—he pours together historians and torment in a new assertion. To emphasize what he is up to, he abandons that antithetic pattern that he has used, however ironically, to order distinctions within each of the first segments in his sentence, and he substitutes for it a rhetoric making a more flamboyant appeal, one that essentially piles "style" on top of "method" and "mature time of life" upon "most advanced reason" without differentiating significantly between them. And his final sentence recapitulates the whole movement, juxtaposing "torment" and "instruct" only to dissolve the antithesis in "synonimous," which spells out Catherine's surrender of sense to feeling.

Seething at his parody, Catherine tries to defend her uniting of "torment" and "instruct," striking back at him with an intense diction and an urgent rhetoric of her own:

> "You think me foolish to call instruction a torment, but if you had been as much used as myself to hear poor little children first learning their letters and then learning to spell, if you had ever seen how stupid they can be for a whole morning together, and how tired my poor mother is at the end of it . . . you would allow that to *torment* and to *instruct* might sometimes be used as synonimous words."
>
> "Very probably. But historians are not accountable for the difficulty of learning to read; and even you yourself, who do not altogether seem particularly friendly to very severe, very intense application, may perhaps be brought to acknowledge that it is very well worth while to be tormented for two or three years of one's life, for the sake of being able to read all the rest of it. Consider —if reading had not been taught, Mrs. Radcliffe would have written in vain—or perhaps might not have written at all."

"Very probably" shows Henry's rational sympathy for her. Nevertheless, he wants to make sure that the distinction he has drawn will stick: thus he again separates "tormented" from "read" while passing specific judgment on Catherine with "you yourself." But of course he must soften his reproof if he is to win her to logic and affection, so he ends with the witty yet gentle turn back to the beginning of the entire conversation.

※※※※※※※※※※※※※※※※※※※※※※※※※※※※※※※

-◄[IV]►-

It would be unfair to leave the impression, however, that Henry devotes himself only to the teaching of Catherine, or that Jane Austen intends every dialogue in *Northanger Abbey* to expose the dangers of unreasonableness. In the one that follows, for instance, she aims at dramatizing Henry's feeling for Catherine, accomplishing the job through the technique of metaphoric indirection that I have mentioned before. Although Henry's manner remains as playful as ever, his underlying appeals reverberate with emotion—and of course his sustained drive throughout the scene to maneuver Catherine into declaring that she likes him implies the degree of his commitment to her. Not only does their talk reveal Henry's intense affection for Catherine, but it also marks, through the values on which he bases his suit, how conventional he is at bottom.[2]

The conversation records the second meeting of the two (pp. 76–78), and it takes place just after John Thorpe has tried to prevent them from dancing together. Henry speaks first, his opening words unequivocally announcing his attraction to Catherine:

> "That gentleman would have put me out of patience, had he staid with you half a minute longer. He has no business to withdraw the attention of my partner from me. We have entered into a contract of mutual agreeableness for the space of an evening, and all our agreeableness belongs solely to each other for that time. Nobody can fasten themselves on the notice of one, without injuring the rights of the other. I consider a country-dance as an emblem of marriage. Fidelity and complaisance are the principal duties of both; and those men who do not chuse to dance or marry themselves, have no business with the partners or wives of their neighbours."

After that plain beginning, Henry tempers his expression to some extent by turning to the "business" metaphor that dominates the sentences immediately following. But although this figure discreetly impersonalizes Catherine as "my partner," and although Henry's very extension of it implies that he is not overwhelmed by his feelings, he develops the figure in such a way that it attaches a number of emotionally potent suggestions to the actual situation: he and Catherine are bound to "mutual agreeableness" by a "contract," and their "agreeableness belongs solely to each other." But apparently Henry does not find this figure resonant enough, for he deserts it to take "a country-dance"—in the figure that recurs throughout the rest of the dialogue—"as an emblem of marriage," the most intense of human relationships. And by the generalizations of his closing sentence Henry insists on the validity of the new figure, not blatantly—after all, one effect of his rhetoric is to keep the halves of the figure distinct—but powerfully for all that, in part through the cumulative rhetorical pattern of the sentence as a whole, and especially by the conceptual terms of his first clause, which fix the moral identity of dancing and "marriage."

Evidently the figure is too risky for the naïve Catherine. At first she rejects it as illogical, and Henry quickly breaks in with "compared" to keep her grounds strictly rational—to keep her, that is, from rejecting as well the feeling implicit in what he has said.

> "But they are such very different things!—"
> "—That you think they cannot be compared together."
> "To be sure not. People that marry can never part, but must go and keep house together. People that dance, only stand opposite each other in a long room for half an hour."

But for all the prosaic sense of Catherine's closing generalizations, their phrasing gives rise to exactly the sort of overtone which Henry has attempted to muffle. Her resolute division between the latently charged "can never part" and the utterly factual "only stand opposite each other" in effect disputes Henry's moral equation and, worse than that from his point of view, denies the emotion that he has worked to import into their situation as dancers.

Henry acknowledges the strictures of her "definition" momentarily, but only to suggest that he can be as fundamentally common-sensical as she has been. Then he immediately pushes on with his emblem to emphasize its emotional values further:

> "And such is your definition of matrimony and dancing. Taken in that light certainly, their resemblance is not striking; but I think I could place them in such a view.—You will allow, that in both, man has the advantage of choice, woman only the power of refusal; that in both, it is an engagement between man and woman, formed for the advantage of each; and that when once entered into, they belong exclusively to each other till the moment of its dissolution; that it is their duty, each to endeavour to give the other no cause for wishing that he or she had bestowed themselves elsewhere, and their best interest to keep their own imaginations from wandering towards the perfections of their neighbours, or fancying that they should have been better off with any one else. You will allow all this?"

Although Henry shows decorous restraint again in substituting the general "man" and "woman" for more particular references to himself and Catherine throughout the body of his remarks, yet by generalizing his claims he also secures a tone of added authority for the personal feeling reflected in so many of them. Perhaps no more than his reasoned agreement with society's rather hardheaded prudence appears in Henry's observation that marriage, like dancing, involves an "engagement . . . formed" to serve the interests of both the man and the woman. But certainly what he expresses through "man has the advantage of choice" is the affection that has moved him to choose Catherine as his partner—for more than a dance, by the terms of the figure. He even transmutes her low-keyed "can never part" into the vivid "belong exclusively to each other till the moment of its dissolution," pointedly reuniting this heightened emotion with dancing. Through all these generalizations the rhetorical pressure keeps building up, for Henry sets them forth in a series of "that" clauses, reaching his climax—appropriately enough—in an appeal to "duty." And it is worth noting, finally, that the "duty" Henry outlines—while it pulls in harness with "interest" to require that both he and Catherine exercise sensible control over their "imaginations"—requires as well that they direct their deepest feelings toward each other. The speech remains witty courtship, to be sure, but at the same time it delivers a sermon on human relationships, and it also urges Catherine to recognize, to respond to, the emotion of her partner.

She will not budge, however:

> "Yes, to be sure, as you state it, all this sounds very well; but still they are so very different.—I cannot look upon them at all in the same light, nor think the same duties belong to them."

Catherine ignores all the nuances with which Henry has colored the figure, either because she regards it too literally or because she objects to his use of "duty." Whichever the case, there is no shade of personal feeling in her language. So Henry undertakes to make his own fondness for Catherine even clearer, though he maintains his proper distance by continuing to manipulate the emblem and to speak impersonally of "man" and "woman":

> "In one respect, there certainly is a difference. In marriage, the man is supposed to provide for the support of the woman; the woman to make the home agreeable to the man; he is to purvey, and she is to smile. But in dancing, their duties are exactly changed; the agreeableness, the compliance are expected from him, while she furnishes the fan and the lavender water. *That*, I suppose, was the difference of duties which struck you, as rendering the conditions incapable of comparison."

Now he points out the inaccuracy of the figure, but as a way to affirm that in dancing, their present activity, it is the man who must show his regard, as Henry himself is doing, in "agreeableness" and "compliance." And his strict antitheses imply that she is showing none in return. When he caricatures Catherine's objection at the end, he does so only because her sense of some "difference of duties" seems to be what has led her to overlook the emotions inherent in his argument—and he must call attention to them somehow.

But Catherine's reaction to all this sounds as flat as ever, so Henry changes his tack to charge her directly with being indifferent toward him:

> "No, indeed, I never thought of that."
> "Then I am quite at a loss. One thing, however, I must observe. This disposition on your side is rather alarming. You totally disallow any similarity in the obligations; and may I not thence infer, that your notions of the duties of the dancing state are not so strict as your partner might wish? Have I not reason to fear, that if the gentleman who spoke to you just now were to return, or if any other gentleman were to address you, there would be nothing to restrain you from conversing with him as long as you chose?"

Henry's "quite at a loss" is alive with regret that Catherine will apparently neither subscribe to his emblem nor take in its drift, and he voices his distress more explicitly in the "alarming" and "fear" that soon follow. All the while his phrasing cuts Catherine off from any share in these emotions, as if he were thus hinting at her lack of concern. He attacks her more sharply by the figure, however, chiding Catherine for neglecting her "duties" as a dancing-partner—which is to say, if we remember Henry's main exposition of them, that she has not shown herself sufficiently attached to him. At the last, he even seems to give up the metaphoric mode itself, though without surrendering the values he has appropriated to dancing. For he moves from the relatively indirect "your notions" and "your partner" to the specific "I" and "you" to tax Catherine openly with preferring other gentlemen to himself, rendering his own lack of favor with special force by the inclusive "there would be nothing."

While the facts that Catherine now recites appear somewhat promising in themselves, her tone remains noncommittal:

> "Mr. Thorpe is such a very particular friend of my brother's, that if he talks to me, I must talk to him again; but there are hardly three young men in the room besides him, that I have any acquaintance with."
> "And is that to be my only security? alas, alas!"

So Henry is finally compelled to ask her straight out for some real assurance that she likes him. Of course, by "alas, alas!" he consciously exaggerates the feelings behind his plea, but in order to keep the public expression of them decorous he must objectify them—and in some new way, given the dismal failure of his efforts to communicate with Catherine through the emblem.

Fortunately for him, she is stirred at long last to the handsomest of answers: "Nay, I am sure you cannot have a better; for if I do not know any body, it is impossible for me to talk to them; and, besides, I do not *want* to talk to any body." In the first clauses she still holds fast to common sense; perhaps she even labors her logic deliberately here to suggest how unreasonable Henry is in demanding that she declare her emotions. But she concludes with the sort of direct, personal statement that he has been after all along, and he knows how to value it: "Now you have given me a security worth having; and I shall proceed with courage." It is no accident that Henry repeats "security," now employing it as a metaphor, for he thus converts Catherine's pledge from a group of words into something concrete, something utterly real. And he does indeed "proceed with courage," right to the end of the novel.

The entire scene richly illustrates Jane Austen's technique of treating a social situation in metaphorical terms to dramatize the emotions of her characters. Here she allows Henry to invent the specific emblem, and we have seen how fully he uses it: not only to make known his affection for Catherine but also to formulate it with appropriate restraint. Through the double life of Henry's figure, Jane Austen creates the virtual life of the scene. And by letting him break with the emblem finally to utter his feelings more directly, Jane Austen only reaffirms what she has rendered throughout the passage—that this virtual life is vigorously emotional. In the sustained vivacity of the dialogue as a whole, in Jane Austen's delicate control of its multiple meanings, we begin to breathe the air of *Pride and Prejudice.*

❧❧❧❧❧❧❧❧❧❧❧❧❧❧❧❧❧❧❧❧❧❧❧❧❧❧❧❧❧❧

1. Whether *Northanger Abbey* as we have it represents fundamentally earlier or later work than our *Sense and Sensibility* is a bibliographical problem that cannot be solved decisively. We know only that the early novels went through several versions before publication. We can make fairly sound guesses about the dates of revision, but we cannot say how far Jane Austen revised in any given case. I am venturing to take up *Northanger Abbey* after *Sense and Sensibility* mainly because its dialogue sounds technically more mature to my ear. Yet there is some scholarly warrant for treating it as later work. For one thing, if we may believe Cassandra Austen's memorandum, the original of *Northanger Abbey* postdates a dramatic version of *Sense and Sensibility,* itself the reworking of an epistolary *Elinor and Marianne,* and indeed one version of *Pride and Prejudice* (see R. W. Chapman's Introductory Note to *Sense and Sensibility,* p. xiii). So one could argue that *Northanger Abbey,* even in its initial form, would probably have benefited from Jane Austen's earlier experiences with a dramatic genre to the extent of being technically more assured. It might also be added that several scholars—among them Chapman in his *Jane Austen: Facts and Problems* (Oxford, 1948), p. 75 —have suggested the possibility of Jane Austen doing some revising of *Northanger Abbey* as late as 1816, though this new date hardly supports my placing of the novel where I have. In any case, it is certain that *Northanger Abbey* never had to fight its way out of an epistolary form as *Sense and Sensibility* did.

2. Mudrick writes that Henry "cannot speak except in irony" (*Jane Austen,* p. 50), a finding that seems to me conditioned less by the text of *Northanger Abbey* than by the critic's rather complicated psychological interpretation of it. Taking the novel as an attack on all social conventions and personal feeling, he senses in its pages the "need" of the youthful Jane Austen "to assert her own non-commitment" (p. 51). She supposedly satisfies this compulsion by identifying herself in large part with Henry, whom Mudrick views as the implacable enemy of convention and apparently of personal feeling as well. But we have already heard how earnestly Henry rebukes Catherine for her unorthodox conception of General Tilney, and in the dialogue that I am now to analyze I think his liking for Catherine comes clear—indeed he expresses it directly in his first sentence.

5 *Pride and Prejudice*
Vitality and a Dramatic Mode

Few readers would question that *Pride and Prejudice* is the most brilliant of Jane Austen's novels. Perhaps it is less neatly turned than *Emma,* to name a work which has recently found increasing favor among critics because of its technical finesse, but *Pride and Prejudice* has a vibrancy and a rich dramatic texture all its own. Especially through the first half of the novel, Jane Austen recreates the quality of our social experience, that sense we often have of the ambiguities inherent in behavior. She accomplishes this partly through engaging us, alongside the vivacious Elizabeth Bennet, in making out a number of characters largely on the basis of what they say and do in public. In addition, she shows us that the motives are themselves mixed which impel Elizabeth to misjudge the novel's hero for so long, to find Darcy insufferably arrogant and nothing more. But the author's major success here is with Darcy, who seems to me a far cry from the two-dimensional Fanny Burneyan figure that he is so often taken to be. For Jane Austen endows him with mixed motives of his own—pride, shyness, a liking for Elizabeth—at the same time that she keeps prompting us to share the prejudiced Elizabeth's flattened interpretation of him. And through the second half of the story, although Elizabeth and Darcy are now coming to terms with each other, Jane Austen refuses to thin the motives of either one. Elizabeth sacrifices none of her wit and charm in making her peace with Darcy's values, and Darcy attains a more amiable manner without giving up the substance of his pride. In thus ripening, as it were, both Elizabeth and Darcy express the theme of *Pride and Prejudice,* which again is grounded in the heroine's progress from blindness to insight, and which again argues that the individual must mitigate the demands of personal feeling—whether Elizabeth's prejudice or Darcy's pride—and reconcile them with the claims of sense. Yet by ripening within the contours of personality established for them from the start of the novel, the hero and heroine bear witness to Jane Austen's integrity as an artist.

Both the variety of Darcy's character and Jane Austen's virtuosity in representing it are easy enough to overlook on our first reading of *Pride and Prejudice,* or even on later ones. For one thing, Elizabeth so wins the hearts of us all that we feel no urge to disagree with her, particularly about anyone as stuffy as Darcy appears to be. For another, Jane Austen must keep us pretty much in the dark about him—as she does by screening most of our impressions through Elizabeth—in order to bring off the chief dramatic effect of the story: overwhelming surprise at his first proposal. It is reactions like these, I suspect, that have combined to produce what seems to be the usual opinion of Darcy: that he is a cold man, implacably proud, who unexpectedly shows a new face from the first proposal on, yet remains altogether too unconvincing a character to make a fitting partner for the lively Elizabeth. But to my mind this opinion does no justice to the Darcy whom Jane Austen has created, and the main purpose of my chapter is to revise it. First off, as a kind of reintroduction to the story, I want to indicate how pervasively Jane Austen manipulates our view of Darcy. Next, I shall take up some of the novel's characters in greater detail, paying special attention to Elizabeth in hopes of showing that she readjusts herself at least as radically as Darcy does. Then, in the final section, we must turn to the most brilliant dialogues between Elizabeth and Darcy, where I shall aim at making the vitality of his courtship clear. If through all this I seem less than fair to other figures, particularly Elizabeth, it will be because of trying to make out as strong a case for Darcy as the novel allows.

◄[II]►

In *Pride and Prejudice* our point of view is much more subtly managed than in either of the novels we have already examined. *Sense and Sensibility*'s Elinor proved reliable almost without exception. And though we saw the action of *Northanger Abbey* along with Catherine, Henry Tilney was always near at hand to correct any false impressions that might arise. But in *Pride and Prejudice* there is no one on whom we can depend for a true account. Rather, we are for the most part confined to Elizabeth's deeply biased perceptions, and Jane Austen tempts us to accept her heroine's view of Darcy at every turn, though just as consistently leaving the door open to a more favorable interpretation of his behavior.

At his introduction, we do not hear him speak until the "great admiration" he initially stirs has given way to a general "disgust" with his "manners"—that is, until Jane Austen has planted society's judgment, based wholly on appearances, in our minds, and perhaps in Elizabeth's as well. So the real ambiguity of his opening remarks catches us with our guard down. When Bingley urges him to dance, we overlook what may be Darcy's protestation of shyness in "You know how I detest it, unless I am particularly acquainted with my partner," even though it supplies a clear logic for the mention of Bingley's "sisters" that follows: "Your sisters are engaged, and there is not another woman in the room, whom it would not be a punishment to me to stand up with" (p. 11). Instead of entertaining the possibility that Darcy's tone reveals the instinctive irritation of a shy person at an aggressive invasion of his privacy, we seize on his whole reply as betraying an absolute contempt engendered by pride. Our listening to this with Elizabeth does not help a bit, for her prejudice is fixed when he goes on in as sharp a tone to reject Bingley's offer of introducing him to her—though it is an open question whether Darcy realizes that she can hear him.[1]

These first glimpses of him, so carefully slanted by Jane Austen, condition us to minimize every hint that he might be less of a monster than Elizabeth supposes. Thus her sister Jane's report—that Darcy "never speaks much unless among his intimate acquaintance. With *them* he is remarkably agreeable" (p. 19)—we discount readily enough, even though it echoes the ambiguity of Darcy's first speeches, because it has originated with the disagreeable Caroline Bingley. We refuse to set any store by Elizabeth's profession that she herself is biased, " . . . I could easily forgive *his* pride, if he had not mortified *mine*" (p. 20), because her phrasing sounds witty and open-minded. And by the time Darcy actually invites her to dance, first at the home of the Lucases and later at Netherfield, we have become so acclimatized to her dislike that we are almost as suspicious as she is of his intentions, as content to ignore the most plausible motive behind his requests, and as hopeful as she is that he will be discomfited by her ironic "Mr. Darcy is all politeness" (p. 26) or " . . . I do not want to dance a reel at all—and now despise me if you dare" (p. 52).[2]

Occasionally in these opening chapters Jane Austen lets us escape from Elizabeth's perspective to a more omniscient view of Darcy, but without encouraging us to give up Elizabeth's opinion. When the author describes Darcy's growing attachment, she narrates it in such a way that we are less aware of his affection than of his pride, less struck by his "discovery" of a "beautiful expression" in Elizabeth's eyes than by his finding the discovery "mortifying" (p. 23). Sometimes the rhetoric itself of Jane Austen's comments on Darcy inclines us toward Elizabeth's prejudice while it slyly permits him a richer blend of motives: for example, in stating that Elizabeth "attracted him more than he liked—and Miss Bingley was uncivil to *her*, and more teasing than usual to himself" (pp. 59–60), Jane Austen buries Darcy's sympathy for Elizabeth in the first half of the antithesis, completing the structure—as she has begun the sentence—with claims relating to his sense of himself. Even when she puts Darcy in action for us during Elizabeth's absence, as in his quarrels with Miss Bingley about Elizabeth's "fine eyes" (pp. 27, 36), we cannot tell for sure whether he wants to praise Elizabeth or to provoke her rival or to demonstrate haughtily that he is Miss Bingley's superior by turning down her bids to entangle him in a community of opinion.

Most of the time, however, Jane Austen forces us to look on with Elizabeth at what is happening, which means that Darcy is inevitably distorted. If Elizabeth notices, for instance, "how frequently Mr. Darcy's eyes were fixed on her," she immediately transforms the fact into a fancy that "there was a something about her more wrong and reprehensible, according to his ideas of right, than in any other person present" (p. 51). Indeed we often hardly realize that what seems an objective account of Darcy's behavior by a detached author has really been filtered through Elizabeth's perceptions. When Mr. Collins leaves her to pay his respects to Lady Catherine's nephew, addressing himself to Darcy twice, we are told:

> —It vexed her to see him expose himself to such a man. Mr. Darcy was eyeing him with unrestrained wonder, and when at last Mr. Collins allowed him time to speak, replied with an air of distant civility. . . . Mr. Darcy's contempt seemed abundantly increasing with the length of his second speech, and at the end of it he only made him a slight bow, and moved another way.
>
> (p. 98)

The terms that color Darcy here—"wonder," "distant civility," and "contempt"—belong to Elizabeth, so to speak, and are perhaps heightened because she is "vexed" to start with.

By maneuvers like these, Jane Austen obscures Darcy's real nature through half of *Pride and Prejudice*. And, while we can no longer doubt his love for Elizabeth after the first proposal scene, the author tries to prevent us from settling his character decisively until the conclusion of the story. Thus, the housekeeper at Pemberley may commend him warmly, but Jane Austen undercuts the tribute by mentioning Mrs. Reynolds' "pride or attachment . . . in talking of her master" (p. 248). When Darcy himself turns up, Elizabeth keeps protesting about the amazing "alteration in his manner" (p. 252), although by this time we may well suspect that much of the alteration is in Elizabeth herself, who has been surrendering her prejudice against him. Even the favorable testimony of the Gardiners, who have given us for the first time in the novel a relatively unbiased reaction to Darcy (p. 257), is invalidated somewhat by their wish to see Elizabeth marry him (p. 264). Only at the end of *Pride and Prejudice* does Jane Austen permit Darcy to reveal his character completely and explicitly, although by restricting us still to her heroine's point of view in the closing chapters, she teases us about his feelings a good deal less than she does Elizabeth.

In detailing some of the tricks by which Jane Austen controls our perspective on Darcy, I am not implying that he is really without pride. Rather, I want to suggest how constantly in the interest of the novel's dramatic effect she highlights his pride, making him appear something of a humor character by keeping his other qualities hidden in shadow. But the very limitations of our point of view here should caution us to cling fast to the dialogues as our surest source of truth, about Darcy, Elizabeth, or anyone else. In them we can discover a three-dimensional Darcy, as I shall try to show more fully in the last section of this chapter. In the meantime, we must look closely at some of Elizabeth's verbal encounters, mainly to find out how she changes in the course of the novel, but partly to get a sense of some other figures as well, who display their own varieties of pride and prejudice.

◄[III]►

Our best general guide to Elizabeth's development, and for that matter to Darcy's, is the insight she offers us late in the novel: "It was an union that must have been to the advantage of both; by her ease and liveliness, his mind might have been softened, his manners improved, and from his judgment, information, and knowledge of the world, she must have received benefit of greater importance" (p. 312). For the passage makes clear that Darcy changes in manner, not in essentials, and it implies that Elizabeth has been biased by her emotions. Yet she has always believed that she speaks cool sense, a sense which she thinks she can rely on because it owes so little to conventional opinion. Thus convinced that her mind is unclouded by prejudice of any sort, she invariably trusts herself to her immediate perceptions. And she is constantly exercising them to decide on some particular case, sure that her judgment will do fuller justice to its merits than any other. Of course, this assurance and unconventionality combine with the very real sense that she has to make almost everything she says sparkle with wit—though unfortunately I must ignore her wit from now on to make another point. For her speeches also reveal something that Elizabeth is quite unaware of: the fact that warm feeling rather than cool sense informs many of her decisions, and not only those concerning Darcy.

Early in the novel, for instance, when the relationship between Bingley and Jane Bennet engages the attention of most of the characters, Elizabeth has a set-to with her friend Charlotte Lucas about Jane's placid behavior to her suitor (pp. 21–23). The prudent Charlotte takes the position that Jane risks losing Bingley unless she shows her feelings more openly. Charlotte builds her case largely on hardheaded generalizations, though she sounds a more compassionate note in the first sentence that follows: "We can all *begin* freely—a slight preference is natural enough; but there are very few of us who have heart enough to be really in love without encouragement. In nine cases out of ten, a woman had better shew *more* affection than she feels." But Elizabeth brushes aside such reasoning to cite her own experience of the situation at hand: "If *I* can perceive her regard for him, he must be a simpleton indeed not to discover it too." She seems confident of uttering nothing but plain sense here, yet "simpleton" marks her typical intensity, and obviously the whole reply is inspired by sympathy for her sister. When Charlotte counters by observing rationally enough that Bingley cannot "know Jane's disposition as you do," Elizabeth refuses to retreat. Instead, she leaps to a generalization—"But if a woman is partial to a man, and does not endeavour to conceal it, he must find it out"—in order to confirm what she has said before, but surely this new claim stems at least as much from Elizabeth's private concern for Jane as it does from impartial reason. The exchange goes on in this vein, Elizabeth becoming so impatient with the prudence of her opponent that she finally breaks out in open sarcasm. This moves Charlotte to restate her position in generalizations that set out as severe version of marriage as ever, though they do not inhibit her own sympathy for Jane: [3]

> "Well . . . I wish Jane success with all my heart; and if she were married to him to-morrow, I should think she had as good a chance of happiness, as if she were to be studying his character for a twelve-month. Happiness in marriage is entirely a matter of chance. If the dispositions of the parties are ever so well known to each other, or ever so similar before-hand, it does not advance their felicity in the least. They always continue to grow sufficiently unlike afterwards to have their share of vexation; and it is better to know as little as possible of the defects of the person with whom you are to pass your life."
> "You make me laugh, Charlotte; but it is not sound. You know it is not sound, and that you would never act in this way yourself."

Again Elizabeth scoffs at Charlotte for being unreasonable, closing the argument with the splendid assertion that she knows Charlotte better than Charlotte knows herself. But the facts of the novel scoff at Elizabeth: one of Darcy's major reasons for intervening between Bingley and Jane is that she does not seem strongly attached; and Charlotte does adhere to her principles in marrying Mr. Collins. This is not by any means to say that we should approve of Charlotte's act or that she speaks more truly than Elizabeth in the passage under discussion. But it is to say that Elizabeth frequently misjudges, failing to recognize that her reasoning is biased by feelings, here her affection for Jane and her disdain for Charlotte's prudence.

The same motives and the same sort of misjudgment crop

up when Elizabeth talks over with Jane the apparently permanent removal of Bingley to London, for which he has offered
no explanation, and the engagement of Charlotte to Mr. Collins
(pp. 134–37). Jane, of course, cannot bear to think badly of
anyone, and she never speaks without revealing how completely her benevolent feelings determine her decisions. Indeed,
a remark she makes at one point, "Let me take it in the best
light, in the light in which it may be understood" (p. 137),
might well serve as her motto. But refined as Jane's feelings are,
her thoroughgoing dependence on them is a form of prejudice
as settled as Charlotte's prudence. And Elizabeth is as eager to
expose the one extreme as the other, still assured that her own
sense is immune to any such error. So when Jane excuses
Bingley much too charitably, blaming herself instead for having
wrongly imagined that he liked her, Elizabeth first praises her
sister as "angelic," but then proclaims her own superior wisdom
in a rhetoric that assigns Jane to one camp and herself to another:

> "Do not be afraid of my running into any excess, of my en-
> croaching on your privilege of universal good will. . . . There
> are few people whom I really love, and still fewer of whom I
> think well. The more I see of the world, the more am I dissatis-
> fied with it; and every day confirms my belief of the inconsist-
> ency of all human characters, and of the little dependence that
> can be placed on the appearance of either merit or sense. I have
> met with two instances lately; one I will not mention; the other
> is Charlotte's marriage. It is unaccountable! in every view it is
> unaccountable!"

By distinguishing so dispassionately between the "few" whom
she can "really love" and "still fewer of whom" she can "think
well," Elizabeth presumably guards herself against Jane's emotional "excess." But the generalization about "inconsistency"
actually arises from her dissatisfaction with "the world," and her
"two instances" bear this out. Of Bingley she will say nothing
at the moment out of affection for Jane, but Charlotte is another matter. Although Elizabeth protests, by "unaccountable"

and "in every view," that her own verdict is purely rational, the repetition of phrase betrays her pique. And in fact the verdict is conditioned by her dislike for Mr. Collins and by her irritation with Charlotte—whom we saw accounting for herself in detail—for proving Elizabeth's earlier assessment of how her friend would behave quite incorrect. Perhaps it is mildly ironic that Jane should put her finger on the element endangering Elizabeth's judgment, begging her sister not to "give way to such feelings as these." In any event, Jane goes on typically enough to interpret the whole affair too generously:

> "Consider Mr. Collins's respectability, and Charlotte's prudent, steady character. Remember that she is one of a large family; that as to fortune, it is a most eligible match; and be ready to believe, for every body's sake, that she may feel something like regard and esteem for our cousin."

This is too much for Elizabeth, who belabors first Charlotte, then Mr. Collins, and concludes with a powerful array of conceptual terms to rebuke Jane for being irresponsible:

> "You shall not defend her, though it is Charlotte Lucas. You shall not, for the sake of one individual, change the meaning of principle and integrity, nor endeavour to persuade yourself or me, that selfishness is prudence, and insensibility of danger, security for happiness."

Again the effect of the rhetoric is to play off Jane's singularity against her own reliance on "principle and integrity," and certainly Jane deserves the rebuke. But the fundamental irony turns against Elizabeth once more. She is too irked by Jane's attitude and too positive of her own integrity to realize that her fixed prejudice against Darcy lays her open to the same charge time and again through the first half of the novel at least, most obviously in her decisions about Darcy himself and in her misjudgment of Wickham.

About the first of her suitors, however, Elizabeth has no illusions. Only Mrs. Bennet could, and perhaps Lady Catherine de Bourgh, for Mr. Collins never deviates from absurdity. Certainly his overly formal rhetoric, constant polysyllables, and especially those notorious ripe metaphors are laughable enough, but we must look behind these traits to get at the essential absurdity of Mr. Collins' verbal manner. On one level he uses language quite consciously: we remember him telling Mr. Bennet about working out "little elegant compliments" in his spare moments. Yet Mr. Collins remains completely unaware that, by the time he has strung his phrases together, they develop an inflated tone which is at best ridiculously disproportionate to whatever he wants to say—and at the worst contradicts his claims. In his classic proposal to Elizabeth, for instance, he spins out a highly formal announcement about being in the grip of overpowering emotions: "And now nothing remains for me but to assure you in the most animated language of the violence of my affection" (p. 106). Diverting as this sort of verbal idiocy may be, the equivalent contradiction at the core of Mr. Collins' nature—humility become pride—makes him sometimes inane and sometimes frightening.[4] If he tries for sense, he comes closer to nonsense: " . . . I consider the clerical office as equal in point of dignity with the highest rank in the kingdom— provided that a proper humility of behaviour is at the same time maintained" (p. 97). And when he vents his feelings, as on learning of Lydia Bennet's elopement, the result is a ghastly parody of a clergyman's sympathy, his "comfort" for Mr. Bennet consisting in encouraging him to disown his daughter. But everything he says and does reflects his irresponsibility so clearly that Elizabeth never stands in danger of misreading him.

The case is rather different with Wickham, who also courts Elizabeth's favor. Her antagonism toward Darcy predisposes her to find "truth" in the "looks" of his enemy (p. 86), and she unhesitatingly accepts Wickham's story about being cut off from his rightful inheritance by a jealous Darcy. What does not register with Elizabeth until much later, after Darcy has told her the truth of the whole business, is that Wickham's verbal manner reveals a contradiction of its own. It is one more subtle than anything Mr. Collins can show, but just as firm a clue to

❋❋❋❋❋❋❋❋❋❋❋❋❋❋❋❋❋❋❋❋❋❋❋❋❋❋❋❋❋❋❋❋❋❋

irresponsibility. This false note is struck during Wickham's first conversation with Elizabeth. While he pretends to honor the de- mands of propriety in holding himself back, he in fact converts decorum into a backdrop to set off his own particular and un- restrained dislike for Darcy: "I have no right to give *my* opinion . . . . I am not qualified to form one. I have known him too long and too well to be a fair judge. It is impossible for *me* to be impartial" (p. 77). Wickham exploits these two roles throughout the scene. As soon as he knows that Elizabeth shares his dislike, he really opens up against Darcy, playing to the hilt the part of a man whose feelings are too strong to be kept back—indeed describing himself at one point as a person of "warm, unguarded temper" (p. 80). Along with these outbursts, sometimes almost in the same breath, Wickham makes a series of appeals to the generalizations of propriety, such as "I cannot pretend to be sorry . . . that he or that any man should not be estimated beyond their deserts" (p. 78), or "A man of honour could not have doubted the intention, but Mr. Darcy chose to doubt it" (p. 79). But Wickham's emotional exhibitionism is simply incongruent with his professions of decorum, a fact which Eliza- beth can formulate only when she has learned to think better of Darcy (p. 207). Until then, blinded by her prejudice, she is completely taken in by Wickham's artful inversions of his own appearance and reality, and of Darcy's.

All the encounters in which we have seen Elizabeth involved so far, however, seem like minor engagements when compared to her running battle with Darcy himself. In their clashes, she remains supremely confident of her perceptions as an individual. While Darcy does not undervalue his opinions either, he does go to work in a different fashion. No less interested than Eliza- beth in arriving at the merits of the particular case, he starts out, at least, with generalizations, often those of society. And along the way he appears more careful than she to ally himself with objective reason. Certainly he sounds as self-assured in making his judgments as she does, though whether because of a peevish sense of superiority—as Elizabeth feels—or a proper pride is harder to determine. Their characteristic tones and methods are illustrated in various dialogues: the argument about Bingley's impetuosity (pp. 48–50), for example, or about Darcy's pride (pp. 57–58). But the scene in which ladies' accomplishments come up for discussion has some special advantages for our purposes. It will show us a little of two other characters, Bingley and his sister Caroline. More important, it will introduce us to the word that lies at the heart of the novel's meaning, *performance*, a concept we will be much concerned with in the final section of this chapter. For the present, though, we need only be aware that the sense of *performance* extends from a mere display of skill to a deed expressive of one's whole being, and that at the start of the conversation before us the word is equated with "accomplished," the alternate term thus acquiring exactly the same range of meaning and, in fact, taking the place of "performance" throughout this scene (pp. 38–40).

The words are put in play by Caroline Bingley, who sets out as usual to bind herself and Darcy together in an exclusive community of opinion, this time by rhapsodizing about his sister's "accomplished . . . performance" on the piano:

> "Such a countenance, such manners! and so extremely accomplished for her age! Her performance on the piano-forte is exquisite."
> "It is amazing to me," said Bingley, "how young ladies can have patience to be so very accomplished, as they all are."
> "All young ladies accomplished! My dear Charles, what do you mean?"
> "Yes, all of them, I think. They all paint tables, cover skreens and net purses. I scarcely know any one who cannot do all this, and I am sure I never heard a young lady spoken of for the first time, without being informed that she was very accomplished."

Clearly Caroline means the words in a narrow sense only, to denote the skills of the aristocratic, so she becomes angry when her brother devaluates such pursuits by allowing all "young ladies" to be "so very accomplished." Bingley himself speaks with that indiscriminating generosity which is so typical of him and which makes him the perfect partner for Jane. His generalizations flow straight from his feelings, but he praises the whole class of "young ladies" for trivial achievements.

As we might expect, Darcy seizes the opportunity to be discriminating about "accomplishments," yet we should beware of identifying his motives with Caroline's:

> "Your list of the common extent of accomplishments . . . has too much truth. The word is applied to many a woman who deserves it no otherwise than by netting a purse, or covering a skreen. But I am very far from agreeing with you in your estimation of ladies in general. I cannot boast of knowing more than half a dozen, in the whole range of my acquaintance, that are really accomplished."

He begins with Bingley's generalization and proceeds to test it in the light of his own observation. Maybe it would be risky to decide at the moment whether his distinction between "common extent" and "really accomplished" is inspired by a snobbish commitment like Caroline's to the superficial sense of the word or by a rational grasp of its whole meaning. But certainly when he replies to Elizabeth's "you must comprehend a great deal in your idea of an accomplished woman" with "Yes; I do comprehend a great deal in it," he accents the weight of the "accomplishments," though perhaps a chance remains that he is being merely haughty. His next remark, however, removes even this ambiguity. After Caroline has reeled off a host of refinements like "drawing," "the modern languages," and "a certain . . . air and manner of walking" which the truly accomplished woman commands, thus hoping to deny the name to Elizabeth and all except the elegant, Darcy comments, "All this she must possess . . . and to all this she must yet add something more substantial, in the improvement of her mind by extensive reading." His generalization insists on a fuller sense of "accomplished," the "more substantial" integrating refined behavior with the reason that comes from "reading." Yet Darcy's words strike a more personal note as well, for a little earlier Caroline has nastily characterized Elizabeth as "a great reader"; so this becomes a compliment to

Elizabeth by offering her an entree into the select category that
Caroline has been jealously hugging to herself.

But the only voice Elizabeth listens to is her antipathy toward Darcy, and characteristically, it compels her to translate his
claim into an extreme:

> "I am no longer surprised at your knowing *only* six accom-
> plished women. I rather wonder now at your knowing *any*."
> "Are you so severe upon your own sex, as to doubt the possi-
> bility of all this?"
> "*I* never saw such a woman. *I* never saw such capacity, and
> taste, and application, and elegance, as you describe, united."

Again Darcy assigns the richest meaning to "accomplished," and
on one level his answer seems strictly rational. But it pays another compliment to the "sex" of which Elizabeth is a member.
Furthermore, he echoes here one of her earlier attacks on him,
"You are severe on us" (p. 24); thus Darcy may also be attempting to clear himself while hinting gently that she is the biased
one. How much of this Elizabeth takes in we cannot tell; we can
only be sure that she rejects both him and his sense of "accomplished" to assert the priority of her own experience. The dialogue has shown, however, that Darcy sets as high a value on
personal experience in making judgments; that he seems, in addition, rather more scrupulous than Elizabeth about observing
the place of reason in generalizations, either his own or those of
others; finally, that he manages all this without slighting his particular feeling for her.

Darcy's feeling reaches its peak, of course, when he disregards
Elizabeth's inferior social status and his low opinion of her family to propose to her, and Elizabeth's animosity comes to a boil at
the same point. What she actually objects to, although she denies it to him (p. 192), is the mode of his proposal, to which she
reverts again and again (pp. 193, 212, 224). And indeed the
mode is all that Darcy ever really apologizes for (p. 367), having
learned from Elizabeth's rebuff, not that he must change his convictions, but that he must modify the confidence and stiffness of
his manner if he is to please. His letter explaining his dealings

with Bingley and Wickham teaches Elizabeth, in her turn, how "wretchedly blind" her prejudice has made her to him and to herself. In fact, as she comes to see Darcy more clearly in the second half of the story, she even takes over from time to time something like his verbal method in presenting her judgments, though she remains quite capable of being witty. As for his opinion of her family, Elizabeth may resent it while he speaks, but she has censured them freely before the proposal (p. 101), and does so on several occasions later on, one of which we will glance at after a moment.

It is not very surprising that Elizabeth should feel a bit uncomfortable about all her immediate family except Jane, whom Darcy also exempts from his reproaches. Mrs. Bennet, to name first the most blatantly indecorous of the group, stands condemned every time she opens her mouth. Her fairly frequent metaphors, intensively particular terms, and abrupt rhythms show that she can never subdue her emotions—the source of her generalizations as well—and cannot therefore respond appropriately to the situations confronting her:

> "My dear, dear Lydia! . . . This is delightful indeed!—She will be married!—I shall see her again!—She will be married at sixteen!—My good, kind brother!—I knew how it would be—I knew he would manage every thing. How I long to see her! and to see dear Wickham too! But the clothes, the wedding clothes! I will write to my sister Gardiner about them directly." (p. 306)

In the flow of her feelings, she treats Lydia, marriage "at sixteen," the aid of Mr. Gardiner, Wickham, and the "wedding clothes" as of equal importance. And obviously Mrs. Bennet is so possessed by her ruling passion, to get her daughters married as soon as possible, that she has no qualms at all about the circumstances of Lydia's elopement. Naturally Lydia herself has none. She shares, in fact, much of her mother's nature and most of her verbal traits, the only difference being that Lydia's tone usually sounds more unconcerned, rather as if she has not yet experienced the strain in satisfying her desires that Mrs. Bennet feels so often.

Although the wit of Mr. Bennet's conversation makes him a good deal more bearable than his wife or Lydia, his conduct really comes no nearer decorum than theirs. The emotional detachment which he cultivates so assiduously proves as crippling as their emotional involvement. Indeed he responds to life as predictably as they do, for whatever the situation, he encounters it with a joke—and pretty much the same joke at that. The essence of his wit lies in that literalistic manner by means of which he converts whatever is said to him and whatever happens into absurdity—thus indulging his superior wisdom. The trick is amusing enough when he plays it on the silly Mrs. Bennet, as in referring to her "poor nerves" as "my old friends" (p. 5). But he seems heartless, even imperceptive, when he talks to Elizabeth of Jane's separation from Bingley in the same fashion: " . . . your sister is crossed in love I find. I congratulate her. Next to being married, a girl likes to be crossed in love a little now and then. It is something to think of, and gives her a sort of distinction among her companions" (pp. 137–38). In the last analysis, Mr. Bennet's mode has the same effect as his wife's, prohibiting him from distinguishing between the trivial and the significant. It is peculiarly appropriate that his one attempt in the novel to express straight sense and straight feeling—when he dissuades Elizabeth from marrying Darcy (p. 376)—should coincide with Mr. Bennet's complete mistaking of his daughter, the person he has depended on knowing best.

The mind of Elizabeth, needless to say, is more flexible than her father's. She possesses altogether finer capacities than any of her family, and she has always behaved with a keener awareness of herself in relation to other people. Once Darcy's letter has cleared her insight, she does not hesitate to judge herself firmly. In the passage that follows, for instance, Elizabeth founds her generalizations in reason alone, and—in another reversal of her earlier ways with language—she levels the generalizations straight at her prejudice rather than considering herself an exceptional case beyond their reach:

"And yet I meant to be uncommonly clever in taking so decided
a dislike to him, without any reason. It is such a spur to one's

genius, such an opening for wit to have a dislike of that kind. One may be continually abusive without saying any thing just; but one cannot be always laughing at a man without now and then stumbling on something witty." (pp. 225–26)

Here she may be remembering Darcy's previous warning, which she spurned at the time, about how easy it is for "a person whose first object in life is a joke" to render "ridiculous" the "wisest and the best of men" (p. 57).

But she adopts his verbal manner itself when she, alone among the Bennets, opposes Lydia's trip to Brighton and tries to persuade her father—who thinks Elizabeth selfishly hoping to preserve her own credit with her suitors—of its impropriety:

> "It is not of peculiar, but of general evils, which I am now complaining. Our importance, our respectability in the world, must be affected by the wild volatility, the assurance and disdain of all restraint which mark Lydia's character. . . . If you, my dear father, will not take the trouble of checking her exuberant spirits . . . she will soon be beyond the reach of amendment. Her character will be fixed . . . . A flirt . . . in the worst and meanest degree of flirtation; without any attraction beyond youth and a tolerable person; and from the ignorance and emptiness of her mind, wholly unable to ward off any portion of that universal contempt which her rage for admiration will excite." (p. 231)

First Elizabeth differentiates carefully between the "peculiar" and the "general"; then she sets out the moral generalization that covers the case; last of all, she measures Lydia in the light of steadfast concepts. Method, vocabulary, the decision itself—all might be Darcy's.

It seems especially fitting, though, that Elizabeth should use a method approaching his—integrated with her own wit—to gain her brilliant triumph over his aunt when that lady forbids her to think of marrying Darcy. Lady Catherine de Bourgh represents the extreme of pride; we might say that her motives really are what Elizabeth has imagined her nephew's to be during the first part of the story. Obsessed with her rank, Lady Catherine cannot distinguish between her own whims and general principles.

This equation dominates her speeches, perhaps never more unpleasantly than when she berates Elizabeth for not giving way to her own project of uniting Darcy with her daughter: "Are you lost to every feeling of propriety and delicacy? Have you not heard me say, that from his earliest hours he was destined for his cousin?" (p. 355). But Elizabeth puts Lady Catherine to rout by discriminating between wishes, facts, and moral obligations:

> "If there is no other objection to my marrying your nephew, I shall certainly not be kept from it, by knowing that his mother and aunt wished him to marry Miss De Bourgh. You both did as much as you could, in planning the marriage. Its completion depended on others. If Mr. Darcy is neither by honour nor inclination confined to his cousin, why is not he to make another choice? And if I am that choice, why may not I accept him?"
>
> (p. 355)

Her controlled reasoning, here and throughout the dialogue, lays bare the bias of her opponent's arguments in reducing them to nonsense. And of course Elizabeth's victory in the scene, once Lady Catherine has reported their discussion to Darcy, brings on his second, successful proposal.

As a result of failing the first time, however, Darcy has forsaken his domineering manner for a mildness typified by his invitation to Elizabeth when they next meet, at Pemberley:

> "There is also one other person in the party . . . who more particularly wishes to be known to you,—Will you allow me, or do I ask too much, to introduce my sister to your acquaintance during your stay at Lambton?" (p. 256)

Indeed "Mr. Darcy is all politeness," almost excessively so in refusing to presume on Elizabeth in any way and in reserving all wishes to his sister and himself. Yet in spite of his more subdued tone, Darcy's habit of differentiating remains unaltered, as is evident in one of his last talks with Elizabeth:

> "*Your* retrospections must be so totally void of reproach, that the contentment arising from them, is not of philosophy, but what is

much better, of ignorance. But with *me,* it is not so. Painful rec-
ollections will intrude, which cannot, which ought not to be re-
pelled. I have been a selfish being all my life, in practice, though
not in principle. As a child I was taught what was *right,* but I
was not taught to correct my temper. . . . I was spoilt by my
parents, who . . . almost taught me to be selfish and overbear-
ing . . . to think meanly of all the rest of the world, to *wish* at
least to think meanly of their sense and worth compared with my
own. . . . You taught me a lesson, hard indeed at first, but most
advantageous. . . . You shewed me how insufficient were all
my pretensions to please a woman worthy of being pleased."
                                                                    (p. 369)

While he compliments Elizabeth by elevating "ignorance" above
"philosophy" and then proceeds to judge himself harshly,
Darcy's speech still bristles with discriminations: between "cannot" and "ought not," "practice" and "principle," "to think" and
"to wish," "hard" and "advantageous," appearance and reality. If
the passage shows that Darcy has come to see himself in a new
light much as Elizabeth did, it also declares that his fundamental
beliefs have not altered.

◄[IV]►

   The verbal traits of all the characters whom we have been re-
viewing, then, reveal how they form their judgments and how
they behave. Bringing the two together, we can go on to say that
the theme of *Pride and Prejudice* concerns judging from behavior and behaving with judgment. These crucial issues are caught
together in the word *performance*—whose meaning, as I suggested earlier, ranges from a show, an exhibition, to a total act, a
deed integrated with one's entire nature. For the term amounts
to more than a convenient ambiguity which allows Jane Austen
to contrast Elizabeth and Darcy by associating her with the thin-
ner sense and him with the deeper one. The word refers to behavior itself: a person can be known only by the qualities of his

performance, whichever kind it may be, and in either sort of performance one mediates between society and oneself. The concept stands, in all its variety, at the very center of the novel's meaning, and it takes its life from the most brilliant dialogues between Elizabeth and Darcy. To these we must turn at last, searching out in them a Darcy who is less disagreeable and more emotional than we usually imagine.

The first conversation between them sets the tone of their relationship and introduces us to the pivotal concept (p. 24). After a moment we shall see Elizabeth interpreting it in a limited sense, but her immediate behavior makes the same point. For, urged on by Charlotte Lucas, she is provoked by the presence of Darcy to put on an exhibitionistic performance for him:

> "Did not you think, Mr. Darcy, that I expressed myself uncommonly well just now, when I was teazing Colonel Forster to give us a ball at Meryton?"
> "With great energy;—but it is a subject which always makes a lady energetic."

She proclaims that she is unconventional by "uncommonly well" and that she is feminine by "teazing." Darcy's "great energy" acknowledges her uniqueness, but he then backs off to a generalization, either to avoid the impropriety of noticing her too personally or to pronounce sternly on the frivolity of ladies. Elizabeth reacts only to the second possibility and accuses him of being stuffy: "You are severe on us." Although her "us" may seem at first a decorous retreat to the anonymity of a class, it really flaunts the opposition of all her sex to Darcy.

Her antagonism swells when Charlotte, a little concerned for Darcy, teases her in turn about the actual performance that is to follow. Elizabeth may pretend to take account of propriety in calling Charlotte "strange," yet she directs attention to her own "vanity" in the act of denying that it has "taken a musical turn":

> "You are a very strange creature by way of a friend!—always wanting me to play and sing before any body and every body!— If my vanity had taken a musical turn, you would have been in-

valuable, but as it is, I would really rather not sit down before those who must be in the habit of hearing the very best performers. . . . Very well; if it must be so, it must." And gravely glancing at Mr. Darcy, "There is a fine old saying, which every body here is of course familiar with—'Keep your breath to cool your porridge,'—and I shall keep mine to swell my song."

Indeed she puts her individuality on parade all through the speech, closing with her most striking flourish at Darcy. Not content with having sneered at him obliquely by "any body and every body," Elizabeth becomes downright specific in her final saucy maxim—and whets its edge by the generalization that separates him from "every body here," from her circle of acquaintance. She is speaking ironically, of course, when she includes herself among the "performers" who entertain the idle rich with their skills. Nevertheless, Elizabeth clearly understands by *performance* nothing more than the kind of conscious self-display in which she has just been indulging.

We observed earlier in this chapter how Darcy identifies himself with the fuller sense of the concept in discussing ladies' accomplishments, and we saw that he does so without disregarding his own feelings for Elizabeth. In the dialogues that follow, we shall find him taking more and more delighted notice of her. When they meet at the Netherfield ball (pp. 91–94), for instance, Darcy surprises her into dancing with him, a high compliment if we recall his earlier comments on the pastime, but Elizabeth,

suddenly fancying that it would be the greater punishment to her partner to oblige him to talk . . . made some slight observation on the dance. He replied, and was again silent. After a pause of some minutes she addressed him a second time with
"It is *your* turn to say something now, Mr. Darcy.—I talked about the dance, and *you* ought to make some kind of remark on the size of the room, or the number of couples."

She taunts him with another show of willfulness, weighing the silence that she reads as offensive pride against her own propriety, which she ironically pretends to, in conversing. Though she is off on another performance, Darcy yields to her with perfect politeness:

> He smiled, and assured her that whatever she wished him to say should be said.
> "Very well.—That reply will do for the present.—Perhaps by and bye I may observe that private balls are much pleasanter than public ones.—But *now* we may be silent."
> "Do you talk by rule then, while you are dancing?"

When she parodies decorum to make his stubbornness clear, he tries to cut through her exhibition to her real self, asking that they overthrow the "rule" of convention and be emotionally direct with each other.

Predictably, Elizabeth desires only to put Darcy in his place. Her first generalizations carefully set up the barrier of impersonal propriety again:

> "Sometimes. One must speak a little, you know. It would look odd to be entirely silent for half an hour together, and yet for the advantage of *some*, conversation ought to be so arranged as that they may have the trouble of saying as little as possible."

And her final generalization keeps Darcy apart from her by assigning them different standards, at the same time that it scarcely masks her disdain for him. Yet he responds with a more personal appeal, one that brushes aside the barrier of decorum to get at their private emotions:

> "Are you consulting your own feelings in the present case, or do you imagine that you are gratifying mine?"
> "Both," replied Elizabeth archly; "for I have always seen a great similarity in the turn of our minds.—We are each of an unsocial, taciturn disposition, unwilling to speak, unless we expect to say something that will amaze the whole room, and be handed down to posterity with all the eclat of a proverb."

But Elizabeth turns down his plea. She can spell out his arrogance if she condemns herself as well, though obviously she means her words to sound absurd when applied to herself.

✳✳

Darcy rejects her typical move to the extreme in order to pursue the truth. But the compliment with which he begins and the warning in his last sentence that she is liable to error make no impression on her:

> "This is no very striking resemblance of your own character, I am sure," said he. "How near it may be to *mine,* I cannot pretend to say.—*You* think it a faithful portrait undoubtedly."
> "I must not decide on my own performance."

Elizabeth uses the term in its narrow sense only, carrying on the figure that "portrait" implies to announce her propriety once more. Yet the total meaning of the word measures her behavior to Darcy with sharp irony, for she is unaware that the role she keeps playing is itself a decision—or that this continuing performance expresses the opposition of her whole nature to Darcy rather than controlled reason, as she supposes. And she remains oblivious through the rest of the scene, blithely acting out what she thinks of him while ignoring what he reveals of himself. When she presses him about Wickham, for example, she fails to realize that her advice is better suited to herself: "It is particularly incumbent on those who never change their opinion, to be secure of judging properly at first." Finally, Darcy resurrects "performance" to hint at her folly: " . . . I could wish, Miss Bennet, that you were not to sketch my character at the present moment, as there is reason to fear that the performance would reflect no credit on either." Nevertheless, he hopes to bring her nearer him by combining their senses of the word. The "performance" he mentions is surely a sketch, but to reproduce reality demands clear insight, which in turn depends on the artist's responsible, unbiased behavior. So, when Elizabeth insists on indulging her skill rather than judging the reality, Darcy shows his anger:

> "But if I do not take your likeness now, I may never have another opportunity."
> "I would by no means suspend any pleasure of yours," he coldly replied.

The word "pleasure" goes only with a light accomplishment. Since Elizabeth has blocked every advance toward mutual understanding and a community of feeling, Darcy ends their talk by handing her one-sided interpretation of the term back to her.

So far Jane Austen has used *performance* as something like a gauge for behavior, letting her characters define the range of the concept in their speeches. Throughout the scene at Rosings (pp. 174–76), she anchors the word in Elizabeth's actual playing of the piano. Now the speakers can keep up an appearance of decorum by pretending to talk of the literal situation, while in fact they treat it metaphorically, thus betraying their most intense emotions. It is the artistic device that we have observed Jane Austen working with in the earlier novels, and we will see it again in the novels to come, but she never manages the device more beautifully, with more moving effect, than she does here.

The conversation opens when Elizabeth accosts Darcy "at the first convenient pause" in her playing; as always, she assumes that he intends to be contemptuous:

> "You mean to frighten me, Mr. Darcy, by coming in all this state to hear me? But I will not be alarmed though your sister *does* play so well. There is a stubbornness about me that never can bear to be frightened at the will of others. My courage always rises with every attempt to intimidate me."

Elizabeth's "hear me" and "play so well" maintain decorum, for they seem to speak only of piano-playing. Yet her final, fully emotional generalizations leave no doubt that she is challenging him personally. Although Darcy answers with conspicuous politeness, he also distinguishes—characteristically enough—between the real and the professed:

> "I shall not say that you are mistaken," he replied, "because you could not really believe me to entertain any design of alarming you; and I have had the pleasure of your acquaintance long enough to know, that you find great enjoyment in occasionally professing opinions which in fact are not your own."

※※※※※※※※※※※※※※※※※※※※※※※※※※※※※※

Literally he is accusing Elizabeth of her usual self-willed performance, warning or begging her to recognize the truth about
himself.

Elizabeth may appear to joke at this as a false sketch, ironically accepting what Darcy has said while she circumspectly addresses herself to Colonel Fitzwilliam. But she bitterly resents
the thrust as another proof of Darcy's nastiness:

> Elizabeth laughed heartily at this picture of herself, and said to
> Colonel Fitzwilliam, "Your cousin will give you a very pretty no-
> tion of me, and teach you not to believe a word I say. I am par-
> ticularly unlucky in meeting with a person so well able to expose
> my real character, in a part of the world, where I had hoped to
> pass myself off with some degree of credit. Indeed, Mr. Darcy,
> it is very ungenerous in you to mention all that you knew to my
> disadvantage in Hertfordshire—and, give me leave to say, very
> impolitic too—for it is provoking me to retaliate, and such things
> may come out, as will shock your relations to hear."

The phrase "pass myself off" reflects Elizabeth's view of what
Darcy tried to do at Netherfield. And she couples "ungenerous"
with the threat of laying bare his disagreeable past to attack him
more directly. Her "impolitic" is just right, for it implies that she
has more sense than Darcy, and it does so without weakening
the emotional power of her assault. Yet he remains utterly polite, and something more: " 'I am not afraid of you,' said he, smil-
ingly." Darcy is "not afraid," either because he feels so confident
of his integrity that he assumes it must win out over Elizabeth's
willful misinterpretations or because he trusts in the ultimate integrity of her sense and feeling. In either case he puts himself
completely in her hands, a real measure of his affection for her.

When Colonel Fitzwilliam invites her to go on, Elizabeth
strikes a tone of parody that thinly disguises her indictment of
Darcy:

> "You shall hear then—but prepare yourself for something very
> dreadful. The first time of my ever seeing him in Hertfordshire,
> you must know, was at a ball—and at this ball, what do you

think he did? He danced only four dances! I am sorry to pain you —but so it was. He danced only four dances, though gentlemen were scarce; and, to my certain knowledge, more than one young lady was sitting down in want of a partner. Mr. Darcy, you cannot deny the fact."

Such phrases as "to my certain knowledge" and "the fact" allege that Darcy was haughty in refusing to dance with her, though Elizabeth still protects her own feelings by generalizing about "more than one young lady." This deed is the foundation of her prejudice, the reality that she is positive Darcy "cannot deny." But he does. At least he redefines what Elizabeth has always taken to be pride as shyness: "I had not at that time the honour of knowing any lady in the assembly beyond my own party." In effect he is saying, "You have interpreted my performance wrongly—as a mere exhibition—because you ignore my total character."

Elizabeth refuses his explanation, polishing him off with a clearly absurd generalization, and then she turns to his friend:

> "True; and nobody can ever be introduced in a ball room. Well, Colonel Fitzwilliam, what do I play next? My fingers wait your orders."
>
> "Perhaps," said Darcy, "I should have judged better, had I sought an introduction, but I am ill qualified to recommend myself to strangers."

Yet Darcy insists on his shyness, even admitting that feeling may have swayed his judgment. So, though Elizabeth keeps her tone light by speaking to Colonel Fitzwilliam, she attacks with even more authority, counting on her impersonal phrasing to provide an air of sense that will decide finally against Darcy:

> "Shall we ask your cousin the reason of this?" said Elizabeth, still addressing Colonel Fitzwilliam. "Shall we ask him why a man of sense and education, and who has lived in the world, is ill qualified to recommend himself to strangers?"
>
> . . . .
>
> "I certainly have not the talent which some people possess,"

※※※※※※※※※※※※※※※※※※※※※※※※※※※※※※※※※※※

said Darcy, "of conversing easily with those I have never seen before. I cannot catch their tone of conversation, or appear interested in their concerns, as I often see done."

But the hostility of Elizabeth still lurks in the bias of her rhetorical question. And Darcy, because he remains unsatisfied that her
formula takes account of his real nature, refers to his shyness for
the third time, again declaring that he cannot put on a skilled
performance, that he must enact his convictions.

Elizabeth finally resorts to her literal performance on the piano in order to carry the day. She uses it metaphorically so that
her thrust may seem decorously oblique, yet she aims her words
straight at Darcy's stubbornness:

> "My fingers . . . do not move over this instrument in the mas-
> terly manner which I see so many women's do. They have not
> the same force or rapidity, and do not produce the same expres-
> sion. But then I have always supposed it to be my own fault—
> because I would not take the trouble of practising. It is not that
> I do not believe *my* fingers as capable as any other woman's of
> superior execution."

At the same time, of course, this is one of Elizabeth's typical self-
displays. But there is a further point: since Elizabeth creates the
metaphor consciously, making the social situation into a vehicle
for illustration, she must still be thinking of *performance* in its
flattest sense.

This allegiance on her part fills Darcy's reply with reverberations:

> Darcy smiled and said, "You are perfectly right. You have em-
> ployed your time much better. No one admitted to the privilege
> of hearing you, can think any thing wanting. We neither of us
> perform to strangers."

He expresses his deepest attachment to her in these sentences.
The first refuses to dispute her judgment of him, which is to say
that Darcy cheerfully sacrifices the real motives he has been explaining. His second sentence must be sheer feeling, for it con-

tradicts the logic both of Elizabeth's metaphor and of what Darcy himself has said earlier: after all, he praises his sister at the beginning of the scene because she "practises very constantly," and Elizabeth has just reproached herself for not practicing more often. Darcy can only mean that her behavior toward him, no matter how prejudiced, is more valuable than her piano-playing. In the third sentence he reverts to the metaphor by "hearing you," which plainly stands for "being with you," but only to keep his extravagant generalization about her charm within the bounds of propriety. Yet his last sentence crowns the others. Perhaps, as a gallant gesture, he is straining to use "perform" in Elizabeth's narrow sense—straining fearfully, if he really wants this meaning, for she is indeed playing to "strangers." But actually, I think, Darcy is calling here on his deeper sense of the word while uttering his most impassioned plea for intimacy, a plea all the more fervent in that it quite irrationally disregards— as a paraphrase shows—the blindness which has marked Elizabeth all along: "We reserve our fullest selves, perfectly understood by both of us, for each other." It is his final, almost desperate attempt before the first proposal to come to terms with her.

But that proposal soon follows, and the letter revealing Darcy to Elizabeth. With both of them now making the necessary personal adjustments and becoming surer of one another's behavior, the play with *performance* disappears from the novel. By the last pages of *Pride and Prejudice,* the earlier tense misunderstandings between them have given way to an exchange like the following, begun by Elizabeth, which ends with them cozily enjoying a joke that takes their true motives for granted:

"Why, especially, when you called, did you look as if you did not care about me?"

"Because you were grave and silent, and gave me no encouragement."

"But I was embarrassed."

"And so was I."

"You might have talked to me more when you came to dinner."

"A man who had felt less, might."

"How unlucky that you should have a reasonable answer to give, and that I should be so reasonable as to admit it!" (p. 381)

※※※※※※※※※※※※※※※※※※※※※※※※※※※※※※※※※

In spite of its lower tension, this bit of dialogue measures how far the characters have traveled since the start of the story. Darcy still defends himself by pointing to his shyness, but he can reckon the liabilities of his behavior. And Elizabeth, though she still puts on something of a show in ironically suggesting that she is disappointed in reason, nevertheless declares the reasonableness of them both. Certainly the lighter tone of the passage should not beguile us into imagining that Darcy has renounced his sense of status, of prudence, of reason, of decorum—those conventional social values which have prompted so many of his previous actions. Indeed, Elizabeth herself comes to endorse these values, as I tried to suggest before, comes to approve the foundations of Darcy's performance.[5] What he has found out— and it is important enough—is that one's total performance may be unacceptable unless it is softened by a gracious display. And Elizabeth has discovered that her own behavior has been lacking in integrity—that the sort of performance in which she has so often acted out her judgment of Darcy has been grounded in a prejudice that distorts reason. The concept, which Jane Austen brings so vividly to life in dialogue, epitomizes the theme of the novel.

1. Mary Lascelles speaks for many critics when she objects to this incident, contending that the Darcy it presents is "inconsistent" with the one "described and developed in the rest of the book" (*Jane Austen,* p. 22). But I think she misses the full psychology behind Darcy's remarks and the artistry of Jane Austen, who sets up here a hero antipathetic to Elizabeth without completely sacrificing his character in the process. Darcy's letter to Elizabeth after his first proposal has also been called in question by Miss Lascelles—and other critics—on much the same grounds: she feels it "not . . . quite plausible" that "so much, and such, information would . . . be volunteered by a proud and reserved man—unless under pressure from his author" (p. 162). But Darcy says himself in it that "my character required it to be written and read" (p. 196), that he will tell Elizabeth what he has done because an "explanation . . . is due to myself" (p. 197). Indeed the letter seems to me almost the only unequivocal instance in the novel of the pride usually attributed to Darcy.

※※※※※※※※※※※※※※※※※※※※※※※※※※※※※※※※※※※※※

2. Reuben Brower has analyzed these dialogues magnificently in his essay on *Pride and Prejudice* in *The Fields of Light* (New York, 1951), pp. 164–81. His chapter contains the most exciting exposition of Jane Austen's methods that I know, and he is the only critic who has done justice to her portrait of Darcy. Brower shows how Darcy's offers to dance convey a variety of motives, ranging from insufferable pride to serious interest in Elizabeth.

3. By pointing out Charlotte's capacity to feel, which also shows up in other parts of *Pride and Prejudice,* I am hoping to suggest only that Jane Austen makes her a somewhat fuller character than we ordinarily imagine, influenced as we are by the hard attitude toward marriage that Charlotte preaches and then puts in practice by accepting Mr. Collins: " . . . it was the only honourable provision for well-educated young women of small fortune, and however uncertain of giving happiness, must be their pleasantest preservative from want" (pp. 122–23). Perhaps it is worth noting, however, that such undeniably sympathetic characters as Mrs. Gardiner and Colonel Fitzwilliam advance a prudent view of marriage themselves (pp. 144, 183).

4. Dorothy Van Ghent makes out the most persuasive case for taking the verbal manner of Mr. Collins as an index to his character, noting at one point that "The elaborate language in which Mr. Collins gets himself fairly *stuck* is a mimesis of an action of the soul, the soul that becomes self dishonest through failure to know itself, and that overrates itself at the expense of the social context, just as it overrates verbalism at the expense of meaning" (*The English Novel*, p. 106).

5. Although Mudrick acknowledges the pressures of society in *Pride and Prejudice,* the general tendencies of his commentary on the novel seem to me misleading. He divides its characters into the simple and the complex, arguing that this is the "first decision" Elizabeth makes about any person and that the decision "is not moral but psychological" (*Jane Austen,* p. 95). The simple personalities, he maintains, are beneath "moral judgment" (p. 123). The "complex individual" is marked by his capacity for "choice" and by his "freedom": a freedom which makes him at bottom "isolated" from his society; a choice which Elizabeth, at least, must exercise by settling on a husband who is "undefeated by his social role" (pp. 124–25). In all this Mudrick seriously underrates, so I think, both Elizabeth's responsiveness to the values of society and the influence of conventional morality in the novel. Dorothy Van Ghent takes a stand somewhat like Mudrick's in treating *Pride and Prejudice* as organized about a clash between the "feelings" of the individual and the "utility interests" of society (*The English Novel*, p. 102). She finds the latter embodied in Jane Austen's "materialistic" vocabulary and offers a number of wonderfully perceptive stylistic analyses. Yet I am not quite sure whether she means to suggest ultimately that Jane Austen was really reacting against such language and its implications, though tied down by history to the words and meanings "inherited from her culture" (p. 109), or that

the author accepted her society and its language. The critic's closing judgment of what goes on in the novel itself is completely unequivocal, however, and I feel that it lies nearer to my own view than to Mudrick's: "The final fought-for recognitions of value are recognitions of the unity of experience—a unity between the common culture and the individual development" (p. 111).

6 Mansfield Park
Ethical Rigor and an
Emblematic Mode

To anyone fresh from the bracing air of *Pride and Prejudice*, it seems as if a heavy frost sets in with *Mansfield Park*. In fact the novel is disappointing to many readers and critics of Jane Austen, who find it uncharacteristic. Yet, though *Mansfield Park* undeniably feels chilly when compared with the rest of her work, my underlying argument in the following pages will be that its moral climate remains, in all essentials, exactly the one that we find everywhere in Jane Austen's writings. But before pursuing that matter, we might stop for a moment to notice what makes the temperature drop so sharply.

One reason for it is Jane Austen's handling of our point of view in *Mansfield Park*. Here she makes her nearest approach to the convention of the omniscient author, letting us see many of the characters in action apart from the heroine, judging them for us, all in all presiding more solemnly, I think more openly, than in her other novels. Of course we do look at a good deal of what happens with and through Fanny Price. But we have almost no sense of being dramatically implicated in a partial, perhaps unreliable, view of what is going on, and certainly no sense that the meaning of *Mansfield Park* hinges in any significant way on the limits of Fanny's perceptions as an individual. In these respects the novel differs radically from *Pride and Prejudice* or *Emma*, even from *Northanger Abbey,* and in another respect as well, for Fanny—unlike Elizabeth Bennet, Emma Woodhouse, or Catherine Morland—does not undergo any real change in the course of the story. Rather, her consciousness seems gradually to open out, its quality to become progressively clearer to us, as she more and more obviously takes on the function of the moral norm by which the other characters are to be evaluated. We would have to go back to *Sense and Sensibility* to find a heroine whose moral presence and perspective on events are allowed to be anything like so unequivocally trustworthy as Fanny's, but even Elinor Dashwood is represented as developing to some degree. Not until *Persuasion* will we come on a heroine who changes as little as Fanny; by then, however, Jane Austen has resolved her two tendencies in managing our point of view: though we are dramatically involved in Anne Elliot's limited perceptions, she proves a thoroughly sound judge.

But Anne is so warm, so taking, that no reader feels tempted to hold the soundness of her decisions against her. Nothing of the sort can be said for Fanny; indeed her personality has a good deal to do with the chilliness of *Mansfield Park*. For no one can ignore the fact that she is something less than attractive. Sickly, quiescent, easily and constantly oppressed, she leaves the impression at moments of being Jane Austen's study in inferiority. Yet if Fanny's emotional sensitivity causes her to suffer acutely on practically every occasion, this sensitivity also fosters—somewhat as in the case of Anne Elliot—an almost unrelievedly accurate set of judgments. The combination is certainly unappealing, and I think Jane Austen recognized the fact, for from time to time she works hard to humanize her heroine, going out of her way, for instance, to insist that Henry Crawford's suit would have succeeded if Fanny were not already devoted to Edmund Bertram (p. 231), or showing Fanny to be jealous of Mary Crawford (pp. 67, 74, 159, 199, 279). But efforts like these to make Fanny a more sympathetic figure hardly temper the major sense of her that emerges from the novel as a whole, a sense of unalloyed righteousness, of a nearly infallible judgment.

Although these qualities may keep Fanny from winning the heart of the reader, they also place her at the moral center of the story. And she stands quite alone there, for *Mansfield Park* makes it clear that her feelings, unlike those of any other character, are securely moored in conscience. No matter how intense her emotional experience, she retains that degree of objectivity which allows her to judge herself. In direct contrast, everyone else in the novel is represented as trapped to some extent within feelings oriented toward satisfaction of the self alone, and all these other characters tend, under pressure of such emotions, not to view the world about them as it is, but to recreate it in the image of their desires. This inability to transcend the purely self-regarding element in feeling is what *Mansfield Park* takes under attack, treating it as a moral failure on the part of the individual and arguing that self-interest of this sort—rather as we have seen in the earlier works—results inevitably in folly and blindness. The sheer number of such misjudgments that Jane Austen records here is staggering; in importance, they range from so trivial a matter as Yates's idiotic assumption that Sir Thomas Bertram will approve of the acting scheme, through the more serious mistaking of Maria Bertram by Aunt Norris, to such crucial misconceptions as Edmund's of the Crawfords, or Sir Thomas' of Fanny and of his own family. The malady disables everyone but Fanny at some time or other, and even she shows symptoms of it once, though they clear up quickly. Since it does strike so many characters and, by my reading of *Mansfield Park*, leaves so great a variety of them in morally critical condition, I feel a little uneasy about the interpretation of the novel which finds in it primarily a conflict between worlds—the Bertrams' Mansfield Park vs. the Crawfords' London vs. the Prices' Portsmouth—with the world of the Bertrams winning out because of its moral superiority.[1] Rather, as I have already suggested, *Mansfield Park* seems to me concerned fundamentally with defining moral integrity, a subject it explores by contrasting the self-centered behavior of all the other characters with Fanny's unselfishness. Although the righteousness of the heroine, the gravity with which Jane Austen treats her materials here (such as the acting episode or the affair of Edmund's ordination), and the pervasively somber tone of the novel all combine to make *Mansfield Park* almost Victorian in mood, yet Jane Austen's theme remains very much what it has always been.

This theme is mirrored in the action of *Mansfield Park*, which springs largely from misjudgments of the kind I have mentioned, and in its conversations, which dramatize in their own way the moral obtuseness of the characters. One of the chief clues to personality that these dialogues provide is the individual's estimate of what does or does not seem to be the case, of what is or is not likely to happen—a decision that reveals the degree to which his wishes govern his insight and thus measures his objectivity for us. How frequently such estimates crop up in *Mansfield Park* will emerge, I hope, in the following pages. But my main job will be, first, to set down some of the large lines along which the narrative develops, meanwhile sketching in a few of the minor characters; then to explore the interaction between Edmund, Fanny, and the Crawfords; finally, to show the variation that is worked here on the technique of metaphoric indirection that we have seen Jane Austen using in the dialogues of earlier novels.

·⟨ II ⟩·

It is Mrs. Norris who gets the story started by engineering the invitation of Fanny to settle at Mansfield. And it is Mrs. Norris who introduces us almost immediately to the sort of misjudgment which the novel everywhere condemns; for her zeal to carry her project with Sir Thomas leads her to dismiss with scorn the possibility of any attachment arising between Fanny and either of his sons: " . . . do not you know that of all things upon earth *that* is the least likely to happen . . . ? It is morally impossible. I never knew an instance of it. It is, in fact, the only sure way of providing against the connection" (pp. 6–7). Of course the absurdity of this prediction is demonstrated by the union of Fanny with Edmund at the end of *Mansfield Park*, but so severe an irony is hardly felt as inappropriate, for Mrs. Norris emerges as one of the most disagreeable characters in the book. Although she frequently professes her benevolence and charity, the officiousness with which she prosecutes the schemes that fill her mind shows her need to assert herself at the expense of others. Indeed she betrays her fundamental egocentricity in almost every sentence. Since Sir Thomas is her social superior, she must at least affect discretion when she generalizes to him: "A niece of our's . . . I may say, or, at least of *your's*, would not grow up in this neighbourhood without many advantages" (p. 6). But with inferiors she deals ruthlessly, presuming to generalize with the social authority of the Bertrams while in fact revealing her own snobbishness, and, in the following excerpt, her dislike for Fanny as well: " . . . there is no real occasion for your going into company in this sort of way, or ever dining out at all; and it is what you must not depend upon ever being repeated" (p. 220). Perhaps the actual feelings of Mrs. Norris come clearest, however, in her use of particular terms. When addressing Fanny, she simply gives a free rein to her nasty temper, berating her niece in this passage for resting instead of sewing: "I am sure I almost broke my back by cutting it out. You should learn to think of other people; . . . it is a shocking trick for a young person to be always lolling upon a sofa" (p. 71). To Sir Thomas she speaks in a different tone, yet I think her particular diction—now describing her sympathy for a coachman—still expresses the urge of Mrs. Norris to dominate: " . . . my heart quite ached for him at every jolt, and when we got into the rough lanes . . . I was quite in an agony about him. And then the poor horses too! —To see them straining away!" (p. 189). It is as if, unable to compete with Sir Thomas socially, Mrs. Norris must stake out her own claim to superiority in the realms of sensitivity and unselfishness. Obviously the claim is exploded by her words and deeds throughout the story: far from projecting herself into others, Mrs. Norris stands convicted of being so enslaved by her will that she can see only what she wants to see.

The same charge applies to the favorite of Mrs. Norris, Maria Bertram, whose intrigue with Henry Crawford takes up much of the narrative foreground in the first part of the novel. Sir Thomas' trip to Antigua has given Mrs. Norris her finest chance to exercise her talents at Mansfield, and she distinguishes herself typically, both by promoting Maria's engagement to the rich but insipid Mr. Rushworth and by remaining blind to the subsequent flirtation between her niece and Henry. The absence of their father acts like a tonic on all the young Bertrams, stirring

Maria to behave even more imperiously than usual in adjusting facts to the demands of her will. Thus when Henry Crawford appears, so much more fascinating than Mr. Rushworth, Maria surmises: "There could be no harm in her liking an agreeable man—every body knew her situation—Mr. Crawford must take care of himself" (p. 44). After minimizing her feelings in the first clause, she contrives to shift the responsibility for proper conduct from herself to "every body," especially "Mr. Crawford," while by her arrogant close she implies, ludicrously enough, that she will be far more attractive to him than he to her. Even in the rhythm of Maria's clauses, itself abrupt and assertive, we can hear something of her willfulness. As Jane Austen has just remarked, "She did not want to see or understand." Much the same comment might be made about Tom and Julia Bertram, who share to a large extent their sister's self-indulgence, but Maria's case is the most serious for she has accepted her engagement to Mr. Rushworth willingly, if unenthusiastically. Yet she seizes every opportunity to set herself for Henry Crawford, most conspicuously in the outing to Sotherton and in the acting venture—all the while relishing the precedence she gains from being engaged. Her bubble bursts only with the return of her father from Antigua.

Sir Thomas presides over the action in the middle third of *Mansfield Park,* and he proves no more reliable than Mrs. Norris. Jane Austen has introduced him as a man motivated by "principle as well as pride" (p. 4), but it is the fate of Sir Thomas never to realize how readily his pride subverts principle. His sense of himself can be traced in his talk with Mrs. Norris, early in the novel, about "the distinction proper to be made" in bringing up his girls with Fanny:

". . . how to preserve in the minds of my *daughters* the consciousness of what they are, without making them think too lowly of their cousin; and how, without depressing her spirits too far, to make her remember that she is not a *Miss Bertram.* I should wish to see them very good friends . . . but still they cannot be equals. Their rank, fortune, rights, and expectations, will always be different." (pp. 10–11)

In a series of meticulous antitheses Sir Thomas not only weighs his daughters against Fanny but also separates his "wish" for them to be "friends" from his conviction of their inequality. The controlled rhetoric combines with the dominantly conceptual terms to suggest the role that he always fancies himself to play: that of an impartial judge moving in a world of fixed values. Yet I think we are entitled to ask, even at this stage of the story, whether what informs his strict division between Fanny and her cousins is a thoroughly proper distinction or an exorbitant pride in his children. No such question presents itself to Sir Thomas, of course, who constantly supposes his feelings to be so saturated with principle as to guarantee his conduct. This assumption traps him into any number of errors, most spectacularly after he has come back to Mansfield.

When Sir Thomas recognizes his daughter's indifference to Mr. Rushworth, for instance, yet supports Maria in her desire to go through with the marriage, Jane Austen points out his folly—describing him as "too glad to be satisfied perhaps to urge the matter quite so far as his judgment might have dictated to others" (p. 201)—and shows us his wish for Maria's company masquerading as a principle: "A well-disposed young woman, who did not marry for love, was in general but the more attached to her own family, and the nearness of Sotherton to Mansfield must naturally hold out the greatest temptation, and would, in all probability, be a continual supply of the most amiable and innocent enjoyments." A prediction further from the truth would be hard to imagine, inasmuch as Maria accepts Mr. Rushworth in order to escape from home and later destroys her marriage by running off with Henry Crawford. If Sir Thomas deceives himself in the matter of Maria's engagement, he seems absolutely blind when the courting of Fanny by Henry Crawford—the focus of narrative interest in the second part of *Mansfield Park*—develops into a proposal. Although Fanny declares her real feelings, "I—I cannot like him, Sir, well enough to marry him," Sir Thomas in effect denies their existence, beguiled as he is by his wish for so apparently advantageous a match: "I am half inclined to think . . . that you do not quite know your own feel-

ings" (pp. 315–16). And when she stands by her refusal, his am-
bition for the marriage drives Sir Thomas to invert the morality
of the situation even more flagrantly, for he conceives it his
"duty" to reprimand Fanny for being so selfish:

> ". . . you have disappointed every expectation I had formed,
> and proved yourself of a character the very reverse of what I
> had supposed. . . . I had thought you peculiarly free from wil-
> fulness of temper, self-conceit, and every tendency to that inde-
> pendence of spirit, which prevails so much in modern days
> . . . . But you have now shewn me . . . that you can and will
> decide for yourself, without any consideration or deference for
> those who have surely some right to guide you . . . . You think
> only of yourself . . . ." (p. 318)

As usual, the rhetoric sounds judicious, because Sir Thomas separates his statement about feeling "disappointed" from a supposedly reasoned demonstration of Fanny's stubbornness. But
obviously the generalizations and conceptual terms here bear no
relation at all to her case; rather, they express Sir Thomas' cha-
grin as if it were a law. Perhaps by the end of the story, when he
has seen events frustrate so many of his cherished aims, we are to
believe him somewhat chastened. Perhaps—yet Jane Austen's
final words about him still undercut his sense of principle: " . . .
in the general well-doing and success" of the Prices, the author
reports, "Sir Thomas saw repeated, and for ever repeated reason
to rejoice in what he had done for them all, and acknowledge the
advantages of early hardship and discipline, and the consciousness of being born to struggle and endure" (p. 473).

It is the Prices themselves and their squalid home at Portsmouth that make the most vivid impression in the closing third
of the novel. Fanny's visit to them is planned by Sir Thomas,
who secretly hopes it will induce her to marry Henry, and Fanny
looks forward eagerly to being with her family, for once gravely
misinformed by her emotions. Overcome with nostalgia for her
early childhood and depressed by her inferiority to the people at
Mansfield, she imagines that "to be at home again, would heal
every pain," that at Portsmouth she will be "more loved by all

than she had ever been before," will "feel affection without fear or restraint" and "feel herself the equal of those who surrounded her" (p. 370). But the Portsmouth home turns out to be dirty, life there chaotic, and the Prices—with William away at sea—as completely self-centered as the Bertrams. Although Fanny herself never makes so damaging a comparison between the Portsmouth inhabitants and those of Mansfield, though she even seems something of a snob when she later comes to yearn for the placidity of the Park, at least the feelings that she brings with her to Portsmouth do not blind her to the reality of her family— not that the shortcomings of the Prices are hard to discover.

Fanny's mother and father, who set the tone of the Portsmouth scenes, are so self-engrossed that to all intents and purposes they ignore the return of their daughter. The flurried rhythms of Mrs. Price indicate that she is always at the mercy of the moment's emotions:

> "And when did you get anything to eat? And what would you like to have now? . . . And now I am afraid Campbell will be here, before there is time to dress a steak, and we have no butcher at hand. It is very inconvenient to have no butcher in the street. We were better off in our last house. Perhaps you would like some tea, as soon as it can be got." (pp. 378–79)

As the passage makes clear, her own concerns dominate her talk. When she tries to speak of Mansfield with Fanny, she inevitably ends in herself, for such questions as "How did her sister Bertram manage about her servants," so Jane Austen tells us, "soon led her mind away from Northamptonshire, and fixed it on her own domestic grievances" (p. 385). This absorption in herself makes Fanny's mother the Portsmouth counterpart to Lady Bertram, who differs from Mrs. Price only in being absolutely inert and incapable of attempting to consider anyone else. As for Mr. Price, he never interests himself in Fanny in the slightest. The habitual "by G——'s" are symptomatic of his emotional extremism, a private condition which he converts into a public standard when generalizing about Maria's desertion of

Rushworth: "But by G—— if she belonged to me, I'd give her the rope's end as long as I could stand over her. A little flogging for man and woman too, would be the best way of preventing such things" (p. 440). After an outburst like this, it may appear absurd to name Mr. Price in the same breath with the calm Sir Thomas, but we should observe that feeling—feeling determined by their concern with themselves—governs the judgments that both of them pass on what happens around them. Indeed, for all the murkiness of the Portsmouth scenes (nowhere else does Jane Austen heap up such naturalistic details) and for all that serenity which so attracts Fanny to Mansfield, the Prices' world and the Bertrams' seem to me to reveal the same moral debility. Even at the end of the novel, after Fanny has returned to find life at the Park ruffled by Tom's illness and the news of Maria's infidelity, Mansfield seems ready enough to settle back into its usual ways, most of the Bertrams giving little evidence of any deep-seated change in their attitudes despite the catastrophes that have occurred. But Edmund does discover, through his own bitter experience with Mary Crawford, how false an image of her his feelings have created. And Fanny can be rewarded with him at last, in a match which many feel is about what each of them deserves.

·◄[III]►·

The minor figures of *Mansfield Park,* so I have been arguing, are all to some degree blinded by their desires and thus become expressions of the novel's theme, which contrasts the selfishness that results from indulging in one's own wishes with the principled behavior achieved through self-denial. These conflicting modes of being are treated most fully by Jane Austen in her representation of the major characters. At one pole stands the righteous Fanny; at the other, the fundamentally egotistical Crawfords; and in the course of the story Edmund is drawn toward the

Crawfords, freeing himself of their influence only when he finally comes to see them clearly and to understand himself. In this sense the story is more concerned with Edmund than with Fanny, and he will take up much of our attention in the following pages.

Both of them reveal their essential commitments in an early interchange at Mansfield Park, when it appears that Fanny may have to move in with Mrs. Norris. Edmund thinks the plan thoroughly sensible, though kindly hoping that it will not "distress" his cousin. But Fanny is stirred by her experiences with her bullying aunt to a response full of feeling, its intensity marked by the abrupt rhythms and the repeated "I":

> "Indeed it does. I cannot like it. I love this house and every thing in it. I shall love nothing there. You know how uncomfortable I feel with her."
>
> "I can say nothing for her manner to you as a child; but it was the same with us all, or nearly so. She never knew how to be pleasant to children. But you are now of an age to be treated better; I think she *is* behaving better already; and when you are her only companion, you *must* be important to her." (p. 26)

Edmund begins his reply, in a fashion that may remind us of Sir Thomas, with distinctions that are level-headed enough, using them as the basis for a generalization about Mrs. Norris' dealings with all "children." But the logic collapses in the last half of his remarks. In spite of the syllogistic façade—and Edmund almost always takes pains to speak like a precisionist—it does not really follow, from the premise about Fanny's "age," that Mrs. Norris will or even *"is"* treating her niece better. Quite the opposite, in fact. This is not to say that Edmund is stupid; rather, his ardor for what he feels to be a proper relationship between his aunt and Fanny prompts him to gloss over the imperfections of the one and the deep emotions of the other. Throughout the novel his panoply of logic conceals assumptions, usually benevolent enough in themselves, of which he is unaware. The words of Fanny, on the other hand, spring so directly from her feelings that she often sounds sentimental; but her emotional sensitivity itself—so *Mansfield Park* insists, however arbitrarily—empowers her to cut through the assumptions that bedevil Edmund. Indeed the fact that he should so often be disposed to imagine an emotional bias at work in Fanny sets up one of the standard ironies in the story, for it is Edmund who is constantly swayed by his liking for Mary Crawford.

Mary herself breathes confidence, wit, and high spirits, her manner the antithesis of Fanny's; and her effect on Edmund, not surprisingly, is immediate. But the contrast between Mary and Fanny goes beyond manner: they differ in the quality and kind of their feelings. Mary's have shallower roots than Fanny's, a distinction suggested partly by Mary's willingness at moments to make a conscious display of her feelings—in particular terms or figurative language—and partly by her ability to act, to play someone else (whereas Fanny remains bound by her own nature).[2] Furthermore, the novel presents Mary as unable to escape, in her emotional life as an individual, from being influenced by some sense of self or by her demands as a person. This point is hinted at, I think, by the two types of generalization that she employs throughout *Mansfield Park*.[3] One type is the axiom that codifies self-interest (when leavened with taste), the sort of formulation which Mary has absorbed through living in the fashionable world. Not only does she subscribe to the doctrine, but by acting as a spokesman for it she allies herself with a select social group, which means that some sense of her status as a person haunts her use of the axioms. The doctrine itself may crop up in a relatively casual judgment: she thinks the navy a feasible profession "under two circumstances; if it make the fortune, and there be discretion in spending it" (p. 60). But she brings the same kind of axiom to bear when she is under emotional stress, a measure of her belief in the doctrine: while questioning Fanny suspiciously about the sisters of a friend whom Edmund is visiting, Mary stops to observe, "It is every body's duty to do as well for themselves as they can. Sir Thomas Bertram's son is somebody" (p. 289). Her second type of generalization expresses her personal feelings more openly, and, typically, it projects them as a standard, something valid for everyone. Thus, for all the conscious wit in her apology for monopolizing Fanny's horse, "Self-ishness must always be forgiven you know, because there is no hope of a cure" (p. 68), Mary still makes universals of her own feelings and thus, in effect, legalizes them. The process is really the same when she utters a much more generous sentiment, claiming that "No other man" but Edmund "would have thought of" giving Fanny a necklace for the ball (pp. 274–75). Here the generalization articulates Mary's intense delight at the behavior of the man who strongly attracts her. Of course by nagging about Mary's motives in this way I am darkening, perhaps un-fairly, the impression we have of her on reading much of the novel. For she is intelligent and warmhearted. More than that, *Mansfield Park* shows her enduring a severe emotional struggle in her relationship with Edmund: beset on the one hand by her allegiance to the fashionable world, which has its own set of re-quirements concerning a suitor proper for her, and on the other by the commands of her own heart, probably the more compel-ling of the two forces. But whichever the force that dominates Mary at any given moment—and this is what I was trying to sug-gest in analyzing her kinds of generalization—there remains a touch of the self-regarding in all her feelings, and this element differentiates her absolutely, in the context of this novel, from Fanny.

What Mary hardly realizes, or what in her vivacity she will not worry about, is that this element of the purely personal un-dermines her judgments, giving them a base too local, too limited to her private feelings. Many dialogues illustrate her condition, the talk about family prayer, for instance, or the one I shall sum-marize now, in which she, Edmund, and Fanny discuss the cleri-cal profession (pp. 108–12). Mary begins with an ironic thrust at Edmund, accusing him of choosing to be a clergyman for reasons of self-interest, the motive she attributes to any intelligent per-son: "It is fortunate that your inclination and your father's con-venience should accord so well. There is a very good living kept for you, I understand, hereabouts." Edmund will go so far as to admit her charge that he is "biassed," but he reorients it to prove his integrity:

> "There was no natural disinclination to be overcome, and I see
> no reason why a man should make a worse clergyman for know-
> ing that he will have a competence early in life. . . . I hope I
> should not have been influenced myself in a wrong way, and I
> am sure my father was too conscientious to have allowed it. I
> have no doubt that I was biassed, but I think it was blamelessly."

Characteristically, he works his way through a set of distinctions
which defend his behavior, and just as characteristically, he
avoids taking a stand that is unalterably opposed to Mary's.

Edmund holds his ground for about a page, using his controlled rhetoric and exact logic to overturn those generalizations
drawn from the world of fashion on which Mary builds part of
her case against clergymen. But after a time her more personal
feelings flash out in the particular terms and rhetorical series of
the following passage, throughout which Mary formulates her
emotions as general truths: a clergyman, she maintains,

> "has the best intentions of doing nothing all the rest of his days
> but eat, drink, and grow fat. It is indolence Mr. Bertram, indeed.
> Indolence and love of ease—a want of all laudable ambition, of
> taste for good company, or of inclination to take the trouble of
> being agreeable, which make men clergymen. A clergyman has
> nothing to do but to be slovenly and selfish—read the newspa-
> per, watch the weather, and quarrel with his wife."

The immediate source of these generalizations, as will become
clearer in a moment, is Mary's dislike for her brother-in-law, Dr.
Grant. Understandable as her reaction to him is, it plainly cannot validate her blanket condemnation of clergymen here, any
more than could the prevailing attitude toward them in highly
fashionable society. Edmund, sensing the emotional bias in
Mary's remarks, points out the fallacy of generalizing on the basis of limited instances:

> "There are such clergymen, no doubt, but I think they are not so
> common as to justify Miss Crawford in esteeming it their general
> character. I suspect that . . . you are not judging from yourself,
> but from prejudiced persons, whose opinions you have been in

the habit of hearing. . . . You can have been personally acquainted with very few of a set of men you condemn so con-
clusively. You are speaking what you have been told at your uncle's table."

Though he diagrams her error, Edmund's liking for Mary im-
pels him to make every allowance for her that he can, and so he
attributes the opinion to others, trying to divorce her from it.

Finally, his desire to align himself with Mary forces Edmund
to desert, in effect, his defense of the clergy, for she absolutely
refuses to modify her view:

> ". . . I am not entirely without the means of seeing what clergy-
> men are, being at the present time the guest of my own brother,
> Dr. Grant. And though . . . he is really a gentleman . . . and
> often preaches good sermons, and is very respectable, *I* see him to
> be an indolent selfish bon vivant, who must have his palate con-
> sulted in every thing, who will not stir a finger for the conven-
> ience of any one, and who, moreover, if the cook makes a blun-
> der, is out of humour with his excellent wife. . . ."
> "I do not wonder at your disapprobation, upon my word. It is
> a great defect of temper, made worse by a very faulty habit of
> self-indulgence; and to see your sister suffering from it, must be
> exceedingly painful to such feelings as your's. Fanny, it goes
> against us. We cannot attempt to defend Dr. Grant."

The case of Dr. Grant, of course, does not authorize Mary's earlier generalizations about clergymen; rather, it is the single specific instance at the bottom of the generalizations, as the similarities in language and tone reveal. Edmund, however, gives over
his efforts on behalf of the class, content instead to take his place
at Mary's side by remolding her particular attacks on Dr. Grant
in a conceptual vocabulary.

This turn of events proves too much for Fanny, who comes
out of her shell to reclaim both the "profession" and Dr. Grant:

> "No . . . but we need not give up his profession for all that;
> because, whatever profession Dr. Grant had chosen, he would
> have taken a—not a good temper into it; and as he must either in
> the navy or army have had a great many more people under his

command than he has now, I think more would have been made unhappy by him as a sailor or soldier than as a clergyman. Besides, I cannot but suppose that whatever there may be to wish otherwise in Dr. Grant, would have been in a greater danger of becoming worse in a more active and worldly profession . . . where he might have escaped that knowledge of himself, the *frequency*, at least, of that knowledge which it is impossible he should escape as he is now. A man—a sensible man like Dr. Grant, cannot be in the habit of teaching others their duty every week, cannot go to church twice every Sunday and preach such very good sermons in so good a manner as he does, without being the better for it himself."

While the speech may get on our nerves because of its latent antagonism toward Mary, its sentimental echo of Fanny's love for her brother in the navy, and its moral optimism, still its significance in the present context is unmistakable. Whereas Mary has distorted and Edmund momentarily relinquished the class of clergymen, Fanny refuses to lose sight of the "profession" as a whole. And when she turns to the particular case of Dr. Grant, though she says all that can possibly be said for him, she does not close her eyes to his faults but carefully qualifies her estimate of him. Yet Mary's opinion is not to be shaken, and after a pleasant compliment to Fanny she withdraws to another part of the room, leaving Edmund to sing her praises to his cousin.

As Edmund's affection for Mary increases, his hold on the sort of distinctions we have seen him attempting slips more and more, at least where she is concerned, and this fact is discoverable in his behavior as well as in his rhetoric. After he learns that Mary has joined the cast of *Lovers' Vows*, Edmund agrees to take a part himself: abandoning his earlier moral objections to the theatrical venture, he now identifies "wrong" with Mary's uneasiness at the possibility of having to act with a stranger, a situation to which "it would be really wrong to expose her" (p. 155). The change in his rhetoric that the mere thought of her can produce is another measure of his love. To realize fully Mary's impact on him, we should first listen to Edmund receiving Fanny's thanks for the necklace he has given her:

"My dear Fanny, you feel these things a great deal too much. I am most happy that you like the chain, and that it should be here in time for to-morrow: but your thanks are far beyond the occasion. Believe me, I have no pleasure in the world superior to that of contributing to yours. No, I can safely say, I have no pleasure so complete, so unalloyed. It is without a drawback."

(p. 262)

The rhythm is declarative and, above all, relaxed. The fairly equal sentence lengths show Edmund emotionally poised between a gentle reproof of Fanny—in which he weighs his happiness against her "thanks"—and his complacent attachment to her. So at ease is he emotionally that he can pause, in his next to last sentence, to think over his other pleasures in order to assess his satisfaction in gratifying Fanny. But as soon as she announces that Mary has also given her a necklace, one that Fanny wishes to return, Edmund's rhythm and tone are drastically altered:

"Return the necklace! No, my dear Fanny, upon no account. It would be mortifying her severely. There can hardly be a more unpleasant sensation than the having any thing returned on our hands, which we have given with a reasonable hope of its contributing to the comfort of a friend. Why should she lose a pleasure which she has shewn herself so deserving of?" (p. 263)

The two bursts with which he begins; the fourth sentence, which runs on in agitation; the final, almost querulous question —all mark how deeply Mary affects him. Edmund has left his rhetoric of distinctions far behind, a point implied by Jane Austen's description of him a minute earlier as lost "in a reverie of fond reflection, uttering only now and then a few half sentences of praise" for Mary. It need hardly be added that in his overwhelming anxiety for Mary here he completely ignores Fanny's emotions, both her distrust of her rival and her devotion to him.

This is her fate through most of the novel, of course, and one repeated indication of blindness in Edmund, Mary, and Henry is that none of them can conceive of Fanny being in love with her cousin. All three reveal how essentially their feelings center on themselves in the episodes dealing with Henry's pursuit of Fanny. Henry himself bears close resemblances to his sister. He too will use language as a vehicle for conscious self-display, rather more frequently than she does. He may put his wit on parade via metaphor for the amusement of Mary and himself: spending his time with her "would be all recreation and indulgence," he says, "without the wholesome alloy of labour, and I do not like to eat the bread of idleness. No, my plan is to make Fanny Price in love with me" (p. 229). Or he may represent himself as a simpler soul, protesting to Maria on one occasion that he feels much too deeply to be a "man of the world" (p. 98)—while the whole dialogue shows, incongruously enough, his adroit control of implication and his easy manipulation of Maria. When Henry exploits language in this way, often more playfully than in my examples, he appears quite conscious of indulging himself. But he seems unaware that his remarks, when less carefully wrought, betray the same commitment to his private pleasure, the fundamental egotism that he shares with Mary. Thus, the natural environment itself must answer to his will: since he "can never bear to ask," he declares, "I *told* a man . . . that it was Thornton Lacey, and he agreed to it" (p. 241). And so must the human environment, although all the evidence that Henry has given us about his uncle runs counter to the following prediction: "When Fanny is known to him . . . he will doat on her. She is exactly the woman to do away every prejudice of such a man as the Admiral, for she is exactly such a woman as he thinks does not exist" (p. 293). The whole world is cut to the pattern of his desires.

When Henry sets out to conquer Fanny, he intends merely to entertain himself with another flirtation of the sort he has conducted with Maria. Even after he has come to love Fanny, however, the recurrent motif of his speeches remains self-gratification. In announcing his love to his sister, he may joke about the "bitter pill" it will be to Maria and refuse to exaggerate his own attractions, but in the next breath he is exclaiming, "Yes, Mary, my Fanny will feel a difference indeed . . . and it will be the completion of my happiness to know that I am the doer of it, that I am the person to give the consequence so justly her due," and a moment later, "What can Sir Thomas and Edmund together do, what *do* they do for her happiness, comfort, honour, and dignity in the world to what I *shall* do" (p. 297). I do not want to deny Henry the "moral taste" by which the author explains his attraction to Fanny, but the novel insists, relentlessly, that this taste is vitiated by Henry's drive to indulge himself. His rhetoric gives away his condition when he brings Fanny news of the promotion he has engineered for her brother. Henry begins by asserting his unselfishness: "I will not talk of my own happiness . . . great as it is, for I think only of yours. Compared with you, who has a right to be happy?" But, as the breathless rhythms continue, he dwells mainly on what he has done and felt:

> "I have not lost a moment, however. The post was late this morning, but there has not been since, a moment's delay. How impatient, how anxious, how wild I have been on the subject, I will not attempt to describe; how severely mortified, how cruelly disappointed, in not having it finished while I was in London!"
>
> (p. 299)

Even this "glow" of feeling does not seem to penetrate Henry too deeply, however, for on the next page Jane Austen reports him carrying on to Fanny about "the *deepest interest* . . . *twofold motives* . . . *views and wishes more than could be told*"— in short, reverting to the controlled ambiguity he has practiced earlier with Maria. To be sure, *Mansfield Park* damns Henry arbitrarily in the end by involving him in that escapade with Maria, which happens too suddenly and is altogether too foolish to be convincing as behavior, at least as Henry's behavior. Yet there is a degree of moral consistency in the act, for the novel shows Henry always ruled by the wish of the moment and bent on pleasing himself.

The reaction of Mary to Henry's suit for Fanny makes clear that her primary feelings, like his, revolve around herself or mirror limited personal allegiances. Furthermore, she proves herself as blind to Fanny's real emotions as he has. When Henry tells

Mary of his hopes, she immediately desires the match for her own sake, because it will bring her closer to Edmund. Her *"first"* open response expresses both her own social commitment and her adoration for her brother: "Lucky, lucky girl! . . . what a match for her! My dearest Henry, this must be my *first* feeling" (p. 292). Only then does she declare her genuine value for Fanny: " . . . my *second* . . . is that I approve your choice from my soul . . . . " And Mary instantly rushes on to convert her feelings, much as Henry did, into a prediction: " . . . I . . . foresee your happiness as heartily as I wish and desire it." All is now cut to the pattern of Mary's pleasure. But it is a pattern that sometimes minimizes Fanny as a person in making her simply an adjunct to Henry: "Exactly what you deserve." Or at best the pattern takes Fanny's emotions for granted, and in the following passage imposes its own moral order on the world as well: "Your wicked project upon her peace turns out a clever thought indeed. You will both find your good in it" (p. 295). The "good" equals the "clever," the "wicked" being overcome by a verb of transformation.

In saying this, I do not mean that Mary is insensitive, has odious feelings, or really dislikes Fanny. But the novel does propose that she is as unable as Henry to shed the habit of self-indulgence. On her last personal appearance in *Mansfield Park* she tries as hard as she can to win Fanny over to Henry: "And then . . . the glory of fixing one who has been shot at by so many; of having it in one's power to pay off the debts of one's sex! Oh, I am sure it is not in woman's nature to refuse such a triumph" (p. 363). Perhaps the generalizations sound a little like an exhibition of Mary's spiritedness, of the aspirations she can cherish, or perhaps she echoes here the values of fashionable society. In either case, the "woman's nature" she envisions has absolutely nothing to do with the reality of Fanny. The behavior attributed to Mary in the closing pages of *Mansfield Park*—just as in the case of Henry—seems improbable; yet it is morally consistent. In one letter to Fanny she invokes the standard of self-interest in speculating on Tom Bertram's possible death (pp. 433–34). In another, which reports the disappearance of Maria and Henry,

Mary's partiality for her brother compels her to pronounce him "blameless" (p. 437). The judgment Edmund ultimately passes on her—that she lacks "the most valuable knowledge . . . the knowledge of ourselves and of our duty" (p. 459)—is priggishly bitter, but essentially it restates the point implicit in her verbal habits throughout the novel.

Edmund has good reason, by the end of *Mansfield Park*, to dwell on the importance of knowing oneself, for he has previously shown himself to be almost as self-willed as the Crawfords and just as blind concerning Fanny. He reaches the height of his confusion in the long dialogue during which he works to persuade his cousin that she should accept Henry (pp. 346–54). Edmund attempts one distinction after another, most of them plainly undermined by his love for Mary, and he finds himself opposed by a Fanny who speaks out more sharply than anywhere else, carefully reinforcing her feelings with sense. At first Edmund differentiates between how far Fanny has gone—"So far your conduct" in refusing Henry "has been faultless"—and how far he wishes her to go: "But . . . let him succeed at last, Fanny, let him succeed at last." He desires Henry's success, of course, because it will bring Mary closer to him. And even as he grants here that Fanny was "perfectly right" in rejecting Henry, Edmund colors his statement by adding that the rejection makes him "sorry." To all this Fanny responds with a fervent denial that the match is possible: "Oh! never, never, never; he never will succeed with me." Under further pressure from Edmund, including a remark that Fanny is unlike her "rational self," she explains what she thinks about herself and Henry:

> "We are so totally unlike . . . we are so very, very different in all our inclinations and ways, that I consider it as quite impossible we should ever be tolerably happy together, even if I *could* like him. There never were two people more dissimilar. We have not one taste in common. We should be miserable."

For all the emotional intensity with which Fanny predicts the future, her predictions issue from an appraisal of the real dissimilarities between herself and Henry. In making her judgment, moreover, she explicitly takes into account a condition contrary to her present feelings, "even if I *could* like him."

Edmund now pounces on her appraisal, confident that he can distinguish more aptly than she. Initially he contends that Fanny and Henry have a good deal in common, "moral and literary tastes," for instance, though about the best proof he can offer in support of this curious estimate is the rather equivocal example of Henry reading Shakespeare aloud. Then he claims that the main dissimilarity lies in their "tempers," a difference which, as he goes on, becomes a blessing, for it

> "does not in the smallest degree make against the probability of your happiness together: do not imagine it. . . . I am perfectly persuaded that the tempers had better be unlike . . . . Some opposition here is, I am thoroughly convinced, friendly to matrimonial happiness."

By the time Edmund arrives at this last generalization, as the whole context of the dialogue makes perfectly clear, he is actually no longer thinking of Henry and Fanny at all, the case supposedly under consideration, but cheering himself up about his own relation with Mary. In fact his affection for her has informed the whole, presumably scrupulous analysis of Henry. Fanny recognizes as much and replies with a distinction of her own—between Henry's *"temper"* and "character"—that goes deeper than anything Edmund has managed, one which she supports with the evidence of Henry's flirting during the weeks given over to *Lovers' Vows*. But Edmund brushes her charge of impropriety aside, calling the time itself a "period of general folly," blaming his sisters, blaming himself, and readily slurring over Henry's behavior.

The dialogue comes to its climax when Edmund, kindled by thinking of Mary, reveals that he has talked with her and Mrs. Grant about Henry's proposal. In reporting their view, Edmund does not identify himself absolutely with it:

> "That you could refuse such a man as Henry Crawford, seems more than they can understand. I said what I could for you; but

in good truth, as they stated the case—you must prove yourself to be in your senses as soon as you can, by a different conduct; nothing else will satisfy them."

His phrasing suggests, however, that he shares their opinion to some extent. And Fanny is stirred to utter her fullest defense of her own integrity as well as one of her most powerful indictments of Mary. Her opening generalizations expose the limitations of Henry's sisters, the first sentence by measuring their partiality for him against a standard of total sympathy, what "every woman must have felt," and the second sentence by measuring their assumption that the Henry they love "must be acceptable" to Fanny against a more rational evaluation of the possibilities:

"I *should* have thought . . . that every woman must have felt the possibility of a man's not being approved, not being loved by some one of her sex, at least, let him be ever so generally agreeable. Let him have all the perfections in the world, I think it ought not to be set down as certain, that a man must be acceptable to every woman he may happen to like himself. But even supposing it is so, allowing Mr. Crawford to have all the claims which his sisters think he has, how was I to be prepared to meet him with any feeling answerable to his own? . . . How was I to have an attachment at his service, as soon as it was asked for? His sisters should consider me as well as him. . . . And, and—we think very differently of the nature of women, if they can imagine a woman so very soon capable of returning an affection as this seems to imply."

If those generalizations Fanny begins with imply that she thinks more clearly and feels less narrowly than the ladies whom she attacks, the rest of her comments show her exploring the emotional reality of her situation more intensely, more profoundly, than have Mary and Mrs. Grant. The whole speech dramatizes that special, quasi-divine quality in Fanny which sets her apart from all the other characters: her capacity to feel less personally and at the same time more deeply than anyone else. But Edmund, bound by his desire for the engagement, does not attend to what Fanny really says here; instead, he seizes on her conclusion as a proof that she will soon be attached to Henry, the premise he has held to since the start of the conversation.

Till the end of *Mansfield Park,* it is standard procedure for Edmund to misinterpret Fanny's emotions and ignore her insight in relying, as we have so frequently seen him rely, on a logic unconsciously distorted by his love for Mary. Only after the affair between Henry and Maria, when Edmund finds Mary objecting to the "detection" rather than to the "offence" itself (p. 455), to the social appearance rather than to the moral reality, does he recognize his own errors in judgment: "My eyes are opened" (p. 456). Thus cleansed, he can become Jane Austen's gift to the worthy Fanny.

⊰[IV]⊱

Throughout this chapter I have been insisting that every character except Fanny—whether major or minor, whether from Mansfield, London, or Portsmouth—is dominated to some degree by feelings which aim at satisfying the self. That is to say, all these persons are lacking in the capacity to be objective, which explains why *Mansfield Park* reads like a catalogue of misjudgments. The meaning of the novel turns on how accurately one can perceive reality, and this is the essential subject of those dialogues in which Jane Austen employs something like her technique of metaphoric indirection. I should probably call the technique here emblematic rather than metaphoric, for the author presents us with a correspondence between A and B, not with a fusion of them. Whereas some of the conversation in *Pride and Prejudice* operates on a literal and metaphorical level simultaneously, *Mansfield Park* will put two dialogues side by side, one of them a fairly explicit discussion of certain attitudes and the other an oblique representation of the same attitudes. It almost seems as if Jane Austen wants to make sure that no one can miss the moral issues involved.

Several pairs of scenes in the novel illustrate the method: the talk between Fanny and Mary about Edmund's name, which precedes a clash between Mary and Edmund over what is really valuable (pp. 211–14); or the discussion between Henry and Edmund concerning sermons, which is followed by Henry's misappraisal of his own character (pp. 339–44). But the two dialogues I shall take up occur during the outing to Sotherton, Mary and Edmund chatting together while Fanny listens (pp. 91–96). In these conversations Edmund stands his ground pretty firmly (we are still early in the novel), and it is Mary's habits that come under fire.

The first of the pair deals with Edmund's choice of a profession. Mary has recently learned that he is to take orders and, after expressing her "surprise," remarks:

> ". . . it had not occurred to me. And you know there is generally an uncle or a grandfather to leave a fortune to the second son."
>
> "A very praiseworthy practice," said Edmund, "but not quite universal. I am one of the exceptions, and *being* one, must do something for myself."

A normal enough possibility has "not occurred" to Mary because she dislikes clergymen, and her wish that he were richer, could thus become something else, is the actual basis of the generalization that follows. Edmund points out its fallacy by "not quite universal," going on to emphasize the reality of his own situation by the accented *being*. Yet Mary still tries to circumvent the facts, buttressing her argument with another generalization obviously grounded in her aversion to the clergy:

> "But why are you to be a clergyman? I thought *that* was always the lot of the youngest, where there were many to choose before him."
>
> "Do you think the church itself never chosen then?"
>
> "*Never* is a black word. But yes, in the *never* of conversation which means *not very often*, I do think it. For what is to be done in the church? Men love to distinguish themselves, and in . . .

the other lines, distinction may be gained, but not in the church. A clergyman is nothing."

When Edmund's "never" confronts her with the exact logical consequence of her assertion, Mary accuses him of being the illogical one by her own play with *"never"*—though of course she ends up with a generalization more emotionally extreme than any she has earlier advanced.

So Edmund takes it on himself to give her a little lesson in analysis, but, before getting down to his most serious business, he both underlines her error and brings into the open her limited sense of what constitutes distinction:

> "The *nothing* of conversation has its gradations, I hope, as well as the *never*. A clergyman cannot be high in state or fashion. . . . But I cannot call that situation nothing, which has the charge of all that is of the first importance to mankind, individually or collectively considered, temporally and eternally—which has the guardianship of religion and morals, and consequently of the manners which result from their influence. No one here can call the *office* nothing. If the man who holds it is so, it is by the neglect of his duty . . . and stepping out of his place to appear what he ought not to appear."

Although Edmund's rhetoric swells with feeling when he describes the responsibility of the clergy, in his speech as a whole he charts out a series of differentiations: between Mary's view and his, the *"office"* and the "man," appearance and reality. His sentences offer her a model, as it were, of the rational activity that must go hand in hand with generalizing.

But Mary refuses to retract her opinion, and I do not think her fundamental method changes. She may now take the trouble to create a verbal surface which seems more rigorously logical, first by distinguishing between "one" and "I," then by making much of visual evidence:

> "*You* assign greater consequence to the clergyman than one has been used to hear given, or than I can quite comprehend. One does not see much of this influence and importance in society,

and how can it be acquired where they are so seldom seen themselves? How can two sermons a week, even supposing them worth hearing, supposing the preacher to have the sense to prefer Blair's to his own, do all that you speak of . . . ? One scarcely sees a clergyman out of his pulpit."

Yet her contempt for clergymen breaks out again in the clause about Blair's sermons. And, despite the consciously impersonal "One" governing her last generalization, I cannot keep from hearing Mary's typical style here, the style which formulates her own experience as general truth. Perhaps this is unfair to Mary's feelings, but Edmund concerns himself only with her logic, suggesting to her again that a valid generalization needs a broad base:

"*You* are speaking of London, *I* am speaking of the nation at large."
"The metropolis, I imagine, is a pretty fair sample of the rest."

Mary, however, simply reasserts that her logic is inviolable, and, unshaken by another long paragraph of Edmund's distinctions, she restates the feeling that brought on the entire dialogue: "I am just as much surprised now as I was at first that you should intend to take orders." This section of the scene records a number of specific judgments, to be sure. Yet the main subject under discussion, as I have tried to show, is how to make a judgment that closes accurately with reality—a subject which both Edmund and Mary analyze more or less officially.

The different commitments that they have made fairly explicitly in the first conversation are imaged in a second, which occurs some moments later and revolves about the distance they have walked. Mary begins the dialogue by projecting, quite typically, her feeling of "wonder" at not being "tired" into a claim about how far they have gone, and Edmund replies by citing fact:

"I am really not tired, which I almost wonder at; for we must have walked at least a mile in this wood. Do not you think we have?"

✳✳✳✳✳✳✳✳✳✳✳✳✳✳✳✳✳✳✳✳✳✳✳✳✳✳✳✳✳✳✳✳✳✳✳

"Not half a mile," was his sturdy answer; for he was not yet so much in love as to measure distance, or reckon time, with feminine lawlessness.

Before she lets Mary answer, Jane Austen herself intervenes to insure that the reader will view the argument from a proper moral perspective.

And when Mary does continue, she performs on the emblematic level exactly as she has in judging clergymen, interpreting facts subjectively to support her private conviction:

> "Oh! you do not consider how much we have wound about. We have taken such a very serpentine course; and the wood itself must be half a mile long in a straight line, for we have never seen the end of it yet, since we left the first great path."
>
> "But if you remember, before we left that first great path, we saw directly to the end of it. We looked down the whole vista, and saw it closed by iron gates, and it could not have been more than a furlong in length."
>
> "Oh! I know nothing of your furlongs, but I am sure it is a very long wood; and that we have been winding in and out ever since we came into it; and therefore when I say that we have walked a mile in it, I must speak within compass."

Scoffing at the precision of Edmund's "furlongs," Mary discards his objective account to reaffirm what she has said earlier. Although her "therefore" has a reasonable sound, still the root of her whole declaration is the emotional certainty of "I am sure." Even when Edmund comes forward with some corroborating data, she will not back down:

> "We have been exactly a quarter of an hour here," said Edmund, taking out his watch. "Do you think we are walking four miles an hour?"
>
> "Oh! do not attack me with your watch. A watch is always too fast or too slow. I cannot be dictated to by a watch."

Mary remains the intuitionalist impatient with the restrictions imposed by reality.

By the close of the scene, indeed, she will not really admit the evidence in front of her eyes:

> "Now, Miss Crawford, if you will look up the walk, you will convince yourself that it cannot be half a mile long, or half half a mile."
>
> "It is an immense distance," said she; "I see *that* with a glance."
>
> He still reasoned with her, but in vain. She would not calculate, she would not compare. She would only smile and assert.

Clearly both Mary and Edmund are acting out—in all this business about looking at the wood and judging its size—the same principles that they talked over more explicitly in their dispute about clergymen. And Jane Austen's final words here heighten the emblematic quality: they not only spell out again the moral significance of the scene but also, in paralleling her first intrusion, complete the formal frame of the dialogue.

In the tendency of this emblematic method to handle the discussion of principles separately from their embodiment in action and to set up a one-to-one correspondence between the two, we have another reason for the sense of stiffness conveyed by the novel—and another proof of Jane Austen's need in *Mansfield Park* to decide unequivocally and uncompromisingly on questions of morality. If we turn now to *Emma,* we shall find no relaxing of the moral standards, but we will see Jane Austen taking up again a more purely dramatic technique.

---

1. Mudrick's chapter on *Mansfield Park* contains the most sustained account of it as presenting "a collision of worlds" (*Jane Austen,* p. 155). He condemns the novel, essentially on the grounds that Jane Austen abandons her ironic method to take a series of arbitrary moral stands— against the Crawfords, for Fanny, and in favor of the Mansfield world. I cannot agree with Mudrick—one of several points at which I quarrel with his reading of the novel—that the Mansfield characters are rendered so sympathetically as he suggests. A more satisfying critique, to my mind, appears in Lionel Trilling's essay on *Mansfield Park* in *The Opposing Self* (New York, 1955), pp. 206–30. Like Mudrick, he senses a clash between worlds in the novel and suggests that Jane Austen treats the

Mansfield group rather indulgently. But he defends the concept of duty advanced in *Mansfield Park,* discriminating brilliantly between the "insincerity" of the Crawfords and Fanny's integrity, between her principled behavior and "the *style* of sensitivity, virtue, and intelligence" that Mary "cultivates" (p. 220).

2. Lionel Trilling develops a much larger claim of this sort in his discussion of the acting episode in the novel (*The Opposing Self,* pp. 218–20).

3. Mudrick observes that Mary is "impatient with generalities" (*Jane Austen,* p. 162). He is not talking about her verbal habits, to be sure, yet I think his remark needs qualifying, given the number of times Mary herself generalizes. It might be truer to say that she is impatient with any generalizations but her own and those of the fashionable world. And I wonder if another of Mudrick's comments on Mary may not be similarly misleading. He finds that she is "uninfluenced by snobbery or condescension" in approving of the "prospective marriage" between Henry and Fanny (p. 166), and Mudrick illustrates his claim by quoting a passage in the course of which Mary remarks, "Fanny Price—Wonderful—quite wonderful!—That Mansfield should have done so much for—that *you* should have found your fate in Mansfield!" While Mary does wholeheartedly approve of the match, these words suggest that her immediate judgment is a social one. A little later on in my text I shall try to deal with Mary's reaction more fully.

7 Emma
Fluent Irony and the Pains
of Self-Discovery

Jane Austen herself places *Emma* among the novels for us in a letter to the Reverend J. S. Clarke: ". . . I am strongly haunted with the idea that to those readers who have preferred 'Pride and Prejudice' it will appear inferior in wit, and to those who have preferred 'Mansfield Park' inferior in good sense." [1] This second judgment can be accounted for easily enough: not only is Jane Austen writing to a clergyman, but *Emma* certainly does lack the moral fervor that pervades *Mansfield Park*. The grounds of the first judgment are harder to settle. Perhaps Jane Austen is thinking simply of the sparkling repartee in *Pride and Prejudice*. But I wonder if the judgment may not reflect the fact that the rich ambiguity which we and Elizabeth must come to recognize—the union of pride and shyness in Darcy's behavior—has been thinned in *Emma* to an either/or irony which counterpoints the heroine's illusions with reality. This is not to minimize the achievement of the novel, for it remains in many ways Jane Austen's most finished work. She sustains the irony brilliantly, as well as the point of view on which it depends (though in one chapter, the fifth of Volume III, she shifts us from Emma's perspective to Mr. Knightley's in order to show us Jane Fairfax and Frank Churchill more clearly). She not merely sustains the irony, but develops it through a series of increasingly tense misinterpretations to the climactic moment when Emma discovers what she most wants, indeed what her real self is, only to be convinced that she has forfeited Mr. Knightley by her own actions.

The novel is founded, then, in Emma's perspective. Through her we participate in the three main narrative movements: her encouragement of the courtship she imagines Mr. Elton carry-

❊❊❊❊❊❊❊❊❊❊❊❊❊❊❊❊❊❊❊❊❊❊❊❊❊❊❊❊❊❊❊❊❊❊

ing on with Harriet Smith, which results in Mr. Elton propos-
ing to Emma herself; her games with Frank Churchill, whom
she also assigns to Harriet after a time, only to find that he has
been engaged to Jane Fairfax all along; finally, her rivalry with
Harriet over Mr. Knightley, which ends with Emma getting
the man she loves, but not until she has lived some days with
the fear that he prefers Harriet and with the knowledge that she
herself has unwittingly taught her protégée to hope for him.
Jane Austen interlocks these movements beautifully, the new
situation and its characters always beginning to claim our attention before the old movement is quite finished. More than
that, she handles the movements as a whole so that the courses
of Emma and Mr. Knightley gradually converge, so that they
reveal their feelings for each other more and more clearly. I am
thinking of such matters as the early quarrel between them over
Harriet's rejection of Robert Martin; of Mr. Knightley's resentment against Frank Churchill, in the middle stages of the story,
which is matched by Emma's scorn at the suggestion that Jane
Fairfax has attracted Mr. Knightley; and of the anxious misinterpretations which each of them falls into about the feelings
of the other when they meet at last to talk over Frank Churchill's engagement. The details of the relationship between Emma
and Mr. Knightley I shall take up in a later section of this
chapter. But I must first make clear what sort of person Emma
is, largely by placing her against a number of other characters,
and what change she undergoes in the novel.

-❧[II]❧-

Emma's most basic trait is trust in her own judgment. The
story shows, of course, that her measurements of personality are
often sheer fancy—Jane Austen frequently mentions Emma's
active "imagination"—and that her interpretation of an event
is likely to consist of an absolutely false induction. What else is

her misreading of Mr. Elton's behavior toward Harriet and herself; or her fantasy of the attachment that is to flower as a result
of Harriet's rescue by Frank Churchill from the gypsies; or, perhaps the most ironic example, Emma's supposition that some
secret understanding exists between Jane Fairfax and Mr. Dixon
—an edifice which Emma erects on the chance juxtaposition of
the two names in a rambling monologue by the Miss Bates
whom she so disdains? This habit indicates more than perverse
rationality on Emma's part. Her complete reliance on her own
convictions and her ready publication of them mark her need
to dominate. Out of her own brain she fabricates a reality
which she imprints on the world around her, fancying the
progress of one match after another. And time after time, when
imposing her views on others, she congratulates herself on being
the only person who can really see what is going on. Both of
these tendencies betray Emma's compulsion to assert herself,
indeed to prove herself unique.

Emma's aggressiveness seems to have been nourished by her
upbringing, given what we learn of that: if Mr. Knightley has
checked her now and then, both her father and her governess
(who later becomes Mrs. Weston) have indulged her constantly.
The personality of Mr. Woodhouse, of course, has nothing like
the bite of Emma's. But perhaps it is not entirely absurd to find
one source for her self-centeredness in the behavior of her father
—rather as his other daughter, Isabella Knightley, has inherited his concern about health—for he appears almost wholly
engrossed in himself. Long accustomed to a social position that
permits him to have his own way, an old man confirmed in his
distaste for any change and in his worry about illness, Mr.
Woodhouse keeps voicing his whims as universal truths. Thus
he translates his own sadness at the departure of Emma's governess to marry Mr. Weston into a general opinion—"What a pity
it is that Mr. Weston ever thought of her!" (p. 8)—and assumes
thereafter that everyone must agree with him in regarding her
as "poor Miss Taylor," unfortunate because she has left Hartfield. Or he feels that his own diet of thin gruel should be standard for mankind. In fact his ruling passion for health may lead

✳✳✳✳✳✳✳✳✳✳✳✳✳✳✳✳✳✳✳✳✳✳✳✳✳✳✳✳✳✳✳✳✳✳✳✳

him beyond generalizing to an indecorous particularity, as when he hears that Jane Fairfax has been out in the rain: "Young ladies are delicate plants. . . . My dear, did you change your stockings?" (p. 294). This remark will also suggest, however, what is no more than the truth: that Mr. Woodhouse is gentle and kindly for all his selfishness. And most of the time, far from imposing his notions on anyone else, he is merely humored by others, who then proceed to manage him. He serves in the first two-thirds of the novel primarily as a foil to Emma, making her selfishness seem less by his own. Throughout these pages he also has a more positive function, in the sense that Emma shows her better nature, a capacity to love and to serve someone else, in her dealings with him. Yet once, just once, he is allowed a triumph at the expense of Emma. She has been maliciously trying to stir up in him the same contempt that she feels for Mrs. Elton, and she goes about her business by rocking his hobby-horse, appealing to his prejudice against marriage, that signal of change. But Mr. Woodhouse stands firm, holding through a series of statements to the position that proper treatment of Mrs. Elton "is a matter of mere common politeness and good-breeding, and has nothing to do with any encouragement to people to marry" (p. 280). Although the passage sets him off to better advantage than Emma, Mr. Woodhouse has no idea of what she is up to, and he cannot be said to rebuff her here— or anywhere else.

Emma meets with a much higher degree of consciousness in Mrs. Weston, but with the same indulgence. Mrs. Weston is affectionately disposed toward everyone and the reverse of over-bearing. When in her turn she kindly advises Jane Fairfax against walking in the rain, for instance, she refuses to be dictatorial, advancing her opinions as her own and separating her "I" from an autonomous "you": "The spring I always think requires more than common care. Better wait an hour or two, or even half a day for your letters, than run the risk of bringing on your cough again. Now do not you feel that you had? Yes, I am sure you are much too reasonable" (p. 295). The unassertiveness of Mrs. Weston owes a good deal to the "mildness of her temper" which Jane Austen mentions, but I would guess that it also reflects the habit developed by a former governess, by a person somewhat inferior socially. She often seems uneasy about the socially prominent Frank Churchill, and not merely because he is her stepson. Certainly she defers to Emma almost always. But of course she loves Emma, loves her so much that, when on one occasion she is faced with Mr. Knightley's differentiation between the attractions of Emma's "person" and the faults of Emma's "mind," Mrs. Weston glosses over the distinction to praise both the "person" and the "mind" (pp. 39–40). In spite of her partiality for Emma, Mrs. Weston never appears foolish or trivial (as her husband often does). Warm as her feelings are, she accepts their consequences. Thus, when the news breaks of the engagement between Jane Fairfax and Frank Churchill, Emma bursts into a tirade because she has been duped and because she has made indiscreet remarks about his fiancée to him, but Mrs. Weston replies: ". . . as I have always had a thoroughly good opinion of Miss Fairfax, I never could, under any blunder, have spoken ill of her; and as to speaking ill of him, there I must have been safe" (pp. 399–400). She has been "safe" concerning Frank Churchill because she loves her husband and Frank Churchill is his son. The sentence is typical of Mrs. Weston in that it conveys no more, I think, than her declarations about herself. At least I cannot hear in it any reproof for Emma's indiscretion in speaking as she has with Frank Churchill or for her snobbish attitude toward Jane Fairfax.

And Emma is a snob, a snob in her attitude toward many others besides Jane Fairfax. The quality is another expression of Emma's drive for uniqueness. In the act of patronizing others, she elevates herself above them. Yet there is a further point to make. Snobbery, predicated on one's sense of being apart from others, is in the case of Emma the social counterpart of her desire to keep herself emotionally detached as an individual. That she is bent on remaining personally disengaged we can see in her talk about marriage with Harriet (pp. 84–86), in her reveries on Frank Churchill (pp. 261, 265, 315–16), or in this typical meditation: "Harriet rational, Frank Churchill not too much in love, and Mr. Knightley not wanting to quarrel with her, how very happy a summer must be before her!" (p. 332). All this is not to say, by any means, that Emma is incapable of becoming attached. The cause of her compulsive disengagement is her inability to recognize and to admit what she feels for Mr. Knightley. Once she has been shocked into taking a good look at herself by listening to Harriet's words about him, detachment is impossible for Emma. But the reader has understood all along that her stance is a fraud, for in a number of passages like the following (Jane Austen's editor cites several in a note), Emma gives away her real feelings:

> She was more disturbed by Mr. Knightley's not dancing, than by any thing else.—There he was, among the standers-by, where he ought not to be; he ought to be dancing,—not classing himself with the husbands, and fathers, and whist-players . . . so young as he looked!—He could not have appeared to greater advantage perhaps any where, than where he had placed himself.
> (pp. 325–26)

It is the novel's major irony that an Emma so frequently wrapped up in herself, and one who cultivates detachment, should so radically misconceive her real attachment.

Both her snobbery and her wish to keep herself emotionally inviolate condition Emma to seize on Harriet as a companion. By fashioning a career for Harriet, whom Jane Austen presents as a mere "parlour-boarder" in a school for girls and "the natural daughter of somebody," Emma can demonstrate her social authority; and Harriet is altogether too insignificant as a person to make any heavy demands on Emma's emotions. The conversation of Harriet reveals her as artless and rather ignorant. The staple of her talk is facts, facts which demand more often to be reported than interpreted, as we can see in one of her speeches to Emma about Robert Martin:

> "He did not think we ever walked this road. He thought we walked towards Randalls most days. He has not been able to get the Romance of the Forest yet. He was so busy the last time he was at Kingston that he quite forgot it, but he goes again to-

morrow. So very odd we should happen to meet! Well, Miss Woodhouse, is he like what you expected? What do you think of him? Do you think him so very plain?" (p. 32)

Clearly these facts are reported at the pitch of her interest in Robert Martin, and perhaps the even rhythmic units will suggest how far Harriet's feelings are from being threatened by her mind. Invariably she speaks, as it were, to the beat of her heart. Despite this emotional intensity Harriet rarely generalizes, possibly the sign of an utterly naïve involvement in herself, or possibly the sign of her intuition that she is socially inferior. In the following passage her first generalization declares her respect for Emma, who has just foreseen that Harriet will marry Mr. Elton, just as the second one she comes to declares her respect for that gentleman:

> "Whatever you say is always right . . . and therefore I suppose, and believe, and hope it must be so; but otherwise I could not have imagined it. It is so much beyond any thing I deserve. Mr. Elton, who might marry any body! There cannot be two opinions about *him*. He is so very superior. Only think of those sweet verses—'To Miss ———.' Dear me, how clever!—Could it really be meant for me?" (p. 74)

She can adjust herself to the first generalization—in effect, to Emma's opinion—only through the degrees of "suppose, and believe, and hope," and by the close of her remarks she has hardly adjusted herself to the second generalization at all. As the story develops, she learns from Emma to rate herself much higher than she does here, and it seems especially fitting that at last Emma should bring about her own greatest misery by forcing a set of generalizations on her protégée and insisting that Harriet identify herself with them.

Naturally Emma has no qualms herself about generalizing, or, for that matter, about setting Harriet a snobbish example in passing judgment on Robert Martin:

> "A young farmer, whether on horseback or on foot, is the very last sort of person to raise my curiosity. The yeomanry are pre-

✻✻✻✻✻✻✻✻✻✻✻✻✻✻✻✻✻✻✻✻✻✻✻✻✻✻✻✻✻✻✻✻

cisely the order of people with whom I feel I can have nothing to do. . . . But a farmer can need none of my help, and is therefore in one sense as much above my notice as in every other he is below it." (p. 29)

Whereas Harriet's generalizations spoke an ideal which she struggled painfully toward, Emma's generalizations smugly catapult herself to a social elevation almost unapproachable. Her words are informed not only by her desire to appear socially exclusive but also by her irritation with Robert Martin for having attracted Harriet—which is to say that Emma, like her father, unhesitatingly converts private feelings into principles. She reveals the same habit and the same snobbishness when she discusses Mr. Elton with her brother-in-law:

"Mr. Elton's manners are not perfect . . . but where there is a wish to please, one ought to overlook, and one does overlook a great deal. Where a man does his best with only moderate powers, he will have the advantage over negligent superiority. There is such perfect good temper and good will in Mr. Elton as one cannot but value." (pp. 111–12)

While Emma pretends to evaluate Mr. Elton accurately, she in fact describes the sort of man she feels a proper partner for the rather naïve young girl whom Miss Woodhouse has so kindly noticed and thus raised in the world. In addition, this passage conveys the personal detachment mentioned earlier: it is implicit, I think, in Emma's easy settling of Mr. Elton's merits, and indirectly of Harriet's, while allowing each of them a claim on her own good will. This particular house of cards comes tumbling down when Mr. Elton proposes to Emma, naming the realities which she has ignored: the "encouragement" in her manner toward him and the fact that his "visits to Hartfield have been for yourself only" (p. 132).

Really Emma should have been under no illusions about Mr. Elton, for his conversation leaves little doubt about what he is up to. Not the equal of the Woodhouses socially, Mr. Elton keeps trying to boost his status by means of a spirited manner and a willingness to agree, both of these expressed in the phrase with which Jane Austen tags him, "exactly so." Often he displays his verve through a heightened phrasing or diction which sounds modish: "Let me entreat you," "so charming," "How could you," "Is not this room rich in specimens," "inimitable figure-pieces" (p. 43). In generalizing, he is likely to aim at allying himself with his superiors, as in his defense of the portrait Emma has made of Harriet:

> "Oh, no! certainly not too tall . . . . Consider, she is sitting down—which naturally presents a different—which in short gives exactly the idea—and the proportions must be preserved, you know. . . . it gives one exactly the idea of such a height as Miss Smith's. Exactly so indeed!" (p. 48)

Yet these are merely social devices with Mr. Elton. When Emma spurns his proposal, he thumps out his real convictions: "I need not so totally despair of an equal alliance, as to be addressing myself to Miss Smith!" (p. 132). And his sense of his own importance is amply fed by the wife whom he soon brings in triumph to Highbury.

Mrs. Elton is snobbish and pretentious—indeed a vulgar and extreme instance of the tendencies we have noted in Emma herself. In whatever Mrs. Elton says, she is campaigning to establish her prestige. She may generalize, just as Emma does, to articulate the sort of view which proves her socially superior, though Mrs. Elton will frequently add another sentence to make sure that no one misses the significance of the trick: "The advantages of Bath to the young are pretty generally understood. . . . I could immediately secure you some of the best society in the place" (p. 275); "Ah! there is nothing like staying at home, for real comfort. Nobody can be more devoted to home than I am" (p. 274). And, just as Emma does, Mrs. Elton will generalize in order to launch herself into a region where she may shine in lonely majesty: "A bride, you know, must appear like a bride, but my natural taste is all for simplicity . . . . But I am quite in the minority, I believe; few people seem to value simplicity of dress,—shew and finery are every thing" (p. 302). She has the field all to herself in the matter of figurative language. She means it to show her vivacity, but actually it indicates her appalling lack of taste through the wild disproportion between the expression she uses and the situation she describes. She calls herself "cautious as a minister of state" (p. 454), for instance, in affecting to keep back from Emma the word of Jane Fairfax's engagement, and she alludes to her marriage with Mr. Elton in terms of "Hymen's saffron robe" being "put on for us" (p. 308). The same vulgarity is exhibited in Mrs. Elton's particular expressions. With them she may dramatize her supposedly brilliant past. Or by a careless particularity she may underline her present claim to social eminence: not only in addressing an obvious inferior like Jane Fairfax as "You sad girl" (p. 295), but in describing the more prominent Frank Churchill as "without . . . puppyism" (p. 321), and—the trait which offends Emma more than anything—in constantly referring to "Knightley."

Emma herself, however, can be venomously particular, even though she is usually much more careful than Mrs. Elton to preserve some form of propriety. And few things irritate Emma more than her own relations with Jane Fairfax. Her snobbishness breaks out once more after Frank Churchill has in effect threatened her exclusiveness by intimating that she and Jane must be close friends: they are not, Emma assures him, and "I hardly know how it has happened; a little, perhaps, from that wickedness on my side which was prone to take disgust towards a girl so idolized and so cried up as she always was, by her aunt and grandmother, and all their set" (p. 203). Blended with Emma's snobbishness in these particular terms is another ingredient: her personal dislike for Jane. She feels bitter about Jane because, deep in her heart, she regards Jane as her rival, because she finds in Jane, as Mr. Knightley has once observed, "the really accomplished young woman, which she wanted to be thought herself" (p. 166). In the novel, the two of them are juxtaposed both socially and personally.

In spite of her many accomplishments, Jane Fairfax is destined to be a governess, for the remains of her family—deaf Mrs. Bates and talkative Miss Bates—are the next thing to paupers and occupy the lowest rank in Highbury's society. It is Jane's acute social consciousness, at least as much as the engagement she must conceal, which forces her to subdue herself so severely. Perhaps we can best approach her usual manner by way of a very untypical speech, one that she utters in great emotional stress when excusing herself to Emma for leaving the party at Donwell: "I am . . . I am fatigued; but it is not the sort of fatigue—quick walking will refresh me.—Miss Woodhouse, we all know at times what it is to be wearied in spirits. Mine, I confess, are exhausted. The greatest kindness you can show me, will be to let me have my own way" (p. 363). Jane's generalization about "we all know . . ." makes an almost direct plea, though less for Emma's sympathy, perhaps, than for the indulgence of a superior. And the major weight of what she says is still borne by the personal "I's" and "me's." Most of the time Jane keeps herself at a much greater distance from her generalizations, characteristically speaking in her own person and reserving them, as it were, for the opinions of those above her. Her first report on Frank Churchill, for instance, is sprinkled with such phrases as: "She believed he was reckoned a very fine young man"; "He was generally thought so"; "She believed every body found his manners pleasing" (p. 169). Jane talks in this way, I take it, not merely because she wants to hide her interest in Frank Churchill, but because her lack of position makes it improper for her to judge authoritatively. A few pages later, indeed, she explicitly separates herself from "the general opinion" when Mr. Dixon's name comes up: "Oh! as for me, my judgment is worth nothing. Where I have a regard, I always think a person well-looking. But I gave what I believed the general opinion, when I called him plain" (p. 176). If personal pressures condition Jane's rhetoric, forcing her to hide her love for Frank behind generalizations, so do social pressures, which impose on her a rhetoric depending heavily on "I." But when her attachment finally becomes known, removing at least one reason for her reserve, Jane does not hesitate to call up a series of moral generalizations with which to measure her own behavior in agreeing to a secret engagement:

❋❋❋❋❋❋❋❋❋❋❋❋❋❋❋❋❋❋❋❋❋❋❋❋❋❋❋❋❋❋❋❋❋❋

> "The consequence . . . has been a state of perpetual suffering
> to me; and so it ought. But after all the punishment that miscon-
> duct can bring, it is still not less misconduct. . . . I never can be
> blameless. I have been acting contrary to all my sense of right;
> and the fortunate turn that every thing has taken . . . is what
> my conscience tells me ought not to be." (p. 419)

She makes it clear here that she has, since the beginning of the
engagement, accepted full responsibility for her feelings, a point
we must remember when we turn back to Emma after a moment.

But first a few comments on Miss Bates, the aunt of Jane
Fairfax and an irritant in her own right to Emma. Miss Bates
has no accomplishments, only a good will as boundless as her
speeches. These are one of the artistic triumphs in *Emma*. Not
only does Jane Austen develop each monologue in accordance
with some chain of association, thus preventing the talk of Miss
Bates from disintegrating into a host of unrelated phrases,[2] but
she also employs this associative chain brilliantly to convey several buried hints of Frank Churchill's interest in Jane Fairfax
(pp. 323, 329–30, 346). The conversational habits of Miss Bates,
however, do not mark her merely as the bore which Emma
finds her. Surely what in part motivates her to report so many
facts and to speak so often of herself (even more than Jane
does) is Miss Bates's awareness that she and social authority
have nothing at all to do with each other. In the following passage, we can see how quickly she backs up to "I" after her excitement has momentarily betrayed her into a decisive generalization: ". . . if I must speak on this subject, there is no
denying that Mr. Frank Churchill might have—I do not mean
to say that he did not dream it—I am sure I have sometimes the
oddest dreams in the world—but if I am questioned about it, I
must acknowledge that there was such an idea last spring" (pp.
345–46). By and large, however, Miss Bates will generalize only
when moved by her love for Jane—"Nobody could nurse her,
as we should do" (p. 161)—or when paying compliments to the
rest of the world. And underlying those compliments is the deep
gratitude of Miss Bates for the favors which her family has received, a gratitude that she declares more openly in such sen-

tences as: ". . . our friends are only too good to us. If ever there were people who, without having great wealth themselves, had every thing they could wish for, I am sure it is us" (p. 174).

Given the humility of Miss Bates, Emma's joke at her expense during the outing to Box Hill is one of the nastiest bits of behavior in the novel. And, if we bear in mind the continuous judgment to which Jane Fairfax has subjected herself, Emma's reaction to the event at Box Hill becomes specially significant. Charged by Mr. Knightley with having been insolent, Emma retorts: "Nay, how could I help saying what I did?—Nobody could have helped it. It was not so very bad. I dare say she did not understand me" (p. 374). She instinctively shields herself from responsibility by the generalization in her second sentence, her words carrying a more than latent tone of social superiority. With "bad" she offers a moral judgment, but one that still minimizes her offense, and she finally acquits herself by dismissing the incident out of hand.

But Mr. Knightley—whose character provides the major contrast in the novel to Emma's—will not let her off so easily. First he sets out the reality of the affront: "She felt your full meaning. . . . I wish you could have heard how she talked of it—with what candour and generosity" (p. 375). Then he goes on, with the richest union of sense and feeling, to anatomize Emma's new rationalization:

> ". . . you must allow, that what is good and what is ridiculous are most unfortunately blended in her."
> "They are blended," said he, "I acknowledge; and, were she prosperous, I could allow much for the occasional prevalence of the ridiculous over the good. Were she a woman of fortune, I would leave every harmless absurdity to take its chance, I would not quarrel with you for any liberties of manner. Were she your equal in situation—but, Emma, consider how far this is from being the case. She is poor; she has sunk from the comforts she was born to; and, if she live to old age, must probably sink more. Her situation should secure your compassion. It was badly done, indeed!" (p. 375)

Mr. Knightley's sense shows in the basic structure of his reply: its move from a concession of Emma's point, to the entertaining

❋❋❋❋❋❋❋❋❋❋❋❋❋❋❋❋❋❋❋❋❋❋❋❋❋❋❋❋❋❋❋❋

of a hypothesis about Miss Bates, through an examination of her actual case, to an inevitable conclusion. Perhaps his sense is also implied by the fact that through much of his analysis he uses a vocabulary which deals in fixed concepts—and entrusts the primary judgment he arrives at to terms of this sort: "Her situation should secure your compassion." Yet plainly the whole speech is also shot through with feeling. It shows in the accumulation of clauses beginning "were she"; in the metaphor of "sunk," itself repeated in "sink"; and especially in the closing exclamation—"It was badly done, indeed!"—which seems to utter a much more personal reproach than the official judgment preceding it. Everywhere in the novel Mr. Knightley reveals this same sympathy, this same emotional responsiveness, and thus he never strikes us as a prig or a stuffy partisan of reason. Through his fusion of feeling and sense in the passage at hand, he achieves the kind of rounded evaluation impossible for Emma until she has developed an integrity to match his.

The sharp contrast between them that emerges through most of the novel may be suggested by one more brief comparison of passages. The first belongs to Mr. Knightley, who is protesting to Mrs. Weston—in a speech too long to be reproduced in full here—about Emma's influence on Harriet (pp. 38–39). Mr. Knightley builds this speech mainly on an antithetic handling of the two girls, as in: "She knows nothing herself"—"and looks upon Emma as knowing every thing"; "How can Emma imagine she has any thing to learn herself"—"while Harriet is presenting such a delightful inferiority?" And he sustains the major antithesis (while fashioning some new ones) up to the close: Harriet "will grow just refined enough to be uncomfortable with those among whom birth and circumstances have placed her home"—for "I am much mistaken if Emma's doctrines give any strength of mind, or tend at all to make a girl adapt herself rationally to the varieties of her situation in life.—They only give a little polish." In these conclusions, furthermore, Mr. Knightley depends heavily on diction of the type we have heard him use before, words such as "birth," "strength of mind," or "varieties of her situation," which rest his decision on settled categories.

This soberness has been preceded by exasperation, however, for near the beginning of his protest Mr. Knightley was saying, "I think her the very worst sort of companion that Emma could possibly have." Perhaps clearer than this rather muted shift from a mode of feeling to a mode of sense is the change that the text records in the kind of statement made by Mr. Knightley. He starts the body of his speech by referring to the particular Harriet—"But Harriet Smith—I have not half done about Harriet Smith"—and goes on to draw the specific contrast between Emma and Harriet. But he ends up with what amounts to a generalization about the effect that the "doctrines" of Emma will have on "a girl." If these claims about the passage sound a little strained, still I think I have not misrepresented its basic tendencies—or Mr. Knightley.

If we look now at one of Emma's protests, against Harriet's continuing interest in the married Mr. Elton, we can see how radically the case is altered. Emma's rhetoric impulsively piles one verbal unit on another, moving by accumulation rather than through antitheses, until even the real distinctions that she feels between herself and Harriet become blurred, or at least reduced to the difference between "pain" and "greater pain":

"I have not said, exert yourself Harriet for my sake . . . because for your own sake rather, I would wish it to be done, for the sake of what is more important than my comfort, a habit of self-command in you, a consideration of what is your duty, an attention to propriety, an endeavour to avoid the suspicions of others, to save your health and credit, and restore your tranquillity. These are the motives which I have been pressing on you. They are very important—and sorry I am that you cannot feel them sufficiently to act upon them. My being saved from pain is a very secondary consideration. I want you to save yourself from greater pain. Perhaps I may sometimes have felt that Harriet would not forget what was due—or rather what would be kind by me."
(p. 268)

The dissimilarity between this and the speech by Mr. Knightley is not simply a matter of different occasions and different audiences. Certainly Emma wants to persuade Harriet, is to some extent conscious of her audience, but Mr. Knightley's situation was roughly analogous, at least in that he could be as sure as Emma of addressing a woman with strong feelings. Yet instead of concluding with an emotional appeal—to Mrs. Weston's or his own friendly affection for Emma, say, or to their good will for Harriet—Mr. Knightley rested his decision on a highly conceptual vocabulary. But Emma, though using such words freely in the first part of her speech, will not entrust her case to them finally, turning rather to the more directly emotional "pressing," "sorry," and "kind" in her closing sentences. This passage does not provide us, unfortunately, with any statement by Emma that we can properly compare with the trustworthy generalized evaluation we saw Mr. Knightley moving toward concerning the effects of "Emma's doctrines" on "a girl." So maybe it is worth reminding ourselves, by just glancing at another passage, of how unreliably Emma generalizes when evaluating the behavior of someone she is interested in; of Frank Churchill's jaunt to London, presumably to get a haircut, she reflects:

> "I do not know whether it ought to be so, but certainly silly things do cease to be silly if they are done by sensible people in an impudent way. Wickedness is always wickedness, but folly is not always folly.—It depends upon the character of those who handle it." (p. 212)

In spite of the sobriety that she affects by the first clause, Emma's decrees about "silly things" and "folly" have no basis in reason; they are founded solely in her wish to find Frank Churchill pleasing.

Near the end of the novel Emma admits to "a little likeness" between herself and that gentleman. In fact, both of them are self-indulgent, he often more consciously so than Emma—or than his father, whom he also resembles. Of course through most of the story Frank Churchill is playing a role, that of a prodigal, of Emma's gallant, in order to hide his attachment to Jane Fairfax. One way in which he projects this role is by a spirited divergence from some sort of norm. It may be from the opinions and attitudes of those whom he is with, or from a more inclusive generalization, as in his reply on being asked by Emma how he has thought "Miss Fairfax looking":

> "Ill, very ill—that is, if a young lady can ever be allowed to look ill. But the expression is hardly admissable, Mrs. Weston, is it? Ladies can never look ill. And, seriously, Miss Fairfax is naturally so pale, as almost always to give the appearance of ill health. —A most deplorable want of complexion." (p. 199)

Then, too, Frank Churchill can put up a fine show of feeling by using emotionally intense terms. Thus he declares, apropos of arriving at Highbury a day earlier than expected, "It is a great pleasure where one can indulge in it . . . though there are not many houses that I should presume on so far; but in coming *home* I felt I might do any thing" (pp. 190–91). But Frank Churchill seems quite unaware—and in this he reminds one of Henry Crawford—that the part he acts in public is almost indistinguishable from his private self, that he really is the emotionally extravagant, rather wayward young man he pretends to be. When he is deeply upset by a quarrel with Jane, and no longer playing a role with Emma, his sentences reveal the usual emphasis on "I," the emotive words, and the concern with his own gratification: "I am tired of doing nothing. I want a change. I am serious, Miss Woodhouse, whatever your penetrating eyes may fancy—I am sick of England—and would leave it to-morrow, if I could" (p. 365). Indeed Frank Churchill never loses his tone of fatuous vanity, for in one of his very last speeches, after all has come right between himself and Jane, he can still appear far more interested in celebrating and adorning the beauty he has won than in praising Jane's merits:

> "Look at her. Is not she an angel in every gesture? Observe the turn of her throat. Observe her eyes . . . . —You will be glad to hear (inclining his head, and whispering seriously) that my uncle means to give her all my aunt's jewels. They are to be new

✳✳✳✳✳✳✳✳✳✳✳✳✳✳✳✳✳✳✳✳✳✳✳✳✳✳✳✳✳✳✳✳✳✳✳✳✳✳

set. I am resolved to have some in an ornament for the head. Will not it be beautiful in her dark hair?" (p. 479)

If Frank Churchill does not really change in the novel, Emma does, but not until she has been through a crisis brought on by her own self-indulgence and her will to dominate. Largely ignoring the misadventures to which she has exposed Harriet with Robert Martin and Mr. Elton, Emma gaily encourages her protégée in a new attachment, this time—so Emma thinks—with Frank Churchill. "Let no name ever pass our lips," she says piously, affecting to have learned her lesson from the past. But she immediately starts manipulating Harriet by such generalizations as "more wonderful things have taken place, there have been matches of greater disparity" (p. 342). As usual, the fancy in which Emma indulges straightway becomes a law. Appropriately enough, this manipulation of Harriet and these words themselves come back to haunt Emma in that scene when Harriet, who has interpreted all this as her license to aspire to Mr. Knightley, finally reveals her heart to Emma, explains how Emma has taught her to hope, and declares her reasons for imagining herself favored by him.

These disclosures shatter Emma's complacency and, by releasing her true feelings about Mr. Knightley, compel her to see her real self for the first time. Once she has started becoming acquainted with that self, she can also begin to accept the personal responsibility that she has shunned all along. One of Jane Austen's major successes in the novel, it seems to me, is the almost naturalistic accuracy with which she charts Emma's slow progress from snobbish self-absorption toward integrity. The old habits are not easily thrown off. Emma can feel that "there would be no need of *compassion* to the girl who believed herself loved by Mr. Knightley" (p. 408). Even later on, when she imagines that her disappointed friend must be kept away from a Hartfield containing Mr. Knightley and herself, "Emma could not deplore her future absence as any deduction from her own enjoyment. In such a party, Harriet would be rather a dead weight than otherwise" (p. 450). But precisely side by side with

these relics of Emma's earlier attitude are proofs of an invigor-
ated moral sensibility. Thus "a strong sense of justice by Harriet" informs Emma's behavior during the disclosures, and "justice" also demands of Emma that Harriet "should not be made
unhappy by any coldness now" (p. 408). Similarly, she can
continue her reflection on excluding Harriet from Hartfield by
saying: ". . . it seemed a peculiarly cruel necessity that was to
be placing her in such a state of unmerited punishment" (p.
450). Certainly Harriet's recital of her hopes for Mr. Knightley
makes Emma bitterly resentful. But if Emma's musings betray
her animosity toward Harriet, they also show her recognizing to
the full her own guilt: "Who had been at pains to give Harriet
notions of self-consequence but herself? . . . If Harriet, from
being humble, were grown vain, it was her doing too" (p. 414).
More than this, although Emma is under greater emotional
stress than ever in her antagonism to Harriet and her love for
Mr. Knightley, her feelings do not issue in what they always
have before, some prediction or some attempt to mold reality.
For the first time, that is, she accepts the consequences of an error
and submits herself to the course of events—utterly resigned to
taking her chances with Harriet for Mr. Knightley, even though
she fears that Harriet has the advantage.[3] Of course Emma
turns out to be the winner at last, but not until the change in
her nature has become reasonably secure. If we sometimes feel a
little restive in the closing pages when she considers Harriet's
social inferiority, we should at any rate recollect that the status
which Emma now assigns Harriet—no longer fancying her
friend the daughter of some rich gentleman—is the same status
which Mr. Knightley has assigned Harriet from the beginning.
And surely one of the last estimates by Emma of Mr. Knightley
shows not only that she has learned well how to value him but
that she remains conscious of her own failings: "What had she
to wish for? Nothing, but to grow more worthy of him, whose
intentions and judgment had been ever so superior to her own.
Nothing, but that the lessons of her past folly might teach her
humility and circumspection in the future" (p. 475). In her
advance toward integrity, as the passage suggests, Emma be-

※※※※※※※※※※※※※※※※※※※※※※※※※※

comes capable of attaching herself to Mr. Knightley and of orienting herself to the real world.

·{ III }·

This change in Emma's behavior is not merely something asserted by the expository passages in the novel; it is rendered in the dialogue itself. And to see the change most accurately, we must turn at last to some of her conversation with Mr. Knightley. I have already said that he and Emma reveal a more and more intense feeling for each other as the novel goes on, and often they do so in dialogues which exhibit Jane Austen's technique of metaphoric indirection. The prime example in *Emma* is the proposal scene, which I shall be dwelling on in a few moments. But in order to highlight what happens there, I want first to take up briefly one of the early interchanges between Emma and Mr. Knightley, using it to suggest again their typical modes.

The bit of dialogue acts as a prelude to the long quarrel between them over Harriet's refusal of Robert Martin, a refusal engineered by Emma. In the scene as a whole Jane Austen makes some use of metaphoric indirection, for Harriet, the ostensible subject of the talk, off and on becomes a vehicle by which Mr. Knightley and Emma define their attitudes toward each other. As usual, he has reason on his side, but he keeps being exasperated by her foolishness—partly because he likes her so well. And as usual, Emma adopts a calmer manner, the outward proof—so she imagines—of her superior reason, though in fact her thinking reflects her feelings only. Some of these motives and something of the scene's technique appear in its prelude (p. 58), which Mr. Knightley begins with a sensible evaluation of the Harriet whom he expects to marry Robert Martin:

"Her character depends upon those she is with; but in good hands she will turn out a valuable woman."

"I am glad you think so; and the good hands, I hope, may not be wanting."

Probably Mr. Knightley has Robert Martin's "good hands" mainly in mind. But surely the phrase refers as well to Emma, the molder of Harriet. In such a context it seems most likely a reminder of Emma's responsibility, though the entire clause may also compliment Emma very discreetly by praising her friend. She assumes, of course, that he is thinking only of herself. While she pretends to remain properly objective by taking over the oblique phrasing of "good hands," she actually preens herself on her ability and presses him for a franker compliment.

Mr. Knightley brings her desire into the open with characteristic bluntness, but he holds back his own feelings for Emma, deliberately citing a minimal improvement in Harriet:

"Come . . . you are anxious for a compliment, so I will tell you that you have improved her. You have cured her of her school-girl's giggle; she really does you credit."

"Thank you. I should be mortified indeed if I did not believe I had been of some use; but it is not every body who will bestow praise where they may. *You* do not often overpower me with it."

Stung by his refusal to cry her up, Emma at first stands on her dignity with a highly formal phrasing. But then she strikes back with the generalization about "every body"; for just a moment the words sound like a compliment to Mr. Knightley, yet they become, by her last sentence, a measure of his usual perversity. Needless to add, Emma feels convinced that the generalization proves her cool sanity, and indeed her moral superiority, to Mr. Knightley. The same assurance sustains her throughout the quarrel about Harriet that follows. The dialogue moves toward a climax when Emma, having indulged in all her fancies about Harriet's birth and personal attractions, assumes herself to be a better judge of men's taste than Mr. Knightley by proclaiming,

❋❋❋❋❋❋❋❋❋❋❋❋❋❋❋❋❋❋❋❋❋❋❋❋❋❋❋❋❋❋❋❋❋❋❋

over his objections, that "such a girl as Harriet is exactly what every man delights in" (p. 64). But Emma is doing more here than converting her wish into law. Since she has already admitted that Harriet lacks sense, yet still makes her friend the measure of man's delight, Emma's generalization has the effect of thrusting her sensible self—and she has paraded her sense all along—beyond the reach of men. Snugly untouchable, she goes on to declare complacently, "Were you, yourself, ever to marry, she is the very woman for you." It is fitting that this vision should return, after some three hundred pages, to cause Emma her greatest misery.

How much she has altered as a result of discovering her love for Mr. Knightley and how richly human he remains—both of these are unmistakable in the proposal scene (pp. 425–30). The dialogue itself compounds the technique of metaphoric indirection with ambiguity, the major dramatic technique of the novel. To be more specific: through talking about the engagement between Frank Churchill and Jane Fairfax, Mr. Knightley and Emma betray their emotion for each other; yet he suspects that her feelings relate to Frank Churchill, and she suspects that his relate to Harriet. The scene comes about because Mr. Knightley, having learned of the engagement and imagining that it must upset Emma, rushes back from London to comfort her. But Emma, not realizing that he has heard the news, fears that he wants to tell her about an engagement of his own with Harriet.

Yet Emma dreads not knowing his heart even more than knowing it. So she sets about discovering it by announcing the match between Frank Churchill and Jane Fairfax, hoping that the subject of marriage will lead him to show his intentions. Given her purpose, she tries hard to hit a purely informational tone with Mr. Knightley at first:

"You have some news to hear, now you are come back, that will rather surprise you."

"Have I?" said he quietly, and looking at her; "of what nature?"

"Oh! the best nature in the world—a wedding."

He interprets her tone very differently, as her attempt to remain composed in the face of losing Frank Churchill; and he reads her remark as indicating her "surprise" and mortification at having been replaced by Jane Fairfax. The reserved tone in which he himself speaks suggests to us mainly that Mr. Knightley wants to make sure of the facts and of Emma's reaction before responding more fully, and perhaps that he has no wish of encouraging her to grieve deeply over a man whom he has always distrusted. Naturally, his reserve does not help Emma understand his plans, so she pushes on in her last sentence, her tone becoming almost shrilly cheerful. She has to rejoice over "a wedding" because she must convince Mr. Knightley that she approves of them all, will not be hurt, that is, by a marriage between him and Harriet.

That Emma has indeed been trying to draw him out is implied by a tiny logical flaw at the start of the speech to follow. After learning from him that he already knows of the engagement between Jane Fairfax and Frank Churchill, Emma speculates that he was "less surprised than any of us," a phrase that clashes ever so slightly with her earlier mention of "news . . . that will rather surprise" him. More important, in what Emma now goes on to say, a complete reversal of her earlier behavior in the novel begins to make itself apparent:

> "You probably have been less surprised than any of us, for you have had your suspicions.—I have not forgotten that you once tried to give me a caution.—I wish I had attended to it—but— (with a sinking voice and a heavy sigh) I seem to have been doomed to blindness."

Emma both accepts the "blindness" with which she has acted and admits to the superior insight of Mr. Knightley, who has given her a "caution" about Frank Churchill's intimacy with Jane Fairfax. This self-recognition on Emma's part also has highly emotional implications, for she realizes not only that her "blindness" to Frank Churchill has been caused by her fancy, so typical, of matching him with Harriet, but that this scheme

❋❋❋❋❋❋❋❋❋❋❋❋❋❋❋❋❋❋❋❋❋❋❋❋❋❋❋❋❋❋❋❋

has kept her from regarding Harriet as a rival to herself for Mr. Knightley. Especially in the passionate close, Emma betrays how deeply she feels about Mr. Knightley, though her words only plead with him to sympathize as a friend with her faults. Now a suppliant, she has completely abandoned her earlier pose of haughty detachment.

And Mr. Knightley responds to her plea, even though he believes all her distress generated by the loss of Frank Churchill, the man whom he has considered his rival. There may be a touch of irony at Mr. Knightley's expense in the fact that he praises Emma's "sense" here while quite misconceiving her situation:

> "Time, my dearest Emma, time will heal the wound.—Your own excellent sense—your exertions for your father's sake—I know you will not allow yourself—. . . . The feelings of the warmest friendship—Indignation—Abominable scoundrel! . . . I am sorry for *her*. She deserves a better fate."

Yet it is typical of Mr. Knightley that, while betraying intense private emotion by his broken clauses, he should undertake to direct Emma toward her proper reaction of "sense," unselfishness, and justice to Jane Fairfax. But clearly what moves him most deeply is the sight of suffering in the woman he loves— and a lingering resentment against his former rival.

Jane Austen writes that "Emma understood him," but the statement is no more than a half-truth. Emma realizes only that Mr. Knightley thinks her attached to Frank Churchill, and she takes pains to set him right about that in several long speeches. One feature of them is Emma's running distinction between appearance and reality. The following extracts will reveal the trait, most obviously in the contrast Emma draws near the start between her "manners" toward Frank Churchill and her lack of feeling for him, and in her later contrast between the "blind" of his behavior and "his real situation":

> "Mr. Knightley . . . I am in a very extraordinary situation. I cannot let you continue in your error; and yet, perhaps, since my

manners gave such an impression, I have as much reason to be ashamed of confessing that I never have been at all attached to the person we are speaking of, as it might be natural for a woman to feel in confessing exactly the reverse.—But I never have."

.   .   .   .
.

"I have very little to say for my own conduct.—I was tempted by his attentions, and allowed myself to appear pleased.—An old story, probably—a common case—and no more than has happened to hundreds of my sex before; and yet it may not be the more excusable in one who sets up as I do for Understanding. . . . He never wished to attach me. It was merely a blind to conceal his real situation with another.—It was his object to blind all about him; and no one, I am sure, could be more effectually blinded than myself—except that I was *not* blinded—that it was my good fortune—that, in short, I was somehow or other safe from him."

But, if we are struck by Emma's ability to make distinctions here, what of her generalizations? Toward the close of the first extract, she certainly pretends to no more than the level of generic "woman": ". . . I have as much reason to be ashamed . . . as it might be natural for a woman to feel in confessing exactly the reverse." In the second speech, she gives up all claims to uniqueness through linking herself absolutely with "hundreds of my sex," now describing her "case" as "common," "An old story." And in the next breath—". . . it may not be the more excusable in one who sets up as I do for Understanding"—Emma does not generalize to escape responsibility, as she has done so frequently before, but to judge herself. The last lines of the speech show her private feelings welling up, half anger at Frank Churchill, half despair of Mr. Knightley. The emotions are interrelated because Emma's plotting about Frank Churchill has led her to ignore Mr. Knightley, and the interrelationship is dramatized through the shifting logic behind Emma's references to blindness. But in speaking so warmly, Emma comes too near disclosing that the source of her feeling is Mr. Knightley, and so she must break off.

She has at least convinced him, however, that she never gave her heart to Frank Churchill, and Mr. Knightley feels so cheered

❋❋❋❋❋❋❋❋❋❋❋❋❋❋❋❋❋❋❋❋❋❋❋❋❋❋❋❋❋❋❋❋❋❋❋❋

by the information that he immediately raises his estimate of the man somewhat. Although this turnabout has its mild irony for us, the speech as a whole attests again to the integrity of Mr. Knightley, for he will not let Frank Churchill off without further reform, nor will he forget the claims of Jane Fairfax. And he maintains this basically sensible and sensitive grip on reality when he is even more deeply moved—by a remark from Emma about the happiness of the engaged couple. Once more Mr. Knightley can take stock intelligently and firmly of the whole relationship between Frank Churchill and Jane Fairfax, but he speaks so feelingly of them because they are enjoying exactly the happiness that he has yearned to share with Emma and believes an impossibility:

> "He is a most fortunate man! . . . So early in life . . . a period when, if a man chooses a wife, he generally chooses ill. At three and twenty to have drawn such a prize!—What years of felicity that man, in all human calculation, has before him!— Assured of the love of such a woman—the disinterested love, for Jane Fairfax's character vouches for her disinterestedness; every thing in his favour,—equality of situation—I mean, as far as regards society, and all the habits and manners that are important . . . .—A man would always wish to give a woman a better home than the one he takes her from; and he who can do it, where there is no doubt of *her* regard, must, I think, be the happiest of mortals.—Frank Churchill is, indeed, the favourite of fortune. Every thing turns out for his good. . . ."
>
> "You speak as if you envied him."
>
> "And I do envy him, Emma. In one respect he is the object of my envy."

Emma is well aware, obviously, that his words reverberate with emotion. Indeed, she cannot bring herself to reply at all to his last remark, for she imagines him "within half a sentence of Harriet." It is a signal irony that Emma, whom we have seen attempting all through here a clarity of vision unobscured by wishful thinking, should fall victim to this last confusion of appearance and reality.

Thus the groundwork is laid for the multiple ironies that arise when Mr. Knightley addresses himself to Emma more explicitly. For one thing, the principals work at cross purposes,

Mr. Knightley trying to propose in spite of Emma's unencouraging manner, and Emma fending off what she most wants because she fears him to be thinking of Harriet:

> "You will not ask me what is the point of envy.—You are determined, I see, to have no curiosity.—You are wise—but *I* cannot be wise. Emma, I must tell what you will not ask, though I may wish it unsaid the next moment."

A further irony inheres in Mr. Knightley's transposition of the roles to which he and Emma have been assigned through most of the novel. He now presents himself as the one governed by feeling—"*I* cannot be wise," "I must tell," "I may wish"—and Emma as the partisan of reason—"will not ask," "determined . . . to have no curiosity," "wise." In this characterization of Emma, however, Mr. Knightley speaks a truer sense than he perhaps realizes, for she now behaves with the richest integrity. For a brief moment her dread of losing him, perhaps mixed with some antagonism toward Harriet, rules Emma, and she begs Mr. Knightley not to speak. Yet she transcends this selfishness immediately, in part through an act of will, to be sure, but mainly through being almost literally moved beyond herself by her tenderness toward Mr. Knightley, and also by some sense of justice toward Harriet: [4]

> Emma could not bear to give him pain. He was wishing to confide in her—perhaps to consult her;—cost her what it would, she would listen. She might assist his resolution, or reconcile him to it; she might give just praise to Harriet, or, by representing to him his own independence, relieve him from that state of indecision, which must be more intolerable than any alternative to such a mind as his.

Surrendering every chance for her own happiness, as she believes, Emma invites Mr. Knightley to go on. And she then learns, of course, that he loves no one but herself. Yet this fortunate result must not tempt us to undervalue what we have just witnessed: Emma shouldering her responsibilities fully in the gravest crisis that she ever endures.

The entire scene seems to me wonderfully successful in con-

✳✳✳✳✳✳✳✳✳✳✳✳✳✳✳✳✳✳✳✳✳✳✳✳✳✳✳✳✳✳✳✳✳✳✳

veying—through the gestures of speech—the deep emotions of Emma and Mr. Knightley, the principles by which they act, and the moral decisions that they make. In achieving what it does, the scene invites us to question such a commentary on *Emma* and Jane Austen as this: "Here, as always in her work, the moral, or rather the philosophy, is not ethical in the stricter sense; it has to do with manners more than with morals." [5] For the dialogue shows that one's "manners," one's verbal habits, cannot help dramatizing one's "morals," one's ethical commitments.

1. *Letters,* II, 443.

2. Mary Lascelles discusses this point acutely (*Jane Austen,* pp. 94–95).

3. Mudrick describes Emma as a "dominating and uncommitting personality" (*Jane Austen,* p. 192), and he implies that she never really changes in the novel. He speaks at one point of her reaction to Harriet's disclosures as "the act of self-abasement that claims sin, in order to avoid the responsibility of self-knowledge" (p. 189). And he allows Emma to be honest about herself, or nearly honest, only when it costs her nothing emotionally: by telling Frank Churchill of their mutual good fortune in attracting such "superior" persons as Mr. Knightley and Jane Fairfax, Emma reveals, according to Mudrick, that she "has finally—almost—got to know herself; but only because the knowledge is here painless" (p. 205). Yet, as I have tried to point out in my text, the scene between Emma and Harriet insists not only that Emma does see herself clearly but that she accepts the responsibility for having encouraged Harriet as well as the consequences of the act. And surely Emma's insight in the scene, even if one ranks it lower than I do, is accompanied by a good deal of pain. In general, it seems to me that Mudrick overrates Emma's emotional detachment. He treats it as a permanent fact of her personality, a fact that leads her to prefer women to men (p. 192), indeed to be "for a time . . . in love with" Harriet, yet to use Harriet, at the same time, as a "proxy" for herself, as her means of experiencing vicariously what she cannot involve herself in personally (p. 203). According to my view, Emma's detachment is a temporary condition—caused by her failure to realize what she feels for Mr. Knightley—and disappears when her feelings are liberated by the revelations of Harriet.

4. Emma is incapable of tenderness according to Mudrick (*Jane Austen,* pp. 192–94, 200), but it seems to me that her tenderness at this critical moment in the novel is unquestionable.

5. E. A. Baker, *History,* VI, 108.

8 *Persuasion*
In Defense of Sensibility

Every reader of Jane Austen senses immediately that *Persuasion* differs in several ways from her other writings. Indeed the differences are so marked, and so tempting to explore, that I had better begin by saying what this last completed novel has in common with the earlier ones. *Persuasion* attacks egoism again, rewarding Anne Elliot's persevering unselfishness with a Captain Wentworth who comes gradually to qualify his emotional intensity and finally learns to see himself clearly. Through the theme of the novel, then, Jane Austen proposes the same values that she has championed from *Sense and Sensibility* on, and we shall find her relying on the same techniques that she has employed before. But *Persuasion* has its singularities. The most noticeable is its pervasive atmosphere, the atmosphere identified in one critic's description of the story as "purely a cry of feeling," and in the remark of another that the book contains Jane Austen's first sympathetic use of the word *romantic*.[1] *Persuasion* also diverges from the previous novels in that it vindicates completely what can only be called Anne Elliot's major intuitions, those regarding Captain Wentworth and William Elliot; it vindicates, that is, a mode of apprehension essentially emotional and intensely subjective. Finally, Jane Austen creates in Captain Wentworth a hero more vigorously emotional and more dominated by feeling than any other who appears within her work.

In its basic narrative *Persuasion* develops along the simplest lines. Captain Wentworth returns to Anne's neighborhood some seven years after she has been persuaded to break off her engagement to him, and he takes up with Louisa Musgrove, the first movement of the novel coming to a close with Louisa's injury in the scene on the Cobb and Captain Wentworth's re-awakening to Anne. In *Persuasion*'s final movement William Elliot comes forward for a time to pay his attentions to Anne, but she and the Captain at last reach an understanding and renew the pledges given up in the past. The essential drama of the story arises from Captain Wentworth's slowly altering feelings toward Anne and resides in the gradual drawing together of hero and heroine. He is, in fact, the only character in the novel who undergoes any change.[2] And for the most part we see him, as we see the other figures and events in *Persuasion*, from the perspective of a heroine who never changes fundamentally.[3]

Both the qualities of Anne as a person and Captain Wentworth's role as hero exert interesting pressures on Jane Austen's handling of the point of view in this novel. Generally speaking, of course, the author works here much as she has before, establishing many of the characters when they first put in an appearance, and taking over from Anne every now and then to comment impersonally or ironically on the action.[4] But we can observe something unusual going on when Jane Austen introduces the Captain. Plainly he must be a firmly sympathetic character to have attracted Anne in the past, and he must be kept so if they are to be finally united. Thus on our first sight of him, the author is at great pains—even to the degree of violating Anne's point of view—to qualify an apparently insulting remark by him which has been reported to Anne, "You were so altered he should not have known you again" (p. 60):

> Frederick Wentworth had used such words, or something like them, but without an idea that they would be carried round to her. He had thought her wretchedly altered, and, in the first moment of appeal, had spoken as he felt. He had not forgiven Anne Elliot. . . .
> He had been most warmly attached to her, and had never seen a woman since whom he thought her equal; but, except from some natural sensation of curiosity, he had no desire of meeting her again. Her power with him was gone for ever. (p. 61)

If Jane Austen does not justify the offense she at least palliates it. Clearly Captain Wentworth has spoken so vehemently because of his past (or present) feeling for Anne. Not until the author has spelled out this winning motive does she retreat from omniscience—at the "but" in the next to last sentence—to the dramatically ambiguous words of her close, which may tell the truth or mark Captain Wentworth's self-deception.[5] Throughout the novel, however, his main fault lies in reacting so violently to having lost an Anne fully worth his love. And she herself can never be allowed to change in essentials, for it might cast some shadow over her original behavior in giving in to Lady Russell's persuasions against Captain Wentworth. Thus the chief characters severely limit Jane Austen's possibilities for a dramatic narrative. She does what she can by keeping Captain Wentworth himself pretty much in the background, except for speeches that refer only indirectly to Anne, and by confining us largely to the heroine, whose feelings are used by the author to obscure the reality of Captain Wentworth.

Jane Austen exploits the nature of Anne, especially, to create the modicum of suspense in *Persuasion*—and to lay the groundwork for the ambiguities that we will notice later on in what Captain Wentworth says. For instance, Anne interprets his reported refusal to breakfast at the house where she is staying as an absolute desire on his part "to avoid seeing her" (p. 59), even though she has earlier jumped at the chance to avoid him because of her own intense sentiment about their past, and even though his plans do necessitate a stop at her home. If Captain Wentworth relieves her of a bothersome child without comment, Anne cannot feel that he is as embarrassed as she is, but that "he meant to avoid hearing her thanks, and rather sought to testify that her conversation was the last of his wants" (p. 80). And when he maneuvers her into the carriage of the Crofts, the act must show a wholly negative kindness: "He could not forgive her,—but he could not be unfeeling" (p. 91). Such are the shifts which Jane Austen is put to in order to sustain the major drama in *Persuasion,* the breach between Anne and Captain Wentworth. The examples should suggest the very real technical difficulties that arise when the point of view is located in a heroine whose misinterpretations, necessary to keep the story going,

❀❀❀❀❀❀❀❀❀❀❀❀❀❀❀❀❀❀❀❀❀❀❀❀❀❀❀❀❀❀❀

must never invalidate her significant intuitions, and when the main moral/emotional conflict is relegated to a hero in the middle distance.

The conflict of Captain Wentworth, at least the resolution of it, we shall come to in the final section of this chapter, where some dialogues saturated with metaphoric indirection will again be our main concern. But first we need a clearer understanding of Anne's nature, and this will involve us in looking at a number of the other figures in the novel.

-⟨ II ⟩-

The central issue of *Persuasion*, I take it, is the appropriate quality of feeling in the individual. This seems to me the point explored, for example, in Jane Austen's contrast between Captain Wentworth and William Elliot as rivals for Anne; or in the pitting of Anne against the field during the scene on the Cobb; or in the author's indications that the Captain does learn to judge his earlier behavior through courting Anne for the second time. It is Anne herself who provides the rich, the continuing instance of this appropriate feeling, much of the novel being devoted to recording her wonderfully sensitive responses to the world around her, and Jane Austen brings out Anne's nature by juxtaposing the heroine with several groups of characters of very different personal capacities.

One group consists of Anne's immediate family, or, to put it more accurately, that travesty of a family: her father—Sir Walter—and her two sisters, Elizabeth Elliot and Mary Musgrove. None of them pays the slightest attention to Anne as a person, for all three are obsessed with the matter of rank. Sir Walter may speak a trifle more sharply than the two daughters would when he propounds his case against the navy, but they rate the claims of social position—and of beauty, apparently its correlative—just as highly as he does:

". . . I have two strong grounds of objection to it. First, as being the means of bringing persons of obscure birth into undue distinction, and raising men to honours which their fathers and grandfathers never dreamt of; and secondly, as it cuts up a man's youth and vigour most horribly; a sailor grows old sooner than any other man . . . . A man is in greater danger in the navy of being insulted by the rise of one whose father, his father might have disdained to speak to, and of becoming prematurely an object of disgust himself, than in any other line. . . . I shall not easily forget Admiral Baldwin. I never saw quite so wretched an example of what a sea-faring life can do . . . they are all knocked about, and exposed to every climate, and every weather, till they are not fit to be seen. It is a pity they are not knocked on the head at once, before they reach Admiral Baldwin's age."

(pp. 19–20)

Sir Walter's generalizations and particular terms, expressing his preoccupation with rank and his contempt with whatever does not fit in with his ideas, could easily be matched in the speeches of Elizabeth and Mary.

But it is more important to note that the concern of them all with social status is not the effect of even so dubious a motive as the love of tradition for its own sake. Rather, they are obsessed with rank because they are obsessed with themselves. In Sir Walter and Elizabeth, feeling seems almost to have atrophied, but what little remains, instead of flowing out, circles endlessly about the sense that each one has of personal superiority. Both of them retain just enough discretion, when speaking of themselves, to erect the slimmest façade of propriety. Thus Sir Walter will pretend that the ladies of Bath might have been admiring the features of his walking companion rather than his own (p. 142). In the same fashion, when it is suggested to Elizabeth that William Elliot has been begging for an invitation because he feels attracted to her, she pretends—toward the middle of her reply—that his regard is for her father:

"Oh! . . . I have been rather too much used to the game to be soon overcome by a gentleman's hints. However, when I found how excessively he was regretting that he should miss my father this morning, I gave way immediately, for I would never

really omit an opportunity of bringing him and Sir Walter together. They appear to so much advantage in company with
each other! Each behaving so pleasantly! Mr. Elliot looking up
with so much respect!"

.   .   .   .

". . . But, upon my word, I am scarcely sensible of his attentions being beyond those of other men." (p. 213)

By using Sir Walter as a surrogate for herself, Elizabeth can
attribute to William Elliot the intense emotion and the attitude
of reverence which she believes define his reaction to herself.
At the same time, especially in the first and last sentences, she
declares her own detachment, that is, her superiority to William
Elliot. For Elizabeth and Sir Walter, indeed, and in a sense for
Mary as well, the appearance that they present to the world—
or the appearance presented by anyone else—is the reality.

The feelings of Mary have not stagnated to quite the degree
that those of her father and sister have, but they revolve as exclusively around her social position and herself. Her rhythms
usually sound more relentlessly demanding than Sir Walter's or
Elizabeth's. Yet her heritage reveals itself, when she tells Anne
about going to a party, in Mary's utter commitment to the appearances of rank, in her snobbish generalizations expressing
private convictions, and in her disdainful particulars:

"One always knows beforehand what the dinner will be, and
who will be there. And it is so very uncomfortable, not having
a carriage of one's own. Mr. and Mrs. Musgrove took me, and
we were so crowded! They are both so very large, and take up
so much room. . . . So, there was I, crowded into the back seat
with Henrietta and Louisa." (p. 39)

In short, Mary is as self-absorbed as her father or Elizabeth, as
incapable of taking any personal account of Anne. All of them
consider Anne merely as some sort of appendage to themselves,
a fact sufficiently illustrated in Mary's comment when her
parents-in-law do not turn up immediately to greet Anne at
Uppercross Cottage: "They ought to feel what is due to you as

my sister" (p. 40). In their emotional callousness, these Elliots differ from the sensitive Anne as night from day.

No one could complain that feeling does not flow in the Musgroves, the family into which Mary Elliot has married. They come on stage in force after Sir Walter and Elizabeth have departed for Bath, and they make up another group of figures used to differentiate Anne. For the Musgroves, though genial enough and far more warmhearted than the Elliots, are all rather self-centered, and the ladies, particularly, are prone to sentimentality. The real ruling passion of Charles Musgrove, the husband of Mary, seems to be sport, for it determines many of his judgments, even some of those in his other area of special interest, property and finance. He confidently decides, for example, that his cousin will not "value" a new living "as he ought" because he is a man "too cool about sporting" (p. 217). Another of the financial opinions offered by Charles Musgrove reveals in a slightly different way his inability to get outside himself, for he speaks with the consciousness of being "an eldest son" in his own right when he approves of a marriage between his sister Henrietta and his cousin, Charles Hayter:

> "It would not be a *great* match for Henrietta, but Charles . . . you will please to remember, that he is the eldest son; whenever my uncle dies, he steps into very pretty property. . . . I grant you, that any of them but Charles would be a very shocking match for Henrietta, and indeed it could not be; he is the only one that could be possible . . . . " [6] (p. 76)

And if Charles Musgrove protests that his views are really uncolored by his private concerns—to Anne, of all people, who has just defended Captain Benwick as "an excellent young man" —the rest of the speech explodes his protest by showing him astride the hobbyhorse of sport again:

> "Nobody doubts it; and I hope you do not think I am so illiberal as to want every man to have the same objects and pleasures as myself. I have a great value for Benwick . . . . We had a famous set-to at rat-hunting all the morning, in my father's great

barns; and . . . I have liked him the better ever since." (pp. 218–19)

These quotations not only suggest the reasonably good-hearted egotism of Charles Musgrove; they also reveal a tendency in him toward emotional extravagance, in that some of the phrases seem more heightened than the local situation warrants.

His sisters are as generally well-disposed as he is, and similarly engrossed in themselves, but their talk sounds shriller than his, their high spirits bubbling out in one verbal extreme after another. In the following passage, Henrietta speaks of Lady Russell with lavish praise, but she is imagining how the interests of her own fiancé might be furthered by that lady:

> "I have always heard of Lady Russell, as a woman of the greatest influence with every body! I always look upon her as able to persuade a person to any thing! I am afraid of her . . . quite afraid of her, because she is so very clever; but I respect her amazingly, and wish we had such a neighbour at Uppercross."
> (p. 103)

In the same fashion Louisa, caught up within her liking for Captain Wentworth, proclaims vehemently to him how highly she values the power of love: "If I loved a man, as she loves the Admiral, I would be always with him, nothing should ever separate us, and I would rather be overturned by him, than driven safely by anybody else" (p. 85). The instance that Louisa lights on to prove herself at the close is rather absurd, making the whole flood of feeling seem disproportionately energetic, in excess of what the context requires. The identical point is conveyed by her action during the scene on the Cobb, when Louisa childishly indulges in her affection for the Captain by insisting that he jump her down the steps again—and falls when he misses his grip on her.

The same sort of sentimentality—the same excess of feeling, that is, relative to the occasion—crops up in some of the elder Mrs. Musgrove's remarks and behavior. For instance, after Mrs. Croft has described her anxiety during one winter with Admiral

Croft away at sea, Mrs. Musgrove ejaculates: "There is nothing so bad as a separation. I am quite of your opinion. *I* know what it is, for Mr. Musgrove always attends the assizes, and I am so glad when they are over, and he is safe back again" (p. 71). And surely the affair of her lamentations for "poor Dick" Musgrove—the worthless son, long dead, who had served with Captain Wentworth—is intended to emphasize the sentimental tendencies in Mrs. Musgrove. Although Jane Austen's notorious attack on her "fat sighings" is indefensible (p. 68), and although the author handles the whole business about the mother and the dead son tastelessly, still the essential fact seems to be that Mrs. Musgrove's present grief is disproportionate, and not simply to the character assigned "poor Dick." For he has apparently popped into her mind only as a result of her hearing the name of Captain Wentworth, and we are told that her subsequent "reperusal" of her son's letters has "thrown her into greater grief for him than she had known on first hearing of his death" (p. 51). A final point about Mrs. Musgrove: absorbed in her feelings for her son, she a little forgets what is due Captain Wentworth—for example, in calling him "such a good friend" of Dick's (p. 66)—just as she has earlier neglected the claims of Mrs. Croft to press forward with her own in the italicized "*I*" of the quotation given above. Both the self-centeredness of Mrs. Musgrove and her self-indulgence are foreign to Anne's nature.[7]

Admiral Croft and his wife, whom we may take as roughly typical of the naval characters in *Persuasion*, mark another boundary of the story's main issue. In terms of the narrative, their renting of Sir Walter's home supplies Captain Wentworth with the chance to become reacquainted with Anne. As persons in their own right, however, the Crofts are neither so hard-hearted as the Elliots, nor so inclined to sentimentalism as the Musgroves, but fundamentally sensible and bluffly emotional. With them the channels of feeling may be a bit crude, but the current runs straight, for the Crofts respond immediately to the claims of everyone, from the Elliots to the Musgroves. There is a touch of the parochial, of course, in their instinctive reliance on naval figures of speech: "We none of us expect," says Mrs. Croft, "to be in smooth water all our days" (p. 70). And though it happens to be the Admiral who speaks the words that follow, his wife often exhibits the same emotional vigor expressed here by his particular terms: "Here I am, you see, staring at a picture. . . . But what a thing here is, by way of a boat. . . . What queer fellows your fine painters must be, to think that any body would venture their lives in such a shapeless old cockleshell as that" (p. 169). Perhaps the robust feelings of the Crofts come through most clearly in their frequent generalizations, which declare their love for a way of life and for each other. "Never was a better sloop," avows the Admiral, "than the Asp in her day.—For an old built sloop, you would not see her equal"; and after a moment he goes on, "What should a young fellow, like you, do ashore, for half a year together?—If a man has not a wife, he soon wants to be afloat again" (p. 65). Mrs. Croft affirms the same sort of convictions just as positively:

> "When you come to a frigate, of course, you are more confined —though any reasonable woman may be perfectly happy in one of them; and I can safely say, that the happiest part of my life has been spent on board a ship. While we were together, you know, there was nothing to be feared." (p. 70)

But this hearty openness should not suggest that we are to regard the Crofts as mere figures of fun, for their emotions do not prevent them from generalizing sensibly. Mrs. Croft can decide against "uncertain" engagements on perfectly practical grounds (thus to some extent validating, incidentally, Lady Russell's original persuasion of Anne against Captain Wentworth, though Lady Russell was motivated by social prejudice as well): "To begin without knowing that at such a time there will be the means of marrying, I hold to be very unsafe and unwise, and what, I think, all parents should prevent as far as they can" (p. 231). And the Admiral, even though he has hoped that Captain Wentworth would marry Louisa Musgrove and has far more affection for him than for Captain Benwick, yet defends the right of Louisa to change her mind: "If the girl likes another man better, it is very fit she should have him" (p. 172). In contrast both to the Elliots and to the Musgroves, the Crofts personify uninhibited sympathy and basic good sense.

Lady Russell is the final member we must notice at present of the human background against which Anne is displayed. In character, Lady Russell takes her place somewhere between the Elliots and the Crofts, for she is influenced on the one hand by a prejudice of her own for rank and on the other by a genuine attachment to Anne. After her first speech of the book, in which Lady Russell tells Anne that Sir Walter must rent his home to pay his debts even though moving will pain him, we cannot doubt her essential integrity: ". . . though a great deal is due to the feelings of the gentleman, and the head of a house, like your father, there is still more due to the character of an honest man" (p. 12). But, given the self-assurance with which Lady Russell generalizes here—as everywhere in the novel—and given her concern for what is "due" to a "gentleman," it is only a short step for her from a sensible judgment like this to the undiscerning allegiance to tradition that is revealed when she encourages the Elliots to make up to their insipid cousins, the Dowager Viscountess Dalrymple and the Honourable Miss Carteret: "Family connexions were always worth preserving . . . . It was very desirable that the connexion should be renewed, if it could be done, without any compromise of propriety on the side of the Elliots" (p. 149). This is the kind of social bias, mixed with her real regard for Anne's future, that has once led Lady Russell to talk Anne out of her engagement to Captain Wentworth, and the same combination of motives reappears when she urges Anne to think favorably of William Elliot as a suitor: "A most suitable connection every body must consider it —but I think it might be a very happy one" (p. 159). Through most of *Persuasion*, Lady Russell's prejudice for rank is in the ascendant, keeping her from acting up to her capacities as a person. But by the close of the story, when Anne and Captain Wentworth have come to terms with each other, Lady Russell's affection for Anne has affirmed itself as her dominant impulse:

✻✻✻✻✻✻✻✻✻✻✻✻✻✻✻✻✻✻✻✻✻✻✻✻✻✻✻✻✻✻✻✻✻✻

". . . if her second object was to be sensible and well-judging, her first was to see Anne happy. She loved Anne better than she loved her own abilities" (p. 249). What she lacks, according to Jane Austen's final dictum, lacks even in her most sensible moments, is "a quickness of perception . . . a nicety in the discernment of character, a natural penetration . . . which no experience in others can equal," for "Lady Russell had been less gifted in this part of understanding than her young friend" (p. 249). What she lacks, in a word, is Anne's intuition, the product of an extraordinary emotional sensitivity.

All these minor characters, illustrating certain varieties of emotional experience, serve to throw the nature of Anne into high relief. I mean the image to suggest the rather static quality of *Persuasion,* for the story seems less to move narratively than to accumulate an overwhelming impression of Anne's being. She is a creature of sensibility, but triumphantly so. Her insight, so much more precise and penetrating in important matters than that of any other figure in the novel, comes from an instinctive, refined rightness of feeling. For all its rightness, her feeling remains intensely subjective in a way that Fanny Price's never does, and Anne shows an openheartedness, a warm compassion for everyone, alien to the heroine of *Mansfield Park.* Anne's rightness of feeling is grounded, of course, in a traditional morality. Jane Austen certifies the fact by calling attention to Anne's sense of duty again and again, as in these sentences: "Every emendation of Anne's had been on the side of honesty against importance. She wanted more vigorous measures, a more complete reformation . . . a much higher tone of indifference for every thing but justice and equity" (p. 12). But something more than a traditional morality informs the words of Anne when Captain Wentworth lifts an apparently lifeless Louisa from the Lower Cobb and Anne herself is burdened with a fainting Henrietta: "Go to him, go to him . . . for heaven's sake go to him. I can support her myself. Leave me, and go to him. Rub her hands, rub her temples; here are salts,—take them, take them" (p. 110). The repeated "him," referring to the man she believes she has lost to Louisa, dramatizes the flood of selfless feeling, the total sympathy, which enables Anne alone to take firm charge of the entire situation. On a lesser scale, her rush of feeling may disclose itself in so typical a reaction to the sight of Captain Wentworth as this: ". . . she instantly felt that she was the greatest simpleton in the world, the most unaccountable and absurd! For a few minutes she saw nothing before her. It was all confusion. She was lost" (p. 175). But it is the same extreme sensitivity, delicate and basically reliable, which under-lies Anne's every action—which marks, too, a shift in emphasis from Jane Austen's other novels.

Anne's being is exactly rendered in her conversation. For one thing, it proves her acutely responsive to the particulars of ex-perience in her own right, yet at the same time fully—and de-corously—conscious of their effect upon others. When Lady Russell hesitantly proposes a call on the Crofts in Anne's former home, Anne's reply takes account both of the adjustment that she herself has made to the "change" and of the influence on Lady Russell of such a visit: "I think you are very likely to suffer the most of the two; your feelings are less reconciled to the change than mine. By remaining in the neighbourhood, I am become inured to it" (p. 125). But Anne's awareness of the par-ticular does not keep her from generalizing. On the contrary, it is the source from which many of her generalizations spring. At one point, for instance, after Captain Harville has testified to the sentiment that continues to bind him and the fiancé of his dead sister together by declaring that he and Captain Benwick now "cannot part," Anne supports him with, "No . . . that I can easily believe to be impossible; but in time, perhaps—we know what time does in every case of affliction, and you must remember . . . that your friend may yet be called a young mourner" (p. 108). Anne's sympathies are stirred in part be-cause she herself has endured a broken attachment, and, when she generalizes about what "time" will do for Captain Benwick, she is uttering a conviction based on her experience with Cap-tain Wentworth (it is a claim she returns to in the climactic dialogue of the novel): that men, unlike women, can eventually recover from such disappointments. The great majority of

Anne's generalizations have their origin in her sensibility, and the fact that they are not therefore invalid will remind us again how far we are from Marianne Dashwood, or from Emma, for that matter. If Anne speaks the clearest sense, she is as likely as not to appeal explicitly to emotion: "Nursing," she tells Mary, "does not belong to a man, it is not his province. A sick child is always the mother's property, her own feelings generally make it so" (p. 56). And even when she directs—without real cause —a moral generalization against herself, her vigorous phrasing shows her to be in emotional possession of it: "What wild imaginations one forms, where dear self is concerned! How sure to be mistaken!" (p. 201). All of these generalizations express reason saturated with Anne's personal feeling, thus becoming a verbal echo, as it were, of that union of innate sense with emotional sensitivity which I have called her intuition.

It is Anne's intuition, I take it, that has been at work some seven years before the story proper begins, firmly assuring her of the young Captain Wentworth's value even though she allows herself to be persuaded to give him up. Within the novel, her intuition exercises itself most strikingly in her distrust of William Elliot. Some readers have felt that Anne's estimate of him is too arbitrary, a sign to them that Jane Austen has failed to assimilate William Elliot into the fabric of *Persuasion,* but it appears to me that the author intends, at least in part, to present us here with an instance of Anne's active intuition. Not only does Anne's nature suggest as much, but the point seems confirmed by such passages as these (the italics are mine):

> Still, however, *she had the sensation* of there being something more than immediately appeared, in Mr. Elliot's wishing, after an interval of so many years, to be well received by them.
> (p. 140)

> He certainly knew what was right, nor could she fix on any one article of moral duty evidently transgressed; but yet *she would have been afraid to answer for his conduct.* . . . She saw that there had been bad habits . . . and, though he might now think very differently, who could answer for the true sentiments

of a clever, cautious man, grown old enough to appreciate a fair
character? (pp. 160–61)

She felt that she could so much more depend upon the sincerity
of those who sometimes looked or said a careless or a hasty
thing . . . . (p. 161)

All of these quotations insist that Anne is uneasy about William Elliot well before Jane Austen rings in Mrs. Smith to tell
us what a villain he is; (after these disclosures, Anne's instinct
about him is brought up again on pages 200, 207, and 249).
And the kind of decision referred to in the italicized phrases
can only be described as intuitive.

The conversation of William Elliot will allow us to make our
own judgment of him, however. And, since he has verbal habits
in common with Mrs. Clay—the lady who flatters Elizabeth,
pursues Sir Walter, and ends up with William Elliot himself—
we might as well take the two characters up at the same time.
We can move toward them via Anne's claim, just noted, about
William Elliot never saying "a careless or a hasty thing," for the
remarks by him and by Mrs. Clay always have an air of contrivance, the effect of slight incongruities in the local verbal manner. Mrs. Clay, for instance, seems almost to make a fetish of
reasoning carefully in the speech that follows, proceeding from
generalizations about "sailors," supported by her own experience, to a detailed survey of "other professions"; but all this
operates to pay a prodigious—if slightly oblique—compliment to
Sir Walter on his features:

"The sea is no beautifier, certainly; sailors do grow old betimes;
I have often observed it; they soon lose the look of youth. But
then, is not it the same with many other professions, perhaps
most other? Soldiers . . . . The lawyer . . . the physician
. . . the clergyman . . . . In fact . . . it is only the lot of
those who are not obliged to follow any [profession], who can
live in a regular way, in the country . . . on their own property
. . . it is only *their* lot, I say, to hold the blessings of health and
a good appearance to the utmost: I know no other set of men but
what lose something of their personableness when they cease to
be quite young." (pp. 20–21)

The same sense of incongruity arises when William Elliot praises Anne for her translation, offered with apologies, of an Italian song. At first he speaks in a fashion technically more oblique than Mrs. Clay's, though he points his irony so heavily that no one can miss his meaning:

> "I see you know nothing of the matter. You have only knowledge enough of the language, to translate at sight these inverted, transposed, curtailed Italian lines, into clear, comprehensible, elegant English. You need not say anything more of your ignorance.— Here is complete proof." (p. 186)

But, after Anne modestly distinguishes between his courtesy and her ability, he goes on to a prodigious compliment of his own:

> "I will not oppose such kind politeness; but I should be sorry to be examined by a real proficient."
>
> "I have not had the pleasure of visiting in Camden-place so long," replied he, "without knowing something of Miss Anne Elliot; and I do regard her as one who is too modest, for the world in general to be aware of half her accomplishments, and too highly accomplished for modesty to be natural in any other woman." (p. 187)

To my ear, his showy exhibition of Anne by generalizing seems out of tune with the cultivated indirection of his previous speech —and of course his close strikes a jarring note in the context of Anne's delicate reply. Whichever the mode he uses here, William Elliot sounds a little too extravagant, and the words of Mrs. Clay leave us with the same impression.

This tendency toward overstatement on the part of them both is a very different thing from the verbal extremism of the Musgroves, whom we heard simply venting their personal feelings unself-consciously. The touch of extravagance in the comments of William Elliot and Mrs. Clay seems a deliberate verbal maneuver, and thus of a piece with the dominant effect created by all their speeches. Whatever they say appears consciously designed for the particular situation and the particular audience, a façade of words behind which the speaker intrigues for private

ends. The most obvious example is the response of Mrs. Clay
when it suddenly comes out that she has been seen in secret
conference with William Elliot. Momentarily startled, she nevertheless has a verbal manner ready—one very different from her
previous pose as a careful reasoner—which permits her to hide
her real motives behind a spate of assumed emotion and to refer
the interest of Mr. Elliot to Elizabeth:

> "Only think, Miss Elliot, to my great surprise I met with Mr.
> Elliot in Bath-street! I was never more astonished. . . . He
> wanted to know how early he might be admitted to-morrow. He
> was full of "to-morrow;" and it is very evident that I have been
> full of it too . . . or my seeing him could never have gone so
> entirely out of my head." (p. 228)

A more subtle production than this is the speech in which William Elliot undertakes to counter Anne's objections to Lady
Dalrymple. His aims in it are two: first, to persuade Anne to his
own opinion about the high value of rank, and second, to ally
himself with her—since he is laying a groundwork for courting
her—in any way that he can. Anne has told him that her cousins
do not measure up to her own "idea of good company," which
she defines as "clever, well-informed people, who have a great
deal of conversation." William Elliot begins his reply with generalizations that set forth his own view, though smoothing over
his disagreement with Anne by the joke about "a little learning,"
which both takes account of her view and indirectly compliments
her on her taste:

> "Good company requires only birth, education and manners,
> and with regard to education is not very nice. Birth and good
> manners are essential; but a little learning is by no means a dan-
> gerous thing in good company, on the contrary, it will do very
> well. . . . My dear cousin, (sitting down by her) you have a
> better right to be fastidious than almost any other woman I
> know; but will it answer? Will it make you happy? Will it not
> be wiser to accept the society of these good ladies in Laura-place,
> and enjoy all the advantages of the connexion as far as possible?
> You may depend upon it, that they will move in the first set in

Bath this winter, and as rank is rank, your being known to be related to them will have its use in fixing your family (our family let me say) in that degree of consideration which we must all wish for." (p. 150)

By the middle of the speech, he turns to Anne more directly. After the open compliment on her "right to be fastidious," William Elliot tries to gain her emotional assent to his propositions about "good company" through the series of rhetorical questions —none of which, incidentally, would evoke the desired answer from Anne. In the last sentence, he reverts to his earlier generalizations with "as rank is rank," and he makes one final attempt to win Anne to his position—and to associate himself with her personally—by the shift from "your family" to "our family." What all this adds up to is simply the fact that William Elliot keeps using his discourse to manipulate Anne, which implies that he remains, like Mrs. Clay, fundamentally detached.[8] And his detachment would seem to be part and parcel of that insincerity, that lack of openness about him, which Anne has intuited.

If her distrust of William Elliot is the most striking instance of Anne's intuition, its major triumph is her continuing attachment to Captain Wentworth. Appropriately enough, given the qualities of the heroine, he is a person who feels powerfully. Jane Austen tells us as much by introducing him as a man of "warmth"—and of "wit" as well. Yet Captain Wentworth's wit, frequently revealed in the light surface of his conversation, is not a device for the manipulation of others: it does not mark the detachment of a William Elliot, but the Captain's conscious restraint. Both the wit and the warmth show up side by side in a number of his generalizations through the first half of the story, generalizations that betray his feeling for Anne even while he intends them to keep him at a distance from her. In the following passage, he talks with a group including the Musgroves, the Crofts, and Anne; and the naval assignment he speaks about has covered the months—though only he and Anne realize the fact—immediately after the severance of their engagement:

"The admiralty . . . entertain themselves now and then, with sending a few hundred men to sea, in a ship not fit to be employed. But they have a great many to provide for; and among the thousands that may just as well go to the bottom as not, it is impossible for them to distinguish the very set who may be least missed." (p. 65)

The Captain exhibits his self-possession in his mode of generalizing, in the witty exaggeration of his plight as the commander of a leaky ship. And by the irony of his last clause, which points covertly to the broken engagement, he sets himself well apart from Anne. At the same time, however, the whole speech reflects how deeply Captain Wentworth has been involved with her. His description of his dangers is a somewhat cruel, though not entirely intentional, reminder to Anne of his lot on being dismissed by her. And he has got to discuss his lot so unconcernedly in order that Anne may have no reason to think him distressed over their parting. Yet how seriously she has in fact distressed him comes clearer in his next sentences: "I felt my luck" in getting a command, he tells Admiral Croft; "It was a great object with me, at that time, to be at sea,—a very great object. I wanted to be doing something."

As the previous quotation will have suggested, when Captain Wentworth speaks only with warmth, not with wit, he still disciplines his words so that they avoid too specific a notice of Anne and of what has happened between them. In part this is a matter of preserving decorum, and in part his verbal control seems the Captain's way of assuring himself that he has come to terms with his past, has put it well behind him. Yet whenever he talks with fervor, Anne is likely to be imbedded in his thoughts, even though his references are too oblique to be caught by his listeners (except Anne), and even though the Captain himself is perhaps less conscious than the reader of Anne's influence on his remarks. In the course of the dialogue we have just been looking at, he reminisces:

"Ah! those were pleasant days when I had the Laconia! How fast I made money in her.—A friend of mine, and I, had such a lovely cruise together off the Western Islands.—Poor Harville, sister! You know how much he wanted money—worse than myself. He had a wife. . . . I shall never forget his happiness. He felt it all, so much for her sake." (p. 67)

To most of his hearers this sounds merely like an expression of the Captain's sympathy for his friend. But the association of money with marriage, especially in company with the phrase "worse than myself," proves his lingering sensitivity to what Anne has deprived him of.[9] Even when, later on in the novel, he addresses Louisa Musgrove earnestly—so earnestly that Anne, who overhears them, thinks him deeply interested in Louisa— Captain Wentworth's generalizations still have their source in his feelings for Anne, in his resentment that she should once have allowed herself to be persuaded against him:

"It is the worst evil of too yielding and indecisive a character, that no influence over it can be depended on.—You are never sure of a good impression being durable. Every body may sway it; let those who would be happy be firm. . . . My first wish for all, whom I am interested in, is that they should be firm." (p. 88)

All of these speeches reveal that Captain Wentworth, though he may often succeed in controlling his words, cannot escape his sense of the past, much as he wishes to. And the quality of his reaction to the past is very different from Anne's. She has suffered as deeply as he, and is at least as intensely alive to their history, but in a completely selfless fashion. What we have heard from the Captain so far, however, implies that he remains trapped within feelings that regard himself, anger at the broken engagement and bitter disappointment with Anne, those same feelings betrayed in his many scornful allusions to "persuasion." It is this version of self-centeredness, which often becomes self-righteousness in the first half of the novel, that Captain Wentworth must fight his way beyond as the story develops. He begins his breakthrough in the scene on the Cobb. The scene is absolutely central to the novel's theme, not only in illustrating Anne's strength of character, but in providing an almost parodic counterpart to the incident from which the whole narrative springs, that persuading of Anne for which Captain Wentworth has never forgiven her. In the little drama on the Cobb, a lover's resolution does carry the day, as it did not in the case of Captain Wentworth and Anne; yet the firmness of Louisa, which the Captain has been moved to admire as the opposite of the weakness he imagines in Anne, expresses itself here in Louisa's sheerly willful demand to be jumped down the stairs again. And Captain Wentworth is the one who surrenders to persuasion now—yet merely to indulge Louisa. The scene issues, of course, in near disaster. But the injury to Louisa shocks Captain Wentworth into seeing Anne more objectively than he has before and into accepting his responsibility with regard at least to Louisa. He reproaches himself immediately for what has happened, and he continues to judge himself harshly some hours after the event:

> "Don't talk of it, don't talk of it," he cried. "Oh God! that I had not given way to her at the fatal moment! Had I done as I ought! But so eager and so resolute! Dear, sweet Louisa!" (p. 116)

Yet exclamations so passionate as these suggest that Captain Wentworth, while recognizing his guilt, is still caught up within his private response to the experience—remains dominated, that is, by his sense of personal anguish. What he must ultimately learn in the course of rediscovering Anne is to moderate the personal element in his feelings, though without blunting them, and to integrate this refined emotion, as Anne has done, with a total acceptance of responsibility—his responsibility to Anne and for their past. This is no easy job for the Captain. The differences between him and Anne are still apparent far along in *Persuasion*, well after his interest in her has been rekindled, as two dialogues will show.

Prior to the first of these interchanges (pp. 182–84), Captain Wentworth and Anne have been talking over the day of Louisa's accident at Lyme, and, when he broaches the subject of Louisa's engagement to Captain Benwick, Anne replies with: "But it

❋❋❋❋❋❋❋❋❋❋❋❋❋❋❋❋❋❋❋❋❋❋❋❋❋❋❋❋❋❋❋❋❋

appears—I should hope it would be a very happy match. There are on both sides good principles and good temper." Her shift from "it appears" to "I should hope" vividly dramatizes Anne's native delicacy of feeling. She retreats from the authoritatively impersonal to the modestly personal, either to avoid deciding on the "match" with a greater certainty than she can properly claim, or—even more graciously—to keep from speaking with assurance about the happiness of a "match" that may pain the Captain deeply (for she still cannot be sure how much he has felt for Louisa). Whichever Anne's motive, she closes by saying all that can safely be said. Captain Wentworth, however, is by no means so constrained:

> "Yes . . . but there I think ends the resemblance. With all my soul I wish them happy . . . . They have no difficulties to contend with at home, no opposition, no caprice, no delays.—The Musgroves are behaving like themselves . . . only anxious with true parental hearts to promote their daughter's comfort."

"With all my soul" attests to his joy at being released from Louisa, a feeling which merges immediately into another: his distress, so near the surface of his sentences commending the behavior of the Musgroves, over the interference that once cost him Anne. Aware that he treads on dangerous ground, Captain Wentworth tries to beat a retreat toward sense, starting out a new speech by measuring the capacities of Louisa against Captain Benwick's:

> "I confess that I do think there is a disparity, too great a disparity, and in a point no less essential than mind.—I regard Louisa Musgrove as a very amiable, sweet-tempered girl . . . but Benwick is something more. He is a clever man, a reading man—and I confess that I do consider his attaching himself to her, with some surprise. . . . It seems . . . to have been a perfectly spontaneous, untaught feeling on his side, and this surprises me. A man like him, in his situation! With a heart pierced, wounded, almost broken! Fanny Harville was a very superior creature; and his attachment to her was indeed attachment. A man does not recover from such a devotion of the heart to such a woman!—He ought not—he does not."

But his reasoning dissolves in the exclamations and the violently particular terms describing Captain Benwick's past—to say nothing of the fact that Captain Wentworth's subject has shifted completely from "mind" to "heart." And by the close, when he attempts to pull his case together, the Captain's explosive generalizations are based entirely on feeling, his own feeling for Anne.

It is no wonder that their conversation comes to a halt for a few moments, until Anne hits on the somewhat safer topic of Lyme. When she mentions that she would like to visit the place again, however, Captain Wentworth responds with:

> "Indeed! I should not have supposed that you could have found any thing in Lyme to inspire such a feeling. The horror and distress you were involved in—the stretch of mind, the wear of spirits!—I should have thought your last impressions of Lyme must have been strong disgust."
>
> "The last few hours were certainly very painful," replied Anne: "but when pain is over, the remembrance of it often becomes a pleasure. One does not love a place the less for having suffered in it, unless it has been all suffering, nothing but suffering—which was by no means the case at Lyme. We were only in anxiety and distress during the last two hours . . . ."

Again charged particular terms mark the Captain's intensity, and again his limitations, for, as his last sentence about "disgust" makes unmistakably clear, he is still confined within a private reaction to the event, his consciousness of how he must have appeared to Anne. Her generalizations, on the other hand, dramatize a much more inclusive response to the affair, and they also bear the indelible imprint of Anne's emotional maturity. Although they derive from experience as intensely personal as his, they transcend the particular details which he cannot escape. And in thus assimilating the experience within a larger context, especially in repudiating his vision of unalloyed suffering, Anne demonstrates—most movingly, I think—her genuine greatness of spirit.

The previous dialogue has shown Anne's feelings to be more

profound than Captain Wentworth's. The following interchange, which occurs very late in the novel (pp. 244-45), shows
that her sense as well is profounder than his. The Captain has
touched on the matter of "persuasion" in telling Anne how he
feared that she might be influenced a second time—to marry
William Elliot—as she had earlier been influenced against Captain Wentworth himself. This latent reproach, largely uninten-
tional on the Captain's part, spurs Anne to defend herself in an
antithetic rhetoric very untypical of her (I have italicized the
phrases central to three main antitheses):

> "You *should have distinguished* . . . . You *should not have sus-
> pected* me now; the case so different, and my age so different. If
> I was wrong in yielding to *persuasion* once, remember that it was
> to *persuasion* exerted on the side of safety, not of risk. When I
> yielded, I thought it was to *duty*; but *no duty* could be called in
> aid here. In marrying a man indifferent to me, all risk would
> have been incurred, and all duty violated."

The passage also sounds untypical in that Anne rests her distinctions so explicitly on moral and rational grounds, rather than
unobtrusively on her emotions. And her final generalization, almost fiercely decorous, strikes a tone of aggressive certainty quite
unusual for her. Anne is compelled to speak so unequivocally,
of course, because the issue which Captain Wentworth has
raised—the validity of her former "persuasion"—is of crucial importance to her (and to our understanding of the novel). When
the Captain replies, he is just as unequivocal, but differently so
(again the italics are mine):

> "Perhaps I ought to have reasoned thus . . . but I *could not*. I
> *could not* derive benefit from the late knowledge I had acquired
> of your character. I *could not* bring it into play: it was *over-
> whelmed, buried, lost* in those earlier feelings which I had been
> smarting under year after year. I could think of you only as one
> *who* had yielded, *who* had given me up, *who* had been influ-
> enced by any one rather than by me."

Here "ought" and "reasoned" are explicitly vanquished by the
Captain's emotion, which pours out the three groups of triplets

as well as the particular terms, and which culminates in his last, passionately personal generalization. In short, he does not yet give the impression of having appropriately subdued his private feelings, come to terms with the "persuasion," or done full justice to Anne. But we shall put off examining the final ordering of his emotions, his ultimate recognition of himself and his responsibility, until the close of the next section.

⊸[III]⊷

Persuasion supplies us with the most convincing evidence, among Jane Austen's novels, of how basic the technique of metaphoric indirection is to her artistic method. For one thing, such dialogues turn up over and over here, as will have been suggested by the number of Captain Wentworth's speeches that refer obliquely to Anne, whether she is a member of his immediate audience or not. During the scene in which we have already heard him talk with the Musgroves of his naval career, for instance, he gets involved in a verbal tussle with the Crofts when he objects to the presence of women aboard ship; and it is perfectly plain to the reader that the Captain, though he apparently imagines himself taking a high naval line, actually reveals his resentment over losing Anne at every stage of his rather petulant argument (pp. 68–70). Not only does the technique appear frequently in the novel, but Jane Austen entrusts several highly significant scenes to it, including the one briefly quoted from earlier in which Louisa professes her "firmness" of character and the Captain applauds the trait, speaking all the while from his sense of Anne's irresolution and not realizing that she overhears the conversation (pp. 87–88). This dialogue is important, first, because it prepares the way for the multiple ironies of the scene on the Cobb and, second, because it provides the sharpest contrast to the climactic dialogue of *Persuasion*, the one overheard by Captain Wentworth in which Anne, the true heroine of the novel, defends woman's emotional sensitivity and endurance—in short, herself—against the claims of Captain Harville. This climactic scene, itself a fine example of metaphoric indirection, proves decisively Jane Austen's commitment to the technique. For it makes up the major part of the only extensive revision by Jane Austen that we possess, and what she has done is to substitute a dialogue that works obliquely for the clumsy apparatus by which she initially reconciled Captain Wentworth and Anne.

In her first attempt at bringing them together, Jane Austen took her cue from a passage in *Sense and Sensibility*. There, as we may recall, Elinor was forced to act in behalf of an embarrassed Colonel Brandon in offering Edward Ferrars the living that would allow Edward to marry Lucy Steele. In the canceled chapter of *Persuasion*, Captain Wentworth finds himself in a predicament like Elinor's, for Admiral Croft—who has heard that Anne plans to marry William Elliot and that she would like to live in her family home—commissions the Captain to tell Anne that the Crofts stand ready to surrender their lease whenever she wishes. The Captain's offer of Kellynch-hall brings on Anne's denial that she is engaged to William Elliot, which leads the Captain himself to propose. Jane Austen's handling of this first version is epitomized in Anne's response to the offer of her home: "You are misin—the Admiral is misinformed" (p. 258). As if to insure that we have understood the Captain's feelings and do understand Anne's, the author allows her heroine to violate momentarily—by the direct reference to "You"—the fiction so far maintained on the surface of the dialogue that the Admiral is the really interested party. No such violation occurs in the revised version, where Anne speaks as generic woman, and to this extent in a formally discreet manner, for her private feelings reveal themselves only indirectly through her claims about the sex as a whole. Moreover, the new scene is wholly oblique in its conception, since here Anne talks only with Captain Harville, never with Captain Wentworth, who sits composing a letter in another part of the room. But of course he does not miss the import of what she says, and by the end of the dialogue he writes his proposal to her.

Near the start of the conversation between Captain Harville and Anne is an exchange that sets out the fundamental contrast between them developed throughout the scene (pp. 232–35). He is deploring the fact that Captain Benwick, in becoming engaged to Louisa Musgrove, has so quickly forgotten the dead Miss Harville. And Captain Harville's lament for his sister, full of affection as it is, nevertheless bears the marks of an emotional extremism and of a personal urgency that may remind us a little of the Musgrove family, or even of Captain Wentworth. "Poor Fanny! she would not have forgotten him so soon!" exclaims Captain Harville after a series of abrupt sentences informed by his love for his sister, and in a moment he goes on addressing Anne with:

"It was not in her nature. She doated on him."
"It would not be the nature of any woman who truly loved."

The brief declarative rhythm and the intensive "doated" show Captain Harville's warm feelings ruffling the surface of his talk. Anne, on the other hand, affirms the value of Fanny Harville, indeed increases it, by associating her with the admirable class of women "who truly loved." And the generalization reveals something more about Anne's nature: she speaks as she does because she is remembering her own experience with Captain Wentworth, yet clearly she is not imprisoned within her reaction to that experience—she cannot be, inasmuch as her remark itself pays unselfish tribute to Fanny Harville and the very making of it shows Anne's consideration for the feelings of Captain Harville.

Perhaps he is unaccustomed to so penetrating a sensibility as Anne's; at least he puts her generalization in question, smiling,

as much as to say, "Do you claim that for your sex?" and she answered the question, smiling also, "Yes. We certainly do not forget you, so soon as you forget us. It is, perhaps, our fate rather than our merit. We cannot help ourselves. We live at home, quiet, confined, and our feelings prey upon us. You are forced on exertion. You have always a profession, pursuits, business of

❋❋❋❋❋❋❋❋❋❋❋❋❋❋❋❋❋❋❋❋❋❋❋❋❋❋❋❋❋❋❋❋❋❋❋

some sort or other, to take you back into the world immediately, and continual occupation and change soon weaken impressions."

Meeting his challenge with perfect tact, Anne nevertheless firmly advances her convictions about women in general, convictions which again have been thoroughly tested, of course, in her private experience. Her distinction between "fate" and "merit" is especially graceful, Anne refusing to boast about her sex at the same time that she voices her deepest claim, a characteristically emotional one, for woman's sensitivity. And her tone remains completely unassuming throughout her generalizations contrasting woman's condition with man's—a comparison which looks back on Anne's history with Captain Wentworth, to be sure, but which also lays out for the benefit of Captain Harville the evidence supporting her claim about women.

Her more impulsive opponent, however, is not to be won over by the argument she has developed. At first Captain Harville makes out that he objects to it on purely rational grounds, pointing with a flourish to the fact that Anne's generalization about men being absorbed in "business" cannot apply to Captain Benwick, who has been living in seclusion with the Harvilles. Anne readily acknowledges her lapse—admitting that she "did not recollect" the case of Captain Benwick, though without explaining that she forgot him because she was remembering Captain Wentworth—but she then presses on with exact logic to show where Captain Harville's reasoning leads: "If the change be not from outward circumstances, it must be from within; it must be nature, man's nature, which has done the business for Captain Benwick." Now the essential quality of Captain Harville's reaction to the stand that Anne has been taking becomes clearer, his answer no longer striking so logical a note. Rather, his words seem to issue from a context of feelings which relate to the self more narrowly and much more directly than do Anne's, and he speaks with an aggressive intensity such as she never allows herself:

"No, no, it is not man's nature. I will not allow it to be more man's nature than woman's to be inconstant and forget those they do love, or have loved. I believe the reverse. I believe in a true analogy between our bodily frames and our mental; and that as our bodies are the strongest, so are our feelings; capable of bearing most rough usage, and riding out the heaviest weather."

The repeated "I's" suggest that under emotional pressure Captain Harville conceives of the whole argument in far more exclusively personal terms than has Anne (despite her memories of Captain Wentworth), and his relatively crude "analogy" between the "bodily" and the "mental" implies that the sensibility which he brings to bear on the argument is somewhat less refined than hers. That Captain Harville is caught up within a dominantly personal response is proved, I think, by his recourse to naval language at the close of his speech.

Anne's reply to him points up, in effect, the limitations of Captain Harville, for it reveals her to be both in control of her claims (rather than trapped within them) and capable of an utterly outgoing emotion. She starts off by capitalizing on his analogy, drawing out the logical consequences of what he has said:

"Your feelings may be the strongest . . . but the same spirit of analogy will authorise me to assert that ours are the most tender. Man is more robust than woman, but he is not longer-lived; which exactly explains my view of the nature of their attachments. Nay, it would be too hard upon you, if it were otherwise. You have difficulties, and privations, and dangers enough to struggle with. You are always labouring and toiling, exposed to every risk and hardship. Your home, country, friends, all quitted. Neither time, nor health, nor life, to be called your own. It would be too hard indeed" (with a faltering voice) "if woman's feelings were to be added to all this."

But after two sentences she turns, with the characteristically deep sympathy of "Nay, it would be too hard upon you," to the four swelling series which soften the impact of her reasoning. This rhetorical intensity would indicate that she is thinking of Captain Wentworth, even if the cited details did not recall the stories he has told in her presence. Still, it is typical that Anne,

❋❋❋❋❋❋❋❋❋❋❋❋❋❋❋❋❋❋❋❋❋❋❋❋❋❋❋❋❋❋❋❋❋❋❋❋❋❋❋

at a moment when she is engaged in defending herself, should yet take into account most generously the situation of another, even that of a Captain Wentworth who has caused her so much distress. She exhibits a total selflessness here quite beyond the capacity of Captain Harville—or of Captain Wentworth himself, so far in the novel—at the same time that she forcefully maintains her side of the local debate.

Although her words do not convince Captain Harville, they appear to have told on Captain Wentworth, for "a slight noise" from his quarter of the room makes Anne aware that he is listening intently, and the dialogue breaks off momentarily. It resumes when Captain Harville observes:

> "Well . . . we shall never agree I suppose upon this point. No man and woman would, probably. But let me observe that all histories are against you, all stories, prose and verse. . . . I do not think I ever opened a book in my life which had not something to say upon woman's inconstancy. Songs and proverbs, all talk of woman's fickleness. But perhaps you will say, these were all written by men."

Certainly the Captain's tone sounds a good deal more moderate in some of these sentences, his tentative "probably" and "perhaps" showing real consideration for Anne. But something of his earlier extremism still lingers in his "all's" and "ever." And at the risk of being fanciful, I would suggest that the whole speech leaves us with a sense that Captain Harville is straining for evidence, inasmuch as his citation of the fictional seems a little out of tune with the impression conveyed by the earlier exchanges that real experience, deeply felt, lies more or less immediately behind his remarks and Anne's.

Evidently Captain Harville's pursuit of the topic embarrasses Anne, who has been "startled" to discover that Captain Wentworth can overhear what they say, for she now attempts to wind up the controversy as quickly as possible. Her first maneuver—graciousness itself—consists in her pretending to be as willful as Captain Harville imagines her, thus throwing the debate to her opponent:

"Perhaps I shall.—Yes, yes, if you please, no reference to examples in books. Men have had every advantage of us in telling
their own story. Education has been theirs in so much higher a
degree; the pen has been in their hands. I will not allow books
to prove any thing."

In striking this exaggerated pose—note her switch from "Perhaps" to the overly intensive "Yes, yes" and that final, un-
typically demanding "I will not allow"—Anne deliberately re-
signs all claim to the good sense with which she has countered
Captain Harville throughout the dialogue. When he continues
to press, however, she takes another tack in order to close off
the discussion, and her reason for wanting to end it—her consciousness of the man at the desk—becomes unmistakable: [10]

"But how shall we prove any thing?"
"We never shall. We never can expect to prove any thing upon
such a point. It is a difference of opinion which does not admit
of proof. We each begin probably with a little bias towards our
own sex, and upon that bias build every circumstance in favour
of it which has occurred within our own circle; many of which
circumstances (perhaps those very cases which strike us the
most) may be precisely such as cannot be brought forward without betraying a confidence, or in some respect saying what
should not be said."

Anne's allusion to the "cases which strike us the most" and her
talk about discretion leave no doubt that her thoughts are
centered on Captain Wentworth, to whom she must not give
herself away. Thus she tries to conclude the argument with
Captain Harville by insisting that it cannot be settled. Even
here, though, Anne's profound integrity is dramatized, for the
generalization starting out with "We each begin" shows her
encompassing the very processes of bias at work in their conversation—shows her transcending, that is, the limitedly personal.

Captain Harville's answer to her, moving as it is, yet proves
him to be of lesser stature: though his sincerity cannot be
questioned, neither can his partiality. Apparently he hopes, by

❋❋❋❋❋❋❋❋❋❋❋❋❋❋❋❋❋❋❋❋❋❋❋❋❋❋❋❋❋❋❋❋❋❋❋

speaking impersonally of "a man" in what follows, to formulate a claim powerful enough in its generality to climax his argument and carry the day with Anne:

> "Ah! . . . if I could but make you comprehend what a man suffers when he takes a last look at his wife and children, and watches the boat that he has sent them off in, as long as it is in sight, and then turns away and says, "God knows whether we ever meet again!" And then . . . the glow of his soul when he does see them again; when, coming back after a twelvemonth's absence perhaps, and obliged to put into another port, he calculates how soon it be possible to get them there . . . all the while hoping for them twelve hours sooner, and seeing them arrive at last, as if Heaven had given them wings, by many hours sooner still! If I could explain to you all this, and all that a man can bear and do, and glories to do for the sake of these treasures of his existence! I speak, you know, only of such men as have hearts!" pressing his own with emotion.

But his lingering attention to particulars, and the speech is weighed down with them, indicates that Captain Harville is much nearer to voicing an intensely personal experience than an authoritative generalization. If further evidence is needed that he is wrapped up in his immediate feelings, we have only to view his final gesture.

Anne realizes his situation, we must suspect, for his outburst calls forth her finest generosity:

> "Oh! . . . I hope I do justice to all that is felt by you, and by those who resemble you. God forbid that I should undervalue the warm and faithful feelings of any of my fellow-creatures. I should deserve utter contempt if I dared to suppose that true attachment and constancy were known only by woman. No, I believe you capable of every thing great and good in your married lives. I believe you equal to every important exertion, and to every domestic forbearance, so long as—if I may be allowed the expression, so long as you have an object. I mean, while the woman you love lives, and lives for you. All the privilege I claim for my own sex (it is not a very enviable one, you need not covet it) is that of loving longest, when existence or when hope is gone."

It is a totally magnanimous reply. In its first stages, such intensive phrases as "God forbid" and "utter contempt" express Anne's fervently sympathetic response to Captain Harville's experience. As her answer develops, the repeated "I believe you" declares her firm conviction that her opponent is sincere. And at the culmination of her speech, in that fully emotional generalization about the single "privilege" belonging to her "own sex," Anne reveals—in the very act of betraying her personal distress—her ultimate unselfishness by minimizing the "privilege" and by insisting on woman's capacity to love when no return is imaginable. It is little wonder that so poignant a reply should indeed climax the dialogue with Captain Harville and also persuade Captain Wentworth to propose.

Nor, with this example of Anne in front of him, is it surprising that Captain Wentworth should finally come to know and to judge himself in the last conversation of the novel (pp. 246–47). The only surprise is that no such dialogue occurred in the conclusion originally drafted by Jane Austen, which thus left Captain Wentworth's development incomplete and omitted the most penetrating analysis of "persuasion." But the revision supplies these deficiencies with an interchange which Anne begins. Again we should be alert to her utter decorum—in refusing to judge anyone but herself, in taking her stand on what is "right" although she has "suffered from it," and in saying all that can be said for Lady Russell while pointing out that her friend's "advice" was questionable, if not wrong:

> "I have been thinking over the past, and trying impartially to judge of the right and wrong, I mean with regard to myself; and I must believe that I was right, much as I suffered from it, that I was perfectly right in being guided by the friend whom you will love better than you do now. To me, she was in the place of a parent. Do not mistake me, however. I am not saying that she did not err in her advice. It was, perhaps, one of those cases in which advice is good or bad only as the event decides; and for myself, I certainly never should, in any circumstance of tolerable similarity, give such advice. But I mean, that I was right in submitting to her, and that if I had done otherwise, I should have

suffered more in continuing the engagement than I did even in giving it up, because I should have suffered in my conscience. I have now, as far as such a sentiment is allowable in human nature, nothing to reproach myself with; and if I mistake not, a strong sense of duty is no bad part of a woman's portion."

How deeply engrained in Anne's nature this allegiance to decorum is becomes evident, toward the close of the passage, when she discriminates between the distress of breaking off the attachment and the pain of breaking with authority. Even her conduct of the speech itself shows Anne's innate propriety, for it is only after she has verbally acted out this entire commitment to the demands of "conscience"—demands which she has characteristically apprehended through feeling—that she permits herself the luxury of the moral generalization with which she ends, one which modestly justifies her earlier behavior.

And Captain Wentworth is at last ready to meet her on equally fundamental grounds, though he pretends for a moment that Anne has merely been pleading with him to approve of Lady Russell:

> "Not yet. But there are hopes of her being forgiven in time. I trust to being in charity with her soon. But I too have been thinking over the past, and a question has suggested itself, whether there may not have been one person more my enemy even than that lady? My own self. Tell me if, when I returned to England in the year eight, with a few thousand pounds, and was posted into the Laconia, if I had then written to you, would you . . . have renewed the engagement then?"
> "Would I!" . . . .
> "Good God! . . . you would! It is not that I did not think of it . . . . But I was proud, too proud to ask again. I did not understand you. I shut my eyes, and would not understand you, or do you justice. This is a recollection which ought to make me forgive every one sooner than myself."

The witty detachment with which he teases Anne about Lady Russell in the first sentences serves as a guarantee, I take it, of Captain Wentworth's objectivity when he turns his attention to "My own self." Surely he views himself with open eyes throughout the second speech. Here he firmly judges his earlier behavior, a far cry from the almost hysterical self-reproaching by which he indulged his personal anguish when talking with Anne on a previous occasion about Louisa's accident. And here —instead of the passionately personal generalization about Anne's having betrayed him that the Captain was driven to utter when he last discussed "persuasion" with her—here the generalization he comes out with is explicitly moral and explicitly takes account of others besides himself. All this is to suggest that he seems finally to have transcended the sheerly personal element in his feelings, and in doing so has become capable of fully accepting his responsibilities in relation to Anne and to the matter of the "persuasion." Having learned to see himself so clearly, Captain Wentworth has earned the right to evaluate his past and future with charming impudence in his closing words to Anne: "Like other great men under reverses . . . I must endeavour to subdue my mind to my fortune. I must learn to brook being happier than I deserve."

A few more sentences and I shall have done with *Persuasion.* It seems to me imperative that we do not interpret this last conversation as a desperate attempt by Jane Austen to put the best face she can on an incident which she really disapproves of, but without which the story could not exist. On the contrary, this exchange between Anne and Captain Wentworth is the climactic expression of the novel's theme, celebrating the triumph of the more than personal over the merely personal in feeling. For the dialogue insists that Anne, at the crisis brought on by Lady Russell's "persuasion," has felt the pull of her love for Captain Wentworth as well as the pull of duty and has found the latter more compelling, though without therefore ceasing to care for the Captain. One mark of Anne's special quality, indeed, is precisely this ability to live with, to assimilate, the contrarieties of experience without seeking impatiently to dissolve the tensions engendered by them. Thus she can go on loving Captain Wentworth although she has rejected his suit; she can retain all her affection for Lady Russell although she has come to question Lady Russell's advice; she can believe herself justified in having followed the counsel although she disagrees with it. And her loyalty to Lady Russell, her continuing regard for the authority exercised by her adviser, Anne's respect, even, for the prudence contained in the advice itself, all of these indicate that she willingly allies herself with the society she lives in, having worked out an adjustment of her own to its values—which is to say once more that she reveals her commitment to something beyond the self. As for Captain Wentworth, we have seen how the dialogue shows him moving beyond the intense involvement in himself traceable through all his previous speeches. Furthermore, in judging his earlier behavior and in recognizing his responsibility to Anne, the Captain approaches the sort of integration typical of her, for he mediates between the self and the claims of another. In brief, the theme of *Persuasion*—as of the previous novels—is essentially moral, the only difference being that feeling, suspect in the earlier works that vindicated "sense," is here the trustworthy agent of moral perception.

1. Reginald Farrer makes the first observation ("Jane Austen," p. 29), and the second belongs to Mary Lascelles (*Jane Austen*, p. 183).

2. The fact that Captain Wentworth is the only developing character in the novel makes for one of my reservations about Mark Schorer's suggestive commentary on *Persuasion* in "Fiction and the 'Matrix of Analogy.'" He perhaps implies, though I am not sure about this, that Anne herself alters in some way when he writes that "The problem of the novel is" in part "to increase her value" (p. 541), or when he describes her condition in terms of "a stock that has a debased value" (p. 543). It seems to me, however, that Anne's actual worth remains the same from start to finish. According to Schorer, "The novel explicitly asks, what is 'the value of an Anne Elliot' and where is the man who will 'understand' it?" (p. 543); the second question appears to me rather different from the first, for it points less to a possible shift in Anne's "value" than to a change in the capacities of Captain Wentworth. I feel similarly uneasy about the implications when the critic observes: " . . . at last Anne's character is '*fixed* on his mind as perfection itself,'" which is to say that, like a currency, it has been stabilized" (p. 542). Schorer's figure may suggest that Anne's own worth has been shifting about, but the phrase from the novel occurs in a passage which makes it clear that the feelings of the Captain are what have been "stabilized" (p. 241).

Maybe I have been twisting Schorer's comments on Anne into meaning something that he does not intend. Yet I also have some reservations about his acute verbal analyses of *Persuasion*. His main purpose is to search out its "dominant metaphorical quality," which he finds in "a stylistic base derived from commerce and property" (p. 540), and in general he rates the intrinsic significance of dead metaphors much higher than I would think safe. Some of his particular readings seem to me rather strained. For instance, *credit* derives from *credere*, and I would suppose that the word refers to "belief" or "faith" quite as readily as to accounting, even in such a phrase as "take all the charms and perfections of Edward's wife upon *credit* [a little longer]" (p. 541). Surely "prospect" implies nothing but a "looking forward" in "all the *precious* rooms and furniture, groves, and *prospects*" or in " 'the *prospect* of *spending*' two months" (p. 541). Can the *"figure"* in "a face not materially *disfigured"* really call to mind "arithmetic," one of "the two large areas of metaphorical interest" in the novel (p. 541)? And I suspect that the critic himself is inventing the pun on *"interest"* in what follows: "When Anne's blighted romance is called 'this little history of sorrowful *interest*,' we hardly forget that a lack of money was the blight. Is 'a man of principle' by any chance a man of substance?" (p. 542). That last remark appears to me especially misleading, for few novelists can have taken such pains as Jane Austen to define "principle."

But I should add that Schorer's essay—though it strikes me as distorting *Persuasion* somewhat in various particulars—gives valuable evidence to confirm one's general sense of Jane Austen's hardheaded practicality.

3. That the Captain alters has been suggested by Mary Lascelles, who describes the "principal pattern" of the story as "formed by the change in Wentworth's feelings towards Anne"; and Miss Lascelles goes on to identify Anne as our point of view: " . . . of the progress of this change we are allowed to judge only from a train of incidents which comes under her observation" (*Jane Austen*, p. 203). Indeed the critic takes issue with Jane Austen for departing on a couple of occasions from Anne's point of view, and one of these I take up in my text after a moment.

4. Mudrick has written that Anne is "unsubjected to the temper of Jane Austen's irony" (*Jane Austen*, p. 222). Yet we must not be led by his comment to think that Anne and her emotional sensitivity are never exposed to the irony of the author. Several relatively trivial examples might be cited, but irony crops up when Anne is under real stress. The following quotation, for instance, describes her reaction on overhearing the Captain praise the enthusiasm of Louisa Musgrove (the italics are mine): "Anne could not immediately *fall into a quotation* again. The sweet scenes of autumn were for a while put by—unless some *tender* sonnet, *fraught* with the *apt analogy* of the declining year, with declining happiness, and the images of youth and hope, and spring, all gone together, *blessed* her memory" (p. 85). The italicized words are too studied, I think consciously so, to permit us to submerge ourselves in Anne's feelings; and "blessed" underlines the irony, for Anne—however submissive—can hardly be expected to gain exquisite relief from any sugges-

tion that the Captain is lost to her. In this next passage, Anne has been exhilarated by some evidence that Captain Wentworth still loves her (once more the italics are my own): "Prettier musings of *high-wrought love* and *eternal constancy,* could never have passed along the streets of Bath, than Anne was *sporting with* . . . . It was almost enough *to spread purification and perfume* all the way" (p. 192). Mudrick takes the sentences as an expression of "the author's overt sympathy," a "burst of affection" (*Jane Austen,* p. 226). My own feeling is that the phrases in italics are again too strained to ask for our total belief. Certainly the figure in the last sentence, if intended seriously, is wholly out of line with Jane Austen's usual practice, though it might be answered that this is a different sort of novel than she has written before. Still, the word "sporting" certainly undermines the emotional intensity of the passage, thus compelling the reader to disengage himself to some extent. By all this I do not mean that we are really to question Anne in any way; my point is only that Jane Austen still treats her heroine with some irony, if a gentle one.

5. Mary Lascelles considers this omniscient perspective at Captain Wentworth's introduction an "oversight" on the part of the author (*Jane Austen,* p. 204), and she may be perfectly right. I am only voicing a hunch when I say that the passage does not strike me as carelessly conceived. Perhaps the lines would have been revised if Jane Austen had lived. But one can see how they came to be written—which is not to claim that they are artistically defensible.

6. Mudrick—who finds the relationship between Mary and Charles Musgrove figuring a larger "conflict" in *Persuasion* "between the feudal remnant . . . and the rising middle class" (*Jane Austen,* p. 232)— characterizes this speech as a "hypnotic bourgeois incantation of advancement and property" (p. 233). But I wonder if the critic's phrase may not attribute too pure an economic motive here to Charles Musgrove, whose words are conditioned in part by his sense of his personal status. Incidentally, the one outburst by Mary's husband against rank is not fired by class enmity, but merely by his wish—thoroughly typical—to have his own way in going to the theater (pp. 223–24).

7. Certainly Jane Austen treats Mrs. Musgrove very shabbily in the first part of *Persuasion,* but I do not agree with Mudrick that the author, perhaps relenting, presents us in the second half of the novel with "a different Mrs. Musgrove from the one already demolished" (*Jane Austen,* p. 213). For one thing, a harmless enough self-interest seems to have conditioned the warm welcome she tenders Anne when they meet at Bath, for in the passage quoted by Mudrick, Jane Austen writes: " . . . Mrs. Musgrove's real affection had been won by her usefulness when they were in distress" (p. 220), when Anne had helped out with the injured Louisa. And later on, even the gentle heroine shudders a little at the impropriety of Mrs. Musgrove when, full of Henrietta's engagement, she goes into all the details of the marriage settlement with Mrs. Croft: "Minutiæ which, even with every advantage of taste and

delicacy which good Mrs. Musgrove could not give, could be properly interesting only to the principals" (p. 230).

8. Mary Lascelles and Marvin Mudrick feel that Jane Austen handles Mrs. Clay and William Elliot arbitrarily in dismissing them to an affair with each other at the end of *Persuasion*. I agree with the general claim of the critics, though on the grounds that the behavior reported of the two characters at the end of the novel is inconsistent with their earlier performances. The suggestion that Mrs. Clay's feeling for William Elliot has had its way with her, and that his feeling for her may have its way with him (p. 250), simply does not jibe with the detachment, the control, that both of them have shown everywhere else. This seems to me a major case of sabotage in comparison with, say, Jane Austen's management of the Crawfords at the close of *Mansfield Park,* for the Crawfords do reveal a minimal consistency in their final actions.

9. Mudrick uses this speech to document Captain Wentworth's bourgeois interest in money: "Even as a sailor, loving battle and glory, he is still frankly a businessman" (*Jane Austen*, p. 235). I cannot be sure how much the critic means to imply by this, but certainly the Captain is not concerned here with money for its own sake. His interest in it is a derivative of his interest in Anne.

10. Margaret Kennedy has pointed out—in *Jane Austen* (London, 1950)—how Anne's awareness of Captain Wentworth is projected in the speech which I have just quoted in my text: " 'The pen has been in their hands,' she [Anne] says, so turning the phrase unconsciously because in her mind is the picture of the man sitting behind her with a pen in his hand" (p. 89).

9 Conclusion

In devoting so many pages to the ways in which Jane Austen dramatizes her characters through their linguistic habits, I have of course neglected some important qualities of her dialogue. Probably the sheer wit that sparkles in so many of the verbal exchanges is the most memorable feature of her conversations. But they are also distinguished by their lifelike flow. If some of the phrasings sound a little stiff to us today, and some of the sentences rather long, still there is a wonderfully easy movement within the single speech which combines with a natural progress from one speech to the next to give the dialogues an air of artlessness, of truth to life. To what extent the conversational practices of Jane Austen's culture and local environment may have provided her with models for such ease and wit is a question that hardly admits of a decisive answer.[1] But it is at least clear that none of her contemporaries or immediate predecessors among the novelists commands a dialogue at once so fluent and so brilliant as hers. And we would have to travel on to Henry James, I think, to find a writer whose dialogue is anything like so charged with meaning as Jane Austen's—though it cannot approach hers in the matter of verisimilitude.

But the qualities that I have just mentioned are evident to any reader of Jane Austen. In fact they tempt us to overlook the actual depth of the characters that the dialogue reveals—and to ignore the more profound implications of the novels. For the underlying motif in Jane Austen's fiction is surely the disparity between appearance and reality, a problem that has haunted men's minds for centuries—all of which may suggest again that the works are less limited than is often imagined. The motif becomes explicit in one of Jane Austen's favorite figures of speech, "blindness." And each novel, we may recall, traces the development of at least one major character from the blindness brought on by too exclusive a self-interest, of whatever sort, to the operative clarity that results from a greater self-consciousness and rigorous self-evaluation. The evolution of these characters—and they range from Marianne Dashwood to Captain Wentworth—is defined in their speeches; but it is defined as well through the contrasting behavior of the other characters, major and minor, who reveal in their own speeches their different degrees of blindness and enlightenment, their differing capacities to appraise reality truly and thus to take effective moral action. Indeed Jane Austen's dialogue, taken as a whole, dramatizes the varieties of personality and explores the fundamental terms on which man lives with himself and with the world.

In her novels, the reality to be assessed properly by the characters and then engaged with is pre-eminently a social one. The fact is implied, it seems to me, by the vast number of conversations in this fiction. But surer evidence is at hand in the part these conversations play throughout her work and in their very nature. For the dialogues here are not what they so often are in other stories, a mere accompaniment to some chain of intrinsically interesting events. On the contrary, these public encounters take up the foreground of the fiction: they are its events—events, moreover, which constantly show the individual in relation to his society and its conventions. The central importance of the conventional, the patterned, in the world created by Jane Austen is vividly suggested by the image which David Daiches has used in describing her works, and his comments point as well to the latent gravity of the novels:

> There is almost what might be called a ballet movement in many of them—or perhaps something between a ballet and a Mozart opera. The characters circle round each other with appropriate speeches and gestures, and occasionally a grotesque like Mr. Collins joins the dance as a symbol of one kind of fate that threatens the dancers. . . .
>   It is a stately dance on the lawn—but all around there are the dark trees, the shadows. And if you do not dance well, if you

have not been able, by the end of the day, to secure a permanent partner with whom to walk off the lawn, you are left, when the sun sets, alone amid the shadows. We are never allowed to forget that possibility, never allowed to forget what a serious business this dancing is. One false step can be fatal.[2]

But although convention is powerful and omnipresent in this world, the claims of the individual are not therefore repudiated. Rather, Jane Austen affirms, as Dorothy Van Ghent has noted, that the "spiritual creativity" of the individual "will be able to operate only within publicly acceptable modes of deportment" —that "These modes of deportment, however public and traditional, must be made to convey the secret life of the individual spirit . . . ."[3] And in the dialogues informed by the technique of metaphoric indirection, we have seen that the individual acknowledges the demands of propriety while voicing his deepest personal commitments. The scenes dramatize the contending forces that determine behavior in the novels, and the delicately controlled resonance of the lines is Jane Austen's finest achievement in dialogue.

1. The art of social conversation must have greatly deteriorated by Jane Austen's time, according to Donald Davie, because the literary genres nourished by it—the epistolary novel and the familiar letter— were themselves degenerating (*Purity of Diction in English Verse* [London, 1952], p. 25).

2. *A Study of Literature* (Ithaca, N. Y., 1948), pp. 114–15.

3. *The English Novel*, p. 102.